HIDEOUT
IN THE APOCALYPSE

JOHN STAPLETON

Print Edition
ISBN: 978-0-9944791-9-8

Published by A Sense of Place Publishing 2018

Edited by Stafford Sanders
Cover photography by mironov on shutterstock.com
Cover design by Jessica Bell
Interior design by Amie McCracken

NATIONAL LIBRARY OF AUSTRALIA

A catalogue record for this book is available from the National Library of Australia

TABLE OF CONTENTS

ONE BIG LIE

THE NEWS was all bad, there in those fading days of summer.

The darkness came early, settling in over the back fence, making the cluttered, indiscriminate garden instantly cold.

For Old Alex, a retired reporter, every day could seem like a century. This time around he knew there would be no mercy, not for him, and certainly not for the thousands who would die.

His head had begun to swarm weeks before. Frightened of the consequences, of all the things he wished he could not hear, of the fantastical things that swirled through his head, he had done everything he could think of to stop it, smoking too many cigarettes, hiding out deep inside the recesses of his own life, his all too desperately human form. He inserted into random conversations the comment: "A dive into the ordinary." He did not want to be found.

In his waking dreams, his species had lived in fright and flight for millennia, and his most overwhelming desire was to be invisible. Unfortunately the times, destiny, this incarnation had chosen the wrong profession for that, journalism, and there were always whispers in the wind. The world had never been a safe place, not for his kind.

The English had invaded the southern continent on the edge of Western consciousness, killed the indigenous, raped the land for profit, invited the world to trample across the sacred hunting grounds, and sold what was left to the highest bidder. The white ghosts were a cruel race and they brought with them their own gods to pour scorn upon the ancient spirits, to smash the land and its peoples – not just in the physical realm, but in the spiritual.

The invaders built their own societies, only, in the end, to destroy themselves. The land would have its revenge.

At the same time as the days began to shorten in the southern hemisphere time, or more precisely events, began to speed up in other parts of an increasingly hyper-connected, image-saturated world. With the advent of internet technologies, the species was busily turning itself into a hive mind. The ancient gods were taking full advantage. As were governments, gifting themselves powers of mass surveillance and control over their populations. Individual privacy was massacred, public interest journalism also.

Every day might seem like a century, but equally the months were collapsing in on themselves. The beginning of summer had barely been a rain-drenched five minutes ago.

Old Alex could make a shopping list sing if he wanted to; but after writing two books in rapid succession he was burnt out, and unusually for him, lacked the emotional coherence or motivation to write. The lyricism which once flowed so readily through his head, the storytelling which had been one of his sole methods of expression, vanished.

Now he sat barely speaking in the backyard while above the heavens were burning, just out of sight. As if the upper atmosphere had caught alight.

He told no one what he was really thinking.

In a flash of recognition an old mentor once said: "You're like me. You think in pictures."

"Yes."

"Can you imagine what it's like to be an ordinary person? One thought following another. It must be like walking through a large empty warehouse."

They both laughed, although it was no comfort.

But at that point in time, beyond the incendiary sky, there were no pictures at all, just a terrifying blankness.

Alex had not intended to be back in Australia at his age or stage of life, in this remote place. As he had written before, like the convicts of yore, he had done his time.

An unravelling world was portrayed in short, ideologically filtered bursts on television screens, distant events of which he was not a part and to which most people in the area paid zero attention.

All around Sydney's inner west the streets remained quiet, the workers' cottages of days gone by selling now for more than a million dollars each, sanctities of silence, good behaviour, ordered belief, middle class welfare. There were few points of commonality. Students gathered in clots in the park to drink, smoke, gossip and while away the afternoons in the thin winter sun. Middle aged women and gay couples walked their dogs. The only sign of creativity was the graffiti which, being neither political slogan-eering nor creative expression, bore little purpose. Sleep in slumber. I anguish, you yearn.

The population had slumped into a zombie-like state, their society dead-ened by obsessive, overarching regulation.

Ceaseless indoctrination pumped from government-controlled media and the mouths of elected representatives.

"I can't understand anyone who criticises Australia," went the mantra. "We're lucky to live here, why would you want to live anywhere else?"

By 2016 Australian culture had become a whimpering desert, redacted, flattened, crushed into a shadow land. The truth was, Australia's egregious, shameless political castes had failed to act or been complicit in the destruc-tion of the county's traditional culture, betraying the public at the deepest levels.

Rules, pointless, stupid rules, covered every waking moment. The bars were dead, the nightlife non-existent, the streets swept of protest. Conver-sations were conducted in whispers, within a narrow band of social justice concerns in a land where there was no justice. Nobody wanted to be caught holding an unacceptable view.

"It's a Police State," Australians frequently said of their own country. The citizens, subdued under excessive levels of bureaucracy in a failing democ-racy and brainwashed with layers of anodyne, anaemic media, had nothing good to say about their country or their politicians, much less the swathes of government machinery their taxes supported. A defeated population.

Data retention laws and expansion of the Surveillance State, under the threat or excuse of terror, meant the actions of every citizen could now, legally and without warrant, be monitored by a plethora of state agencies. Nowhere to Hide. Bureaucrats without heart or conscience toiled for Big Brother. In a twinkling the society had changed, the only thing to keep the citizens safe a malevolent, suffocating blanket.

The government knew perfectly well when it introduced the panopticon, ubiquitous, universal surveillance into Australia, what the results would be: a frightened, conformist population; a place where dissent and protest was hard to organise under the ever watchful eyes of the county's oft-hated and increasingly questioned secret police, including the Australian Security Intelligence Organisation.

A population that was not just less inquiring, but sicker.

For Alex, "panopticon" was a word he had never heard before.

> Philosopher Jeremy Bentham conceived of his "panopticon" in the late 1700s as a way to build cheaper prisons. His idea was a prison where every inmate could be surveilled at any time, unawares. The inmate would have no choice but to assume that he was always being watched, and would therefore conform. This idea has been used as a metaphor for mass personal data collection, both on the Internet and off.

> On the Internet, surveillance is ubiquitous. All of us are being watched, all the time, and that data is being stored forever. This is what an information-age surveillance state looks like, and it's efficient beyond Bentham's wildest dreams.[1]

The Australian Panopticon had been put in place without consulting the population – those whose every move was now a matter of record, every location they travelled to, every website they visited, every term they searched, every phone call they made, every email they sent, every Facebook post they made, every liaison entered into.

The research was already in. The government knew full well universal surveillance would have not just a serious chilling effect on public debate, but broader consequences for the democracy. It also knew universal surveillance would have a serious impact on health and wellbeing.

> There's a strong physiological basis for privacy. Biologist Peter Watts makes the point that a desire for privacy is innate: mammals in particular don't respond well to surveillance. We consider it a physical threat, because animals in the natural world are surveilled by predators. Surveillance makes us feel like prey, just as it makes the surveillors act like predators.

1 *Data and Goliath: The Hidden Battles to Collect Your Data and Control Your World*, Bruce Schneier, W.W. Norton & Co Inc, 2015.

Psychologists, sociologists, philosophers, novelists, and technologists have all written about the effects of constant surveillance, or even just the perception of constant surveillance. Studies show that we are less healthy, both physically and emotionally. We have feelings of low self-esteem, depression, and anxiety. Surveillance strips us of our dignity. It threatens our very selves as individuals. It's a dehumanising tactic employed in prisons and detention camps around the world.[2]

If Modern Day Australia was not a detention camp, what was?

A friend, trying to cheer him up, wrote from the other side of the world:

The nanny/surveillance state may be Orwellian in its effect, but it's always well to remember that this is not the result of a conspiracy, but of a lot of jobsworths trying to make their miserable little jobs bigger, and that at the other end of the lens it's a tiny petty creature that's wasting its precious life watching you.[3]

The Australian government had enthusiastically adopted its own universal surveillance from the Americans. Ostensibly introduced to prevent terrorism, a glib lie foisted on the Australian people, all it did was intimidate the population and, amongst those disinclined to be intimidated, produced a vociferous reaction of dislike and contempt.

Mass surveillance was the first control instrument reached for by oppressive and totalitarian regimes.

The good legislators of Australia knew what they were doing to a once freedom-loving culture.

As for useful evidence, all it produced was evidence of how people and groups behaved when they knew they were under surveillance. Those with genuine intent got cleverer at avoiding detection; the mass of the population grew more compliant, dissidents grew angrier and more outspoken, those who could not stand the thought of being constantly watched more erratic.

The government had ignored the negative consequences, hoping only for docility.

As journalist Glenn Greenwald wrote in his book on Edward Snowden,

---

2 *Data and Goliath: The Hidden Battles to Collect Your Data and Control Your World*, Bruce *Schneier*, W.W. Norton & Co Inc, 2015.

3 Skype conversation between author and Michael Prato, 24 July, 2016.

No Place To Hide, this model of control had the great advantage of simultaneously creating the illusion of freedom. The compulsion to obedience exists in the individual's mind. Individuals choose on their own to comply, out of fear that they are being watched. This eliminates the need for all the visible hallmarks of compulsion, and thus enables control over people who falsely believe themselves to be free.

> Ubiquitous surveillance not only empowers authorities and compels compliance but also induces Individuals to internalise their watchers. Those who believe they are watched will instinctively choose to do that which is wanted of them without even realising that they are being controlled—the Panopticon induces "in the inmate a state of conscious and permanent visibility that assures the automatic functioning of power." With the control internalised, the overt evidence of repression disappears because it is no longer necessary: "the external power may throw off its physical weight; it tends to be non-corporal; and, the more it approaches this limit, the more constant, profound and permanent are its effects: it is a profound victory that avoids any physical confrontation and which is always decided in advance."[4]

Old Alex might have had an image-flooded head, but the future was even more frightening than he could have ever imagined.

Years of surveillance, and his life became an echo chamber. "You have the power to vanquish your pursuers," he tried to tell himself. But it didn't work, nothing worked.

The aim of the specific programs directed at him, and the broader programs directed at the public, was to silence all dissent. Mindless and extremely cruel, the authorities wanted to create their own Bell Jar, a suffocating place of deadly intent under The Sheltering Sky, a mindless place where they were comfortable:

> "Well act as if all this were a bad dream."
> A bad dream.
> To the person in the bell jar, blank and stopped as a dead baby,
> the world itself is the bad dream.
> A bad dream.

---

4 *No Place to Hide: Edward Snowden, the NSA & The Surveillance State*, Glenn Greenwald, Penguin Books, 2015.

I remembered everything. [5]

Freedom. As a young man Alex had been a naïve and enthusiastic advocate, without realising it meant more than being able to have a joint out the back of a pub without being busted. Freedom depended on the circulation of ideas, which government censorship, facilitated by universal surveillance, stifled.

> Awareness that the Government may be watching chills associational and expressive freedoms. And the Government's unrestrained power to assemble data that reveal private aspects of identity is susceptible to abuse. The net result is . . . by making available at a relatively low cost such a substantial quantity of intimate information about any person whom the Government, in its unfettered discretion, chooses to track—may 'alter the relationship between citizen and government in a way that is inimical to democratic society.'[6]

When it came to mass surveillance, the monitoring and collection of every electronic communication of everyone everywhere was heroically exposed by US whistle-blower Edward Snowden, Australia outstripped even its American mentor.

The chilling of the Great Southern Land occurred at a pace, by connivance and confluence of weak governance and the hapless state of both private and public media, which was driven by click rates, fashionable agendas and financial and political self-interest across multiple platforms.

Ever the reporter, Old Alex became intrigued by the psychological impacts of surveillance even as he experienced it, and began to keep an eye out for potential stories.

That was when he came across one of the world's foremost surveillance experts. Bruce Schneier, who told him: "When we are observed at all times we become conformist, and creativity suffers. There's a reason why surveillance states aren't the ones that flourish; it's profoundly inhumane."[7]

The author of *Data and Goliath: The Hidden Battles to Collect Your Data and Control Your World*, Schneier said most censorship regimes were

---

5 *The Bell Jar*, Sylvia Plath, Harper & Row, 1971.

6 Justice Sonia Sotomayor quoted in *Data and Goliath: The Hidden Battles to Collect Your Data and Control Your World*, Bruce Schneier, W.W. Norton & Co Inc, 2015.

7 The govt is reading what you post online, John Stapleton, *The New Daily*, 9 February, 2016.

enforced by surveillance, which in itself led to self-censorship, the so-called "chilling effect". For all those who said if you are not doing anything wrong there is nothing to be worried about, just try dancing around the house singing along to a new pop song and see how differently you behave if you know someone is watching.

Surveillance is a tactic of intimidation.

When we know everything is being recorded, we are less likely to speak freely and act individually. When we are constantly under the threat of judgement, criticism, and correction for our actions, we become fearful that—either now or in the uncertain future—data we leave behind will be brought back to implicate us, by whatever authority has then become focused upon our once-private and innocent acts. In response, we do nothing out of the ordinary. We lose our individuality, and society stagnates. We don't question or challenge power. We become obedient and submissive.

These chilling effects are especially damaging to political discourse. There is value in dissent. Ubiquitous mass surveillance is the enemy of democracy, liberty, freedom, and progress.[8]

When mass surveillance was introduced into Australia, the authorities, senior bureaucrats and the country's elected representatives, including former Prime Minister Tony Abbott, knew full well their laws would create a docile, fearful population and destroy the country's traditional anti-authoritarian character.

The mere existence of a surveillance state breeds fear and conformity and stifles free expression. There are also numerous psychological studies demonstrating that people who believe they are being watched engage in behaviour far more compliant, conformist and submissive than those who believe they are acting without monitoring. There is a reason governments, corporations, and multiple other entities of authority crave surveillance. It's precisely because the possibility of being monitored radically changes individual and collective behaviour. Specifically, that

8 *Data and Goliath: The Hidden Battles to Collect Your Data and Control Your World*, Bruce Schneier, W.W. Norton & Co, 2015.

possibility breeds fear and fosters collective conformity. That's always been intuitively clear. Now, there is mounting empirical evidence proving it.[9]

PEN America, an organisation representing the interests of writers and journalists, reported that most American writers now assumed that their communications were being monitored and significant numbers had curtailed their activities and engaged in self-censorship as a result:

> In the human rights and free expression communities, it is a widely shared assumption that the explosive growth and prolifering uses of surveillance technologies must be harmful—to intellectual freedom, to creativity, and to social discourse.
>
> Freedom of expression is under threat and, as a result, freedom of information is imperilled as well.
>
> While it may not be surprising that those who rely on free expression for their craft and livelihood feel greater unease about surveillance than most, the impact on the free flow of information should concern us all. As writers continue to restrict their research, correspondence, and writing on certain topics, the public pool of knowledge shrinks.[10]

Key to a new transnational political state and corrosion of power structures kept in place by barriers of secrecy was the internet. But anarchic freedom, like the long theorised Higgs boson, the subatomic particle or field which was said to infuse the universe and allow the formation of atoms but which scientists had found almost impossible to detect, the moment of liberation existed for the briefest of times.

Writing on the future of the internet, Julian Assange warned that the state would leech into the veins and arteries of the new societies, gobbling up every relationship expressed or communicated, every web page read, every message sent and every thought Googled, and then store this knowledge, billions of interceptions a day, undreamed-of power, in vast top secret warehouses, forever.

---

9 New Study Shows Mass Surveillance Breeds Meekness, Fear and Self-Censorship, Glenn Greenwald, *The Intercept*, 29 April, 2016.

10 Chilling Effects: NSA Surveillance drives U.S. writers to Self-Censor, PEN American Centre, November, 2013.

It would go on to mine and mine again this treasure, the collective private intellectual output of humanity, with ever more sophisticated search and pattern finding algorithms, enriching the treasure and maximizing the power imbalance between interceptors and the world of interceptees. And then the state would reflect what it had learned back into the physical world, to start wars, to target drones, to manipulate UN committees and trade deals, and to do favours for its vast connected network of industries, insiders and cronies.

The world is not sliding, but galloping into a new transnational dystopia. This development has not been properly recognised outside of national security circles. It has been hidden by secrecy, complexity and scale. The internet, our greatest tool of emancipation, has been transformed into the most dangerous facilitator of totalitarianism we have ever seen. The internet is a threat to human civilisation.

These transformations have come about silently, because those who know what is going on work in the global surveillance industry and have no incentives to speak out. Left to its own trajectory, within a few years, global civilisation will be a postmodern surveillance dystopia, from which escape for all but the most skilled individuals will be impossible.[11]

And this was before the most advanced artificial intelligences ever devised were unleashed onto the net.

Just as with the Hindu cycle of destruction and rebirth, out of the ruins of every civilisation came a new order.

It suited the Australian government to have a docile population – and part of that was the hapless state of telecommunications. The buffering symbol, a blue rotating circle, was the most common experience of the internet. Mobile phone coverage was abysmal.

In one of the scattered circuit of cafes Old Alex visited, an acquaintance told him he had phones with all three major providers, Optus, Telstra, Vodafone, and still had to walk around the house with his various devices in the hope of picking up a signal.

---

11 A Call to Cryptographic Arms, Julian Assange, from *Cyperpunk: Freedom and the Future of the Internet*, OR Books, 2012.

The man was not in an isolated location.

The idea that Australia was a wealthy First World Country was a government-peddled myth. Four million Australians had no access to the internet at all. Middle class incomes and standards of living were either static or dropping slowly, year on year. Working class morale was at all time lows, disenchantment with government at all time highs.

Nomadic for years, with every attempt to establish a home of his own ending in disaster, Old Alex found himself stabilising for a time in a large white house in the inner-city Sydney suburb of Newtown.

Twenty years before he had lived two short blocks away, and walked his children up the narrow lane at the back of the house to the Australia Street School each morning, passing by what was then a bed and breakfast run by a retired opera diva, Peter, and his partner Declan.

Back then, he never met them.

The kids had long since grown and flown, Alex had left full-time employment after decades in the salt mines of journalism, and he had been determined to roam the world in a state of constant adventure, to become the person he was always meant to be.

Things hadn't quite worked out that way, and he was back in the country of his birth.

There was only a passing sense of refuge. It was as if the tides of fortune had dumped him in the one part of Sydney he was yet to say goodbye to.

The ceiling windows in his attic room opened out to a view down to Botany Bay, where Lieutenant (later Captain) Cook made landfall in 1770, encountering the country's indigenous peoples for the first time. It was an event that lingered now in little more than a tourist information centre, a scattering of old artefacts and the residual oral records of first contact, a story which passed down the ravaged generations ever more diluted. The frightening arrival of the white ghosts in their giant canoes was only the beginning of the destruction of an ancient culture and their ancient land.

Fast forward two centuries and the white ghosts were involved in a different kind of massacre. On the world stage multiple deaths in multiple countries became the new norm, in Ankara, Brussels, Paris, Uganda, Baghdad, Orlando...

Quite how an old journalist like Alex came to be staying in a house with an aging gay man whose obsession with old musicals and old movies was rivalled only by his disinterest in world affairs was the result of one of those quixotic string of events only nomads understand. For beyond the next rise, the next death of an animal, the birth of a child, a coming storm, events and circumstance remain unpredictable. Families huddled in shelters would always be buffeted by uncontrollable events. Safety was only fleeting, at best a dodge, a sidestep on the way of calamity. No hideout lasted forever, no base was permanent.

Those things the West deemed important, the squatting singularity of a suburban house, a place in the world, a place in the hierarchy, a surrounding, terrible silence, none of it he had ever wanted. Let go of all attachment. While Peter was the ultimate materialist, and seemed to know every rich and propertied queen, as gay men had once been known, in the whole of Sydney.

Peter was an ostentatious love-a-chat with upper crust pretensions, and they were an odd "couple", as some people thought they were, the man with the big house cluttered with possessions, crystal glasses in cabinets, objects, paintings, useless things. And Alex, with his old car and generally shambolic air, his head torn apart by static.

"I don't know how you clean this place," he said to the cleaner one day as they commiserated over the clutter.

She shook her head. "I just do my best."

Peter was the most far-gone anglophile Alex had ever come across. Downton Abbey played on the television, Vaughan Williams on the stereo.

"Elegaic," Alex sniffed.

"Anglophiliac," he thought, although there were no such words.

Kindness came in many forms, and oddly enough for a time they were kind to each other.

Peter was lonely after the death of his great love Declan the previous year, and in everything that happened in those long months sadness stood at the forefront. Alex had never met Declan, but one of the university students living in the street, who had known them since he was a toddler, told him: "You would see them out walking their dog. They were always together, always happy, smiling, laughing. They would always stop and say hello, ask how I was doing, congratulate me on passing an exam, getting into university."

Declan died at home, in the same bed where Peter still slept, and afterwards Peter had refused to let the funeral parlour take the body, lying next to his dead lover sobbing for 12 hours.

That was the kind of grief that lingered, pallid in old light, a fog over drab, aging carpet.

But after a time the grief that was everywhere in that house began to dissipate.

"Take care of him," Declan's spirit ordered him one day, clear as a bell in the half morning light. "I know what he's like."

And so from that day on, rather than despairing over pretentiousness, the dullness of the aspiring middle classes, the brainless self-congratulatory bitchiness and vanity of Sydney's affluent gay world, Alex settled into a half comfortable home, and became instantly productive.

He had the run of the house, and for once was sleeping like a normal person.

"I don't know why people get up so early and go to work every day when they don't have to," Peter said one morning, dodging the gardener and the cleaner. "It's ridiculous."

"Not everybody's a trust fund baby," Alex replied.

He began to call him Lord Fauntleroy, only to discover that the deceased Declan had called him the same name.

On the question of the war that was enveloping the globe, a war that was all about God, Peter dismissed believers as fools stupid enough to invest their faith in imaginary friends.

"I refuse to listen to it anymore," Peter insisted. "The Muslims can all kill themselves for all I care. I don't want to know about it anymore. Write about something that's fun. I want to have fun."

Old Alex kept his mouth shut. In any case, it was difficult to get a word in edgeways.

It wasn't just the old opera diva turning off. Australian politicians liked to boast that they were the second largest international contributor to the war in the Middle East, but the country as a whole had become immured. Australian taxpayers were going to work to pay for the bombs being dropped on Iraq and Syria, but with very few exceptions they had no idea their country was actively involved in raining down bombs on Muslim families half a world away. Their nation was killing in secret, and as a result of a deliberately manufactured ignorance, there was no anger against the politicians who had involved them in the fiasco.

The issue was only a live one within the Muslim minority, which universally opposed Australia's involvement in America's foreign engagements. Screaming children, sobbing parents, broken hearted families, so-called "collateral damage", burnt flesh, the shattered bodies of civilians and noble warriors alike, none of it made it into the Australian consciousness.

The world grieved for those massacred in the West, photographs and potted biographies and piles of flower tributes from grieving relatives and strangers alike. They grieved not a drop for the thousands dying on the other side of the ledger, those who had been brave enough to put their lives on the line for something they believed in, those who had no way of dodging the bombs raining down upon them.

Australia had been involved in America's disastrous military campaigns through the Korean, Vietnam, Gulf and Iraq Wars and the prolonged fiasco of Afghanistan – all at considerable cost in treasure and life – while moral, political and international credibility fled out the window. Soldiers wore their physical, emotional and psychological wounds in smothered dignity; those who put the lives of their own citizens in the firing line and proceeded to lie about the reasons bore their corrosive sins in secret. But like acid eating into concrete, the scars persisted into old age, no matter how fine their houses, how high their status, how Missing In Action their consciences.

Each successive conflict came to be seen by history as a tragic mistake. The country learnt nothing. Australia's devotion to the American military industrial complex was concealed from the general public. The rich who ran it grew ever richer; while average living standards continued to drop.

In 2016, within the populace there was no sense of urgency or self-sacrifice, no feeling that the nation was at war, no national breast-beating over the killings. And equally no sense of despair at the deadly quagmire enveloping the Middle East which Australia had so actively participated in creating. Anti-war protests were a phenomenon of decades past. Objection to Australia's military involvements was contained within academic, intelligence and policy circles. Disdain for the military adventurism of politicians and Australia's abrogation of its sovereignty to American foreign policy may have been rife amongst the cognoscenti, but none of it made it to the streets.

The soporific indifference to the nation's military misadventures had been deliberately engineered. The government released almost zero information on its operations from Afghanistan to Iraq and elsewhere. Journalists making inquiries were treated as no better than the enemy.

Australians were going to work to pay taxes to kill Muslims, to make a fraught geopolitical situation on the other side of the world worse. And they simply didn't care. They didn't even know. Several times Alex raised the issue of the hundreds of bombs Australia was responsible for raining down on Iraq with members of the professional class, people who might have been expected to be fully abreast of current affairs.

They expressed surprise, doubt, bewilderment.

"I thought we were just there providing humanitarian help."

A spirit of inquiry was no longer part of the Australian psyche.

There was always a price to pay for ignorance. When it was created by governments, it became, in a very real sense, a crime against the people.

Peter kept up his busy social schedule, a lunch at a fashionable restaurant here, cocktails there, while Alex sat in the garden with the heavens burning above and his stomach churning – from driven to drained, exhausted.

"What are you doing?" he was sometimes asked.

"Practising my thousand-yard stare," he would reply.

"You don't need any practice," would come the response.

Still infected by the idea that he was a plaything of destiny, a flying leaf in a nuclear wind, the last light on a winter's day, a transmission point with the birth personality only a component part, he rekindled an old desire to understand everything, and began reading that doorstopper, *The Great War for Civilisation* by Robert Fisk. There in that Sydney backyard:

> I have a fascination for the documents that blow through the ruins of war, the pages of letters home and the bureaucracy of armies and the now useless instructions on how to fire ground-to-air missiles that flutter across the desert and cover the floors of roofless factories.

And:

> Toyota is good for jihad," my driver said. I could only agree, noting that this was one advertising logo the Toyota company would probably forgo. There was moonlight now and I could see clouds both below us in the ravines and above us, curling round mountaintops, our headlights shining on frozen water-falls and ice-covered pools.[12]

12 *The Great War for Civilisation*, Robert Fisk, Fourth Estate, 2005.

On a personal level, for Alex it had all begun with threat.

When he was fifteen-years-old and the students in his English class were asked to each write a short story as an exercise, he had chosen to write about a young man who would head into town on various adventures each weekend, based on personal experience. He would come home on Friday, change out of his school uniform and be off, returning in the early hours of Monday; and be savagely belted for his adventurous spirit.

On the occasion of the short story he was hauled before the Deputy Principal and told if he ever wrote anything like that again he would be caned.

Head constantly buried in books, his heart enthused with the creative triumphs of literature, he did not respond well to intimidation.

Even with the current projects, he heard all too clearly, and was meant to hear, the derogatory comments of what came to seem like an army of surveillance teams primed for attack, bully girls and bully boys, kindly or understanding souls pushed aside by thugs.

The harassment followed him everywhere – bedroom, bathroom, work station, the pub, the streets. He became increasingly jumpy. It was a tactic known as pressurisation.

As a journalist Old Alex had come under various sorts of public and private surveillance over the years, most of it minor. Not everyone wanted their story told. He had just shrugged it off, this was meant to be a free society. There was only one reason why he was coming under attention, because he was a journalist. The greater their levels of incompetence, the more he knew.

He was yet to hear the term Psyops, to understand that he had become a Targeted Individual. That the state was perfectly prepared to fund this type of intimidation.

If they were prepared to do this to a retired journalist of several decades standing such as himself; one could only speculate what they were doing to everybody else.

A key logger followed every keystroke. The technology now cost less than $50.

He had experienced it all before, when he was living in Bangkok, Thailand, and writing about a mafia-run strip of bars known as *The Twilight Soi*, a narrow street running off a main thoroughfare.

Write something on his computer during the day, and his words would be reflected in the bars at night.

Every key stroke followed.

Information, disinformation, it all resolved into threat. It didn't matter how thoughtful or frivolous, how accurate a documentary style or how fantastical the imagery, it all came straight back.

Mention the word "mafia" and sure enough, in the evening the touts would taunt him: "Mafia, mafia".

The Thais had always been proud of their criminal class, followed their lives with a soap-opera fascination.

The further he got into writing *The Twilight Soi*, the worse the abuse became, long before it was published.

Without their use of key logging technology, the authorities could have saved themselves an awful lot of trouble. Instead they proceeded to stir hatred against him to ridiculous levels. There were many things rotten in the Kingdom. The full detail of the story defied imagination, but now was not the time to tell it. Suffice to say he would not have believed it if it had not happened to him, those days when he could barely walk five feet without hearing the words "mai dee falung", no-good foreigner.

Like many a tourist, he had just wanted to have fun.

As he was to discover, it was amazing how miserable you could become trying to enjoy yourself. The Happiness Trap.

It became a sickly, extremely dangerous game. He had loved Bangkok. There was no other city on Earth like it – as if made for him, the City of Black-eyed Angels.

Once upon a time, in lands far far away, he had always been appreciated, if nothing else, for his writing. Now the very act through which he viewed the world became his greatest enemy.

In the years that followed, he came to regret ever writing *The Twilight Soi*. After his lovely French-colonial style house was torched, he fled Bangkok.

Later, fascinated by the complete lack of guilt Thais felt when robbing foreigners, he wrote a book about tourist safety called *Thailand: Deadly Destination*. That book, which quoted others banned in Thailand, got him barred from the kingdom, quite a feat considering the scumbags the country attracted. Thailand was a magnet for the world's criminals, a giant safe house replete with swimming pools, accomplished sex workers and easily bribed police.

There was one commonality between those circumstances and the present: the powerful or the guilty would defend themselves with any means at hand.

And so, back in Australia, he began to hear it all over again, the reaction to every version of every draft, every sentence, every paragraph.

"You haven't got any friends here, mate. You and your poofter buddies."

It was lucky he was used to working in crowded newsrooms where every sentence was immediately scrutinised, where there were many threats of a different kind.

"None of us wish any harm to come to the children."

As in, we do wish harm to you.

So said an elderly, ultra-conservative relative with whom he had reengaged.

How alarming was that?

He wished wholeheartedly informants would whisper to him, make everything clear, sit down and explain why the hell various things were happening.

The operations were designed to make the targeted individual think they were losing their grip, to erode the boundaries of personality, destroy their finances, credibility, sanity, to hunt them tirelessly from one place to another.

This was government funding. Contracts were easily renewed. There was no reason to stop. They could go on for years, forever if necessary; these invisible torturers, leaving their victims sour, bitter and sad, lashing out at they knew not what.

It was the last thing he expected, to be harassed by the authorities in his own country for something he had written.

But that's exactly what happened.

The only upside was the demonstration that words still had power.

Back in Australia the previous year, astonished by the derelict, rundown nature of the country to which he had returned, Old Alex had begun writing a book called *Workers' Paradise Lost*.

As things progressed, it became impossible to ignore the biggest story of all in the transformation of the country, and thus it was that the book morphed into *Terror in Australia: Workers' Paradise Lost*.

The destruction of the irreverent, freewheeling, freedom-loving country he once held such affection for had happened very quickly. He was no terror expert.

Much of his working life as a general news reporter was just meeting daily deadlines on a dizzying array of subjects; three to five hundred words; press the send button, go home. A job was a job and his had been to pound out the story of the day, make sure he got the names right, not get too involved, above all file on time. Some of them were interesting, some not. Of the many hundreds of pieces he had written over the decades, there were plenty he forgot he ever wrote.

The books, which began in earnest after he left newspapers, were an entirely different affair – longer, more complex, more controversial, and without the protection of multibillion dollar corporations they opened him up to a style of harassment and intimidation he had never experienced before.

For a time the previous year he came to rest, although rest was not the word, in a small apartment at the bottom of Oxford Street: an increasingly derelict entertainment precinct nearby Sydney's Central Business District.

But within days there they were, the Watchers on the Watch, from the bedroom to the bathroom. He could always hear them.

From his own experience, he was in no doubt the authorities misused their power. In contrast to old-time journalists their powers of investigation and analysis were minimal. That year the boofhead, yobbo culture of the Australian Federal Police was the subject of an inquiry and a barrage of excoriating news stories.

The circle of circumstance which led to him becoming the object of a vendetta by the authorities followed him through various parts of Thailand, Laos, Cambodia, Vietnam and finally back to Australia.

As he discovered, these people had much to hide and presented a far more dangerous liaison than the criminals themselves. In the words of one airline official he was forced to deal with: "These are very bad people."

But all that was another very wild story which he had never expected to follow him back to the country of his birth, the Great Southern Land.

The small apartment, with its views across the stately flanks of the old Mark Foy's building and the backyard of Sydney should have been a refuge; but with the level of surveillance he was enduring, it was nothing of the kind. Driven to distraction, fighting invisible enemies, the clustering, the formation, having already begun, in those final dismal weeks he slept on the floor at the end of the bed, sick of being watched, frightened of being shot.

Alex had felt under intense surveillance, could hear the constant derogatory comments. At first he couldn't understand it. He was just a reporter, a humble hack on the highways of print, as he liked to say.

What didn't make sense, at least originally, was that if they were professional sleuths why they would not keep quiet, would so regularly alert him to their presence.

But that wasn't the point of the game they were playing.

They wanted to fuck with his head; that, in this Age of Surveillance, was their profession.

At first, attributing good motive where none lay, he thought higher up the bureaucratic food chain there must be some kindness, or thoughtfulness, someone who might wish him well, who appreciated what he was trying to do; that there might be some level of accountability for the expenditure of public funds. But there was no accountability, no reason from top to bottom.

"Sometimes I think some of them support me," Alex told a friend who knew about these things.

Shaking his head his friend asked: "Stockhausen syndrome, you know what that means?"

"Yes." Of course. "You fall in love with your torturer, come to see them as the only source of sanity, humanity, kindness."

As George Orwell put it in the final paragraph of *Nineteen eighty-four*, his last and most prophetic book:

> He gazed up at the enormous face. Forty years it had taken him to learn what kind of smile was hidden beneath the dark moustache. O cruel, needless misunderstanding! O stubborn, self-willed exile from the loving beast! Two gin-scented tears trickled down the side of his nose. But it was all right, everything was all right, the struggle was finished. He had won the victory over himself. He loved Big Brother.[13]

Alex once believed that the multiple eyes were a protective factor, that it was difficult to commit murder, state-sanctioned or otherwise, when so many interested parties were watching. It may have been unwanted attention, but at least the malevolent actors cancelled each other out. Instead of watching him, they were watching each other over the top of his head. He learnt more about them than they ever did about him. He knew firsthand

---

13 *Nineteen eighty-four*, George Orwell, Martin, Secker and Warburg, 1949.

the level of their incompetence.

Mostly he just remained silent and kept on working, driven by he knew not what. The books were evolving, getting better each time around; but in a sense he did not know where they came from.

At one point during the writing of the terror book he had said out loud: "This one's from God."

An imprecise term. Some of the latest theory suggested the universe itself acted as if it was intelligent. That made sense to him.

Suicide, suicide, the purveyors of Psychological Operations whispered through the long nights. Heart attack, heart attack. In a perfect world, in their perfect world, he would do the job for them.

Now he was under no illusions.

He should have realised writing a book about terror in Australia would attract attention from Australia's banks of secret intelligence organisations, from all the wrong people; that far from being lauded as an essential part of a modern democracy, in the 21st Century journalists were viewed as enemies of the state.

Back the previous year, as he struggled to write the terror book, he had become increasingly frightened. There was a story that should be told, but he simply couldn't find a break in the fabric.

"Safest places on Earth", blared one headline. Iceland was the safest. Alex had always wanted to go there.

As had become his habit when writing a book, he would rise around midnight, consume enough caffeine to help him focus, and proceed down wherever the tunnel took him.

During the writing of *Terror in Australia*, on the way to his temporary office on William Street, he would walk quickly through increasingly empty and dangerous streets of what had once been a vibrant entertainment district, the interconnecting web of streets through Kings Cross, Darling-hurst, Oxford Street. Although a natural walker, sometimes, when he felt particularly unsafe, he would catch a taxi.

The streets had been swept clean, their surfaces glistening when wet, dark shadows in every corner, the Mordor-like sight of men pissing in corners, the increasing stench of urine in a derelict city, all of it spoke of an end of consciousness, of the dark spiritual stain that was flowing through the fabric of things, malevolent, disturbed, extremely dangerous.

His pursuers tried to please their bureaucratic overlords, or worshipped their own dark lords in secret; while he tried to pretend nothing was happening. To hide, so to speak, in the long grass.

Destiny would have it otherwise.

The war on terror to which Australia had so readily signed up had become a war on the people.

An external war promptly became an internal war.

He had never paid much attention to all the fear-mongering over Islamic terrorists ramped up by government over the previous fifteen years.

Like newspaper editors, briefed by security agencies, ever since 9/11 he had expected a mass casualty event in Sydney. But as the years rolled by and nothing happened, his attention shifted elsewhere.

A child of the Vietnam War era, he hadn't agreed with the Iraq War and the seemingly inexplicable accompaniment of America into battle; but like most Australians, it was on the periphery of his understanding. He was busy raising children and making ends meet; the war didn't affect him personally and was happening a long way away, in a part of the world where he had never been and did not understand.

There was no resurrection of the conscription which had galvanised his generation, and in any case he was no longer of an age where he could be forced to fight a war not his own, to kill people with whom he had no beef. All he knew was: In Australia the political class was the criminal class. The barbarism of the English towards their convicts reverberated still. These were the same people who now perpetrated war without conscience, killed without conscience, and then proceeded to pulverise their own culture through exploitation and the quashing of dissent in order to conceal their crimes.

Then along came Islamic State – and the country was being marched back into a discredited conflict in the Middle East which Blind Freddy could see would have been better for Australia to stay out of. The country had joined a military alliance which included some of the most oppressive regimes on the planet: Saudi Arabia and the United Arab Emirates. Even Somalia and Albania had lined up to pledge allegiance to America's bombs. It raised the obvious question of "why?".

Old munitions had to be used up. Military contracts were justified by an enemy. There had to be conflict. The death of a few thousand proles, what did it matter in the grand scheme?

Australia had entered the state of perpetual war George Orwell had warned about.

> The object of waging a war is always to be in a better position in which to wage another war. By their labour the slave populations allow the tempo of continuous warfare to be speeded up. The primary aim of modern warfare . . . is to use up the products of the machine without raising the general standard of living.

> The problem was how to keep the wheels of industry turning without increasing the real wealth of the world. Goods must be produced, but they must not be distributed. And in practice the only way of achieving this was by continuous warfare.

> The essential act of war is destruction, not necessarily of human lives, but of the products of human labour. War is a way of shattering to pieces, or pouring into the stratosphere, or sinking in the depths of the sea, materials which might otherwise be used to make the masses too comfortable, and hence, in the long run, too intelligent.[14]

The last thing the Australian overlords wanted was a more intelligent population. They might start asking questions, like: "Why are we being robbed at every turn by the Tax Office, just to support such rubbish governance?"

And thus the country was signed up to war without end.

The think tank Council for Foreign Relations estimated that in 2015 alone, the U.S. dropped at least 23,144 bombs on six Muslim countries, including Pakistan, Yemen and Somalia.

Of these, 22,110 were dropped in Iraq and Syria. This estimate was based on the fact that the United States conducted 77 percent of all airstrikes in Iraq and Syria. In all there were 28,714 U.S.-led coalition munitions dropped in 2015.[15]

How many were killed?

There were only guesses. No one truly knew.

From the get-go, Australian was a willing ally and participant.

One of the most peculiar, astonishing things Alex came across while

---

14 Ibid.

15 How many bombs did the United States drop in 2015? *Politics, Power, and Preventative Action*, Michael Zenko, 7 January, 2016.

writing *Terror in Australia* was that all the operations, strike forces and task forces of recent times, more than 20 of them, had all been named with pro-jihad tags.

He first noticed it in the pre-Anzac Day raids in Melbourne – where a group of Muslim youths were arrested after plotting to stab and behead a police officer, steal his gun and go on a shooting rampage – to keep on killing until they themselves were shot dead, until they, too, became martyrs crying Allahu Akbar, God is great.

The authorities called their action Operation Rising.

You only had to be on the net for five seconds to spot it everywhere: The Rising of Islam.

Then he looked at the naming of the post-Anzac Day raids, which were named Operation Amberd, a place in modern-day Armenia.

Armenia just happened to be the place which, exactly 100 years before, saw the massacre of 1.5 million Christians during the final stages of the Ottoman Empire, killings which easily rivalled Islamic State for brutality and blood lust. The centenary had received worldwide attention after Pope Francis named it the first genocide of the 20th Century and invited descendants to the Vatican. Turkey promptly withdrew its ambassador.

Then Alex began to look back over the years since Tony Abbott came to power in 2013.

Some of them were obscure, some of them blatant.

Task Force Jericho, after one of the largest Muslim caliphates in history.

Operation Polo. Probably after Marco Polo, one of history's most famous critics of Islam. The traveller and writer often referred to simply as Polo condemned the enslavement of women and murder of infidels.

There was also a blogger known as Polo who incensed believers by peddling a joke along the lines: "How do you tell an extremist Muslim from a moderate Muslim? The extremists behead the infidel; the moderate holds their feet." So many variations crammed the web he couldn't find the original.

One of the most blatant was Operation Coulter, after American columnist Anne Coulter, one of the world's most famous critics of Islam. It was she who coined the famous phrase, "Not all Muslims are terrorists, but all terrorists are Muslims" and "If we could only convince them to stop flying, we could dispense with airport security."

On and on it went.

When he drew the names to the attention of one of Australia's leading terror messaging experts, Professor Anne Aly, she observed: "That's no coincidence."

There was no good reason for them to have names at all.

There they were, the most senior figures in the national security and law enforcement wings of government, fronting banks of television cameras at press conferences, boasting of how they were making Australia safe while naming their operations with pro-jihad tags.

It was no wonder the Muslim population had so little respect for them.

The average Australian was not educated enough and did not have access to sufficiently high quality internet to make the connections.

But Arabic, with its cryptographic, calligraphic, symbol-laden structures, combined with the culture's intense referencing of history, respect for education and strong sense of grievance, meant the Muslims of Australia picked up the references in an instant.

And not one of the Good Muslims within the intelligence and security services bothered to inform their bosses of this most blatant of *faux pas*.

What were they going to call the next operation? Strike Force Jihad?

Might as well, couldn't get any worse.

When he queried the Australian Federal Police Media Unit about the naming of the operations and who was responsible, the answer came back that the government had nothing to do with their naming, an answer so bizarre it was instructive in itself. For if the Australian government had nothing to do with the naming of its own operations, who did?'

It displayed a staggering level of incompetence.

He offered them a way out. Knowing his every typed word was being followed, he explained exactly how the government could solve the obvious problem they had.

His thanks for proffering a solution to an obvious problem was a dramatic and intrusive increase in surveillance.

There was no helping these people.

So in order to protect himself, he used a technique he had used while writing the Thai book: he posted it all up online, hoping his multiple pursuers would become paralysed by their own surveillance, staring at each other over the top of him. They could no more get up to mischief than he could.

That was when all hell broke loose.

He couldn't move five feet without coming across someone talking into their smartphone or staring at him with hostility. The point of all this activity, he presumed, was intimidation, although they were the ones who made the mistake.

The spooks were easy to spot. Most Australians couldn't afford a new iPhone, and certainly not in that part of town.

He felt decidedly unsafe, packed up the apartment, both glad to be out of there and angry at being made homeless, relentlessly pursued; as if he had any choice in what he wrote. He could no more write a lie than fly to the moon, it just wasn't in his nature.

He flew first to Saigon aka Ho Chi Minh City and then on to a tourist island off the coast.

On the third day he found himself booking into a group of cabins overseen by an 84-year-old Frenchman, Michel Desmarquet, who was quick to inform him that he was the author of the once bestselling book *Abduction to the Ninth Planet*. The story of being abducted by aliens was entirely true, he insisted, people were blind. There was a spiritual element to everything. He had been abducted and then returned to tell the world what he saw, but people did not listen.

At one point the book had been outselling *The Celestine Prophecy*, a 1993 bestseller which postulated that human consciousness was moving from a belief that the world was governed by divine forces, through to faith in scientific inquiry, then to a hyper-focus on materialism – and, once a restlessness of soul set in at the finiteness of consumerism, ultimately to another leap into higher modes of cognition.

Michel also had a message of hope, that humanity had much to learn, that a shift in consciousness was in the offing.

"Are you making up the story about being abducted by aliens just to sell books?" television interviewers would ask him.

"Would I make up a story like this and embarrass myself?" was his response. "Why would I do that?"

Michel told the story in such a plausible and simple manner that other tourists who sometimes came to join them would ask him quietly: "Is it true, was he really abducted by aliens?"

Alex would look at them, as if to make sure they recognised their own question, and shrugged: "I don't know. He believes it."

As Michel told the story, in coordinated prayer vigils a million Catholics across America had prayed for the exorcism of his spirit.

No ordinary book of fantasy or science fiction attracted such attention.

"Makaks," Michel said dismissively.

Monkeys.

"Can you believe it? Makaks!!"

However fantastical Desmarquet's claims may or may not have been, he was convinced of them. In the 21st Century after Christ, anything came to seem possible. Where only a short time before no planets were known to be circling other star systems, by 2016 more than 3,200 planets had been confirmed. Experts were now suggesting there could be more planets than stars. Significant numbers could support life.

A population habituated by decades of science fiction seemed to find little remarkable in the death throes of the idea that humans were the peak of evolution, alone amongst all creatures the possessors of souls, central to God. Instead the chances of humans being alone, rather than inhabiting a universe teeming with life in many different forms, came to seem more and more unlikely.

> NASA's Kepler mission has verified 1,284 new planets – the single largest finding of planets to date.

> "This announcement more than doubles the number of confirmed planets from Kepler," said Ellen Stofan, chief scientist at NASA Headquarters in Washington. "This gives us hope that somewhere out there, around a star much like ours, we can eventually discover another Earth."

> In the newly-validated batch of planets, nearly 550 could be rocky planets like Earth, based on their size. Nine of these orbit in their sun's habitable zone, which is the distance from a star where orbiting planets can have surface temperatures that allow liquid water to pool.[16]

Throughout history, man had yearned for the stars.

There were now twenty-one known exoplanets circling habitable zones, places capable of harbouring life. The ultimate aim of the missions was to determine whether or not humans were alone.

Increasing numbers, including Michel, claimed to already know the

---

16 Media Release, NASA's Kepler Mission Announces Largest Collection of Planets Ever Discovered, 11 May, 2016. NASA.

answer.

Alex and Michel immediately hit it off, and each afternoon would convene to play chess. Michel was an uncanny player, a worshipper of the game, and would always allow Alex to win one out of every three times, just to encourage him, adjusting his level of play as Alex's rusty game improved.

Michel told a different story about the origins of chess to those he had previously heard.

Sensing someone who could be trusted, Old Alex quickly told him his problem, that he was struggling to finish a book because he felt his every keystroke was being followed and commented upon. In short, he felt very badly harassed, under siege, intimidated and in danger.

"Stop right there," he would so often hear coming out of the ether; and again those lower down the pay scale would be obliged to relay his dreams, his mutterings, his words. As if it all meant something, as if those re-run dreams and creative musings were a threat worth suppressing.

In his waking dreams he heard someone say, "We tried to connect him with others, but he wouldn't have a bar of them," and if everything went flashing away, if everything was caught in The Places in Between, then so be it, there would be no tomorrows, and a million tomorrows. He wasn't the same as them. It wasn't a natural or acquired gift. He had been planted for a purpose. It was neither comfort, talent nor bliss. He didn't want to be here. He wanted to go home; but had no home.

Michel Desmarquet understood instantly.

With all the grandiosity of which he was so capable the chess champion of the island rose to his full stature and said in his heavily accented English: "You are under my protection."

The impact of the Highly Improbable.

Old Alex instantly relaxed and finished the book.

Predestined, sent there by fate and fortune and the spirits, the island came to seem like the only place on Earth where he could "finish the task at hand".

It did seem as if a protective envelope cloaked the complex of wooden bungalows.

Desmarquet had one of those psychic intelligences that could barely be contained within a human skull; in the night Alex could hear the old Frenchman playing chess in his dreams. "Clack, clack, clack."

And it was nice to give the shifting shifts of the Watchers on the Watch a beachside holiday.

> In the midst of the living beings there was something that looked like burning coals of fire, like torches darting back and forth among the living beings. The fire was bright, and lightning was flashing from the fire....

> And the living beings ran to and fro like bolts of lightning....

> Now over the heads of the living beings there was something like an expanse, like the awesome gleam of crystal, spread out over their heads...[17]

In his waking dreams, the thousands of his kind who had been nominated had all been warned that being seeded into the timeline of a planet known to some of the local populations as Earth was an extremely complex operation. They might be technologically advanced, but it was a certainty not all of them would survive. And amongst those who did, some would be seeded into the wrong part of the timeline, and would just have to wait out their time.

A race of cluster intelligences, they knew their duty.

If the situation had not been so urgent, they would never have undertaken such a mission.

They were not gods, although their technology could make them appear as such to the indigenous. Mistakes would be made. As Arthur C. Clarke had put it: The only way of discovering the limits of the possible is to venture a little way past them into the impossible. Any sufficiently advanced technology is indistinguishable from magic.[18]

In those dreams his family's ship had crash-landed, nowhere near the intended point in time and not all that near to the physical target either.

Even then the atmosphere on Mars was extremely thin, and they could not survive.

His grief-stricken parents loaded him into a capsule and sent him on.

He could feel the wrench of departure even now, that terrible sense of absence.

Or perhaps his youthful obsession with science fiction writers – John

17 Ezekial Chapter 1, Verses 13, 14, 22, New American Standard Bible.

18 Hazards of Prophecy: The Failure of Imagination, *Profiles of the Future*, Arthur C Clarke, Phoenix, 2000. Originally published 1962.

Wyndham, Philip K. Dick, Ray Bradbury, Edgar Alan Poe, H.P. Lovecraft, J.G. Ballard, and in latter years Alastair Reynolds – had simply rendered him unfit for the ordinary.

The book complete after six weeks of working from midnight to 5pm, his time on the island drew to a close.

"You were abducted by aliens and I've been trapped on this planet for a hundred million years," he told the old Frenchman with a kind of homely laugh, as they settled in to play chess at the café for the last time. "We make a great pair. There aren't too many people like us."

On that, they agreed.

But it was increasingly untrue. There was now a network beginning, as new styles of consciousness lit up across the globe. The hidden were waking up everywhere. Conversations were becoming more fantastical, linkages clear.

For every birth a death, every destruction a creation, every extinguishment a rebirth. Every dark age brought its own enlightenment.

There were many divines about in that strange, compelling, confounding time.

> The truth is, the people abide my kind, but no one loves us. There is awe, but no affection. We grow used to the turned shoulder, the retreating back, the bright conversation that sputters to a murmur when we enter a room, the sigh of relief when we leave it. I have never become used to it: the awe the common men have for my kind. I suppose it is because I feel no more than a common man myself. Even less, perhaps. No more than a tool in the hand of an unseen craftsman, something to be used as needed and then cast casually aside. They do not understand that I am given only to see those matters that roil the heavens.[19]

It was only on rare occasions he met a kindred spirit.

"You have on old soul," an acquaintance had said to him in Bangkok several years before. "You meet them sometimes..."

Much, as always, was left unsaid.

For a while they had been curious friends, meeting up around Sukhumvit Soi Seven or Soi Eleven. An old Bangkok hand, his friend eventually dived back into a swirl of drunkenness, a crowded world full of too many words and too much threat, enveloped in the cleverest age in the history of

19 *The Secret Chord*, Geraldine Brooks, Hachette, 2015.

mankind by euphoria and despair and dissolute behaviour; and he would only ever hear, after that, disjointed stories of what had happened to him: "I worry about him falling off his balcony. Some of the people he mixes with."

"See you," Alex said that last time, after they had dinner in a tiny restaurant on one of the tiny alleys running off Soi 11, all new to him, familiar to his friend; that part of town where the end of every alley held the promise of something else. Was he dead now? Quite possibly. An accidental overdose. A premature heart attack. Let go of all attachment, most particularly this life, this flesh. That kind always had trouble with maintenance, jumping out of their skin. Many of his literary heroes had drunk themselves to death. He understood.

It came time to leave the island and to say goodbye to his friend, the chess-playing alien abductee. They had been good company for each other, and he missed him still.

"You will make a fortune, you will be very successful," the old man predicted in those final days. "I can see it."

Alex packed his bags for the umpteenth time in his life, caught a flight to Hanoi and went to visit an old journalist friend Tim, who he had known since 1982.

A year later Tim, facing multiple organ failure, would be hovering close to death in a Hanoi Hospital.

But then, Tim was grandiloquent in his planter's hat and largesse, was drinking too much despite a recent hospitalisation for pancreatitis where he had been warned that if he kept drinking he would surely die. Threat of death was never enough to scare a committed alcoholic. Shortly thereafter Old Tim fell down the stairs at the Foreign Correspondent's Club in Hong Kong and broke his shoulder, returning to Hanoi to convalesce. Like many Australians now wandering the globe, there was no worse fate he could think of than being forced to return to his homeland, Australia.

Old Tim had taken a shine to a motorbike tout and in that particular benevolent way of childless men asked him what he most wanted to do in life.

"Set up a bike shop," came the answer, and so it was that Alex spent evenings sitting on small plastic chairs, watching backpackers negotiating prices for reconditioned motorbikes and listening to Tim's many tales.

They were too old now to live by their youthful mottos, "We're here for a good time, not a long time" and "Live hard, die young, leave a pretty corpse."

For Old Alex the terror book was the most difficult he had ever written, but after he finished the project he felt bereft, with no idea what to do with himself. Nor could he settle. During the day he edited an excruciating book on teenage vampires, purely for the money, and spent the evenings at the bike shop.

After the island Hanoi felt like some frantic beehive filled with a million scratching crickets, all concerned with their own insect lives and caring not a jot for him as he cruised those over-trafficked streets.

It would be weeks before the language around him softened and he would begin to make sense of the city. Alex was a terrible tourist, and wasted what should have been an opportunity.

Soon enough, he spotted a sign outside a travel agent advertising trips to Sapa and comparing the mountain rice terraces to those found in Tibet. He had never heard of it but that was enough, he bought a ticket.

Sapa was a surprisingly large town nestled in the steep valleys of the north, where the passing resemblance to parts of Tibet briefly swirled an old heart. He had expected to climb off the bus into some remote location with a few trekking facilities reminiscent of an ancient hippie trail.

Instead Sapa was a well built up, established regional centre and the tourist industry itself ran like clockwork, with numerous hotels, hostels, touts, stocky determined women from the local villages dogging every turn, all surrounded by some of the most glorious landscape imaginable.

Within days of arriving in Sapa, on a steep, rutted mountain road in poor condition, he fell off a motorbike he had rented for $4 a day. Tourists and locals rushed to pull the bike off him and sit him by the side of the road. A year later he still suffered from a fractured vertebra.

Instead of exploring the magnificent Lord of the Ring-style beauties of the surrounding valleys, he hobbled around the hotel like a crippled ancient, barely able to climb the stairs, staring at the cloud-wreathed valley walls opposite and wondering what the hell he was doing there.

Everybody had their own life but him; instead he was unformed, wandering, or in his case hobbling, in an even more aimless manner than usual. He smoked the raw tobacco bongs of the locals, a Vietnamese custom from one end of the country to the other, anything to kill the pain. His head spun as nicotine flooded his system. The locals thought it a great joke to see a foreigner coughing out their lungs.

It didn't matter where he went anymore, on a plane, in a car, in remote villages, in high places or low, wherever he went he felt hunted and was desperate to be invisible. He looked out from Sapa hotel rooms across valleys, hearing the rise of unfamiliar voices and unfamiliar thoughts from the hotels, houses, restaurants and businesses below. The walks, such as they were in his crippled state, were lonely. He stepped through isolation like treacle. He had lost his place in the world.

As was his want, Old Alex stayed in Sapa long enough to watch the tourist machinery at work, the hikers and backpackers and bikers who came for a day or two or three, spending various entertaining evenings with those who came and went. Fond of someone one day, they were gone the next.

The locals went about their lives as if modern-day tourism hadn't transformed them into zoo exhibits.

There was no precognition. He didn't know, anymore, what would happen next. Vietnam was one of the safest places on Earth to hide out from an impending apocalypse; but that familiar feeling came back, wrong place wrong time.

There was the old saying: "You are where you're meant to be."

Alex felt as out of time and out of place as he had ever done.

He became increasingly irritable, disoriented, distrustful, suspicious and extremely uncommunicative.

"You would be foolish to think there was no cooperation," he said of the terror book to one inquiring intelligence officer who got inside his head, thereby betraying in an instant those who had fed him so much. There on a mountain path.

But in an era where every electronic communication could be tracked, these were all secret, invisible things which, thankfully, could never be proven. They might suspect, but no one would ever know for sure. It was only when the possible was ruled out that the impossible became plausible.

Alex returned to Hanoi. Part of him hoped that he would fall promptly on his feet, find some newspaper job, rent a glorious house by the river... and never return to the Great Southern Land.

"We all know what's waiting for us back there," an elderly Australian man working cheerfully at an upmarket restaurant by West Lake said after joining him at his table, his desire for company self-evident.

And what was waiting for both of them, if they went back, was: isolation, neighbours who couldn't care less whether you lived or died, unfriendly pubs, zero local community, a general distrust, suspicion and unease all around, an aching loneliness stuck in a room watching the dismal offerings on TV. And boredom. Ultimate boredom.

Old Alex had interviewed far too many elderly people to doubt the truth of what the man was saying. The village was lost.

It was not called The Age of Loneliness for nothing. The Western disease.

He had no love for Australia left, and still under surveillance became increasingly haunted.

He was no networker and instead did everything he could to vanish, contained within a single square block, abandoning even walks to the Temple of the Jade Mountain; just going around and around the same block, sleeping, despite his claustrophobia, in crowded dorms to avoid detection, to make himself of zero interest.

In his dreams, he knew a long and troubled history, hunted to the edge of extinction. He wasn't going to be found by anyone, no professional, military trained operatives, no-one. He didn't care how mad such thoughts made him appear, telegraphic thinking, for he knew they already knew.

"They were the military, we're here to clean up their mess," said one of the contractors on his tail.

But he dismissed them too. He didn't know who to trust. They were all on government payrolls.

"I would like to apologise on behalf of all Australians for this man," one of assholes from the Embassy said.

Call it historical memory if you will; trance-like visions, a camera-eye flying through hidden portals told him his kind had hidden in the under-growth for millions of years – and the ability to hide, passed down through thousands of lives, through combinations of DNA and drifting intelligences, had been essential for survival. All the time, across different lands, through forest floors, big Marmoset eyes high in the trees, buried behind green – even, at times, hidden in the depths of the ocean – he had been invisible.

And so instead of doing what common sense dictated, he took up semi-permanent residence in a bar.

He took a drunken dive into the ordinary, entirely lost. But destiny was a torture instrument and time passed all too quickly in such close proximity to the arrhythmic clack of pool balls. Too soon, he arrived back in Australia. Dishevelled, upset, angry at the fact that he had been so closely tailgated, he once again walked along the edges of Lake Illawarra, a once sacred lake turned by progress into a suburban pond.

Black swans, the protective spirits beloved by the indigenous, were few in number, the weather cold.

Swimming in a seaside pool, he watched a plane doing aerobatics above. It was as if he could hear them high up, the elated passenger, the excitement, and even the pilot, seasoned as he was, in a buoyant mood.

In Australia a funny thing happened on the way to the Apocalypse.

He had left with one Prime Minister, Tony Abbott, in power and returned to find another incumbent, Malcolm Turnbull.

During the course of writing *Terror in Australia: Workers' Paradise Lost* Old Alex came to regard Abbott as the most dangerous Prime Minister in the nation's history.

One of the first news stories he was commissioned to write on his return to Australia was headlined: "How Tony Abbott made Australia more dangerous."

There were certainly days when it appeared their noble leader had only one goal, to disillusion the Australian populace with the nature of Earthly government. Riding high in the polls, still riding the euphoria of his 2013 victory over what became the shambles of the left, he had seemed a formidable target.

In contrast Old Alex had been essentially defenceless, a flux of wistful persona beyond their prime.

But it all went badly wrong for Mr Abbott, and only shortly after he finished the book the Prime Minister was deposed in a palace coup. The book became an instant artefact, the record of a moment in time.

Abbott had used national security and the terror threat for his own political and religious purposes. It did not work.

The Australian population had been subjected to decades of pro-multicultural propaganda, and to now have the same government beating up fear of Muslims created a cognitive dissonance which rather than herding them towards the conservative side of politics, engendered a distrust of government, full stop.

And nothing could change their widespread dislike of Abbott the man.

The rhetoric shifted up a gear.

In the final days of his prime-ministership, in early September of 2015, almost a year to the day since Abbott had declared with strutting rooster breast his unwavering support for America's activities in the Middle East, he attracted the ire of Australia's Jewish lobby after declaring Islamic militants worse than Nazis.

In an interview with Sydney commercial radio station 2GB, one of the country's only media outlets still championing his cause, Abbott dismissed suggestions his government was trying to frighten people about Islamic State:

> It's nonsense, turn on your televisions, look at what is happening. The latest atrocity apparently was four young men being strung up and burnt alive.

> The Nazis did terrible evil but they had a sufficient sense of shame to try to hide it. These people boast about their evil, this is the extraordinary thing. They act in the way that medieval barbarians acted, only they broadcast it to the world with an effrontery which is hard to credit.[20]

At a press conference later the same day Abbott said:

> Unlike previous evildoers, whether we're talking about Stalin, Hitler or whoever that tried to cover up their evil, this wretched death cult boasts about it. Every day we see new atrocities broadcast to the world, atrocities of an unspeakable inhumanity. And that's why it's absolutely vital that the decent people of the world unite against this death cult and do everything we reasonably can, as quickly as we can to disrupt, degrade and ultimately destroy...[21]

The following day, again on 2GB, talking to his diehard supporter shock jock Ray Hadley, Abbott, after boasting about having significantly increased funding to intelligence services and changed laws to make it easier to arrest people, said:

> The death cult in the Middle East is a dreadful enemy of Australia;

---

20 Jewish backlash after Tony Abbott says Islamic State terrorists are worse than the Nazis, *Sydney Morning Herald*, 4 September, 2015.

21 Agence Francaise Presse, 3 September, 2015.

it's a dreadful enemy of all decent people. The message of the death cult is: submit or die. And we have seen routinely on our TV screens the terrible deaths that they mete out to people who are just going about their ordinary life. For instance, the public beheading of the curator of the Palmyra ruins. I mean, this was the most shocking thing. For 50 years this man had kept alive the world's cultural heritage, but because there was some impiety in this – according to the death cult – they killed him in the most barbaric way. And this is the thing about this evil, it's a boastful evil, not ashamed or embarrassed about the evil it does – it boasts and this is what gives a special quality of horror to what's happening in the Middle East right now.[22]

Abbott had been repeatedly warned by pundits and terror messaging experts that labelling Islamic State a "death cult" and celebrating their barbarity was attracting, not deterring, adherents. The latest research showed that the extreme violence was cutting through, drawing recruits to the black flag. Followers were drawn as much by the lure of violence as by a sense of religious obligation or anger over political and religious persecution and the West's treatment of Muslims worldwide. Hence the spectacular success of the beheading videos. Hence Islamic State's constantly escalating theatrics as they filmed and then disseminated ritualised killings, burning infidels in cages, dragging them to their deaths behind vehicles, shooting them in large numbers in trenches, crucifying them in village squares and along streets, tossing them off buildings and stoning them to death.

To reference the title of a book on home-grown British jihadism: "We love death as you love life."

Abbott used the term "death cult" many hundreds of times.

Death cult, death cult, death cult. Abbott used the term in press conferences which had nothing to do with national security. He even used it at 'countering violent extremism' conferences in front of some of the world's leading terror-messaging experts, all of whom condemned his style of political rhetoric.

Jacinta Carroll, a counter-terrorism expert with the Australian Strategic Policy Institute, funded by the Defence Department but at some arm's-length from government, reflected widespread views amongst policy

22 PM Transcripts: Transcripts from the Prime Ministers of Australia, Interview with Ray Hadley, 2GB, 4 September, 2015.

aficionados that the depiction of Islamic State as a "death cult" was overly-simplistic and made the terror group appear "cool".

> Describing Islamic State as all things that are evil – that has unintentionally been interpreted as applying to all Muslims.

> It has been seen as that way by some in the Australian community.

> An oversimplification and polarisation of the issue is inaccurate as well as unhelpful.

> What would be helpful is a fulsome discussion countering any notion that this is cool and explaining what is happening in the Middle East.[23]

Carroll said that in the future Australia would face terrorist attacks both in Australia and overseas affecting Australians and Australia's interests. Australians would continue to feature among the perpetrators and supporters of terrorism.

> This is why it is important to establish a more nuanced debate within the media and the community rather than over-simplistic slogans such as 'death cult'. And why it is important to develop a more comprehensive and coherent government strategy than presently exists.[24]

Why did Abbott, a staunch Jesuit-educated Catholic, not listen?

While he himself, having thrown the country headfirst into a latter-day 'crusader' war, was responsible for killing more people, through the country's engagement in the Middle East, than any other Australian Prime Minister since World War Two. That is, until his successor Malcolm Turnbull came along.

> Tony Abbott knew perfectly well when he re-entered the conflicts in Iraq and Syria that it would further radicalise Australia's Muslim minority and increase the domestic terror threat.

> The military adventure in Iraq was sold to the public as making

---

23 Former PM Abbott made Islamic State sound cool, John Stapleton, *The New Daily*, 7 June, 2016.

24 Ibid.

the nation safer. It did not.

The government's 2015 Review of Counter Terrorism Machinery declared further terrorist attacks almost inevitable.

As the authorities know, there are now numerous radical preachers teaching in Australia's mosques and Islamic prayer halls.[25]

In January of that year Australian forces flew 70 sorties over Iraq amounting to 601 hours of flying time. On 53 of those missions, bombs were dropped.

How many mujahedeen, fathers, mothers, children and the elderly were killed, the Australian public would never know.

Abbott was the man most directly responsible, and the man who had championed re-engagement.

In February there were 35 sorties involving munitions drops; in March 63, in April 43, in May 45, in June 42, in July 42, in August 39 and during Abbott's last month in office, 37.

On his final night as Prime Minister Abbott expressed great dissatisfaction that not more of the sorties were resulting in bomb drops.

That is, in the death of Muslims on the opposite side of the world.

Abbott had been briefed on Australia's air campaign and had been bemused when told only 20 per cent of our strike sorties had culminated in the release of a weapon. Most of our aircraft were returning to base without having dropped a bomb.

A combination of highly restrictive rules of engagement and poor training among the supported Iraqi ground forces contributed to this ineffective performance.

Exacerbating such constraints was a pervasive mindset of risk aversion in our Defence bureaucracy.

From their perspective, the primary objective of our military contributions to US-led Coalitions is to be seen as a reliable ally. Tangible military results are considered to be of secondary importance to military diplomacy.[26]

---

25 How Tony Abbott made Australia more dangerous, John Stapleton, *The New Daily*, 7 October, 2015.

26 Abbott's Last Supper: Let them eat Dirt, Catherine McGregor, *Daily Telegraph*, 5 April, 2016.

Abbott grasped all these facts and wanted Australia and the Coalition to escalate the fight against Islamic State.

Who was this lunatic?

Why was he so keen to involve the country in a crusader war in the Middle East? To bring down upon his adopted country the ire of Muslims worldwide? To defy many of the country's leading strategic thinkers? For what end?

Abbott spoke about God passionately at every opportunity, including in his inaugural and final speeches as Prime Minister. But what God was this?

Abbott's military adventurism was roundly criticised by senior members of the military fraternity.

In a beautifully written essay "Firing Line", former Australian Army officer James Brown, who commanded a cavalry troop in southern Iraq, served on the Australian taskforce headquarters in Baghdad and was attached to Special Forces in Afghanistan, condemned the chaotic and misguided military adventurism of Tony Abbott.

> Abbott's stewardship of the ADF presents the clearest case in recent times of a prime minister struggling to grasp the limits of Australian military power. He pushed Australia's small defence force and decision-making structures to their limit.[27]

Abbott issued the following tweet: "James Brown's claims about military adventurism by the Abbott government are just fantasy." The former Prime Minister had never served a day of his life in the military, never stood on a battlefield and watched his friends die, never come home from a deployment to an indifferent or even hostile public, never suffered post-traumatic stress syndrome.

There was national euphoria at the replacement of Abbott by Malcolm Turnbull – the population sick of being treated with contempt, spoken down to, lectured about God, told to be their best persons when so many on the government payroll clearly were not.

Abbott's endless beating of the national security drum failed to save his political skin.

Thirty consecutive results of Newspoll, the most reliable of all the polls, placed the Liberals behind Labor.

27 Election 2016: Inside Tony Abbotts chaotic and misguided military deployments, Paul Toohey, *Daily Telegraph*, 18 June, 2016.

On 14 September 2015 Turnbull resigned from the Cabinet and announced he would challenge for the leadership.

He declared:

> We need a different style of leadership.
>
> We need a style of leadership that explains those challenges and opportunities, explains the challenges and how to seize the opportunities. A style of leadership that respects the people's intelligence, that explains these complex issues and then sets out the course of action we believe we should take and makes a case for it.
>
> We need advocacy, not slogans. We need to respect the intelligence of the Australian people.[28]

The fanciful notion that the intelligence of the Australian people would be treated with respect was quickly dashed. It became, in a sense, the foundation lie.

28 We need to respect the intelligence of the Australian people, SBS, 14 September, 2016.

REAPING THE WHIRLWIND

HE BEGAN to sleep over at the Big White House. It was the same name once given, in another part of town, to the Home for the Incurables.

You arrived one terrible day. You never left.

Not so long before, Alex had spent several months at Lumbini, the birthplace of Buddha, a small, dusty and intensely atmospheric little village on the Terai, the flat plains at the base of the Himalayas.

"Let go of all attachments," the Buddha famously declared. Perhaps, having shed his properties and possessions, Alex had taken the injunction a little too seriously.

There was a different view wherever you stood.

In the Big White House and the narrow thatch of streets surrounding it he kept thinking of those Oscar Wilde lines which, having entered the language, were virtually a cliché: "We are all in the gutter, but some of us are looking at the stars."

If it had not been for his nomadic state, he would never have ended up at that house.

Old Alex didn't know why he was drawn to it, apart from the fact that he had lived with his kids, then four and five, barely 300 metres away some twenty years before. Their mother had just left and it had been a time of intense upheaval.

In The Long Goodbye that was now his relationship with Sydney, those narrow streets at the back of Newtown, constituting an enclave of sorts, were the final parts of the city to which he was yet to say a farewell.

And the final part of the city which had vestiges of the Sydney he once loved so much, the easy camaraderie, the free-wheeling nightlife, the clotted groups full of easy physicality, the ready exchange of political views, the social fluidity.

He had always dreamt of coming from a village, of being able to return, the wandering son – and once more be embraced into a community, a kind of family, full of warmth, good cheer, affection, congratulation for his achievements in the wider world.

The parts of the inner city where he became defined as a young man – Paddington, Kings Cross, Darlinghurst – were now cold, uncomfortable, grasping places, with spiralling house prices, strictly patrolled streets, shuttered nightclubs; the bohemian, Amsterdam-by-the-Pacific charms of Sydney long banished by a new Puritanism. The wowsers had won.

Individuals are most defined by those they know, their histories reflected back at them. We become, as the old Peruvian saying goes, a person amongst persons. But in an unfriendly, callous, shifting, gloating, greedy, self-centred city like Sydney such traditional paths of personality formation were barely possible.

With strangling regulation and excessive tax destroying almost all natural commercial activity, real estate was one of the only markets left. Older communities were constantly being replaced by more sliding gangs of property-obsessed, money-hungry cliques. Sydneysiders established within the first few minutes of meeting each other how much property they owned and where they lived – similar to Indians asking the names of stranger's families to establish where they stood in the caste system. If you stood outside that system you were regarded with suspicion, as being casteless.

Sydney had not always been the sterile, status-obsessed place it was to become.

Richard Neville, the face of Australian radicalism in the 1960s and 1970s, was another to die in that terrible year of 2016. Old Alex once interviewed him many years before, when he had become a prominent publisher. As Neville wrote of that lovely book *Radical Sydney*, it was a city of "defiance, crazy idealism and the trashing of cop shops… of fabulous characters, some fresh from uprisings in Europe, determined to flick away the trappings of avarice and class. Today we are sleepwalkers, compared to these egalitarian-seeking bookworms and brawlers, who sure knew how to paint the town red."[29]

29 Cover notes, *Radical Sydney*, Terry Irving, Rowan Cahill, University of New South Wales Press, 2010.

I hate to sound like an evangelist, but it's like the thing of Plato's cave. I get the feeling that we're living in this cave and we're chained and there are flickering shadows, and after a while you become the shadows.

But if somebody escapes, which they do from time to time, to come out and see the sun and the brightness and the possibilities, then their obligation is to come back and warn the other people who are there.

I think some of this is happening now; there is a deeper plot...[30]

Tributes poured in from around the world for one of Australia's wildest sons. But the ideals he once stood for were already vanquished.

The Sydney Alex grew up in had a population of two million. By 2016 it was heading towards five.

As a result of the government's sustained commitment to high immigration rates, in any given location one ethnic group was constantly being replaced by another. Each incoming wave of migrants meant that as each group became wealthier and more established they moved to more prestigious suburbs, to be replaced by others; the Sudanese replaced the Indians who replaced the Lebanese who replaced the Greeks, Koreans replaced the Chinese who replaced the Vietnamese, the Italians replaced the poor whites... all in various combinations. The South Africans, unused to a life without servants, just headed straight for the city's wealthiest enclaves.

In theory a multicultural society created a rich, vibrant, diverse, tolerant community.

In practice the country was full of resentment and discontent, more closed and intolerant than it had ever been, anti-immigrant sentiment worse than at any time in its history and the city itself increasingly divided into ethnic enclaves.

In conversation people most of all begrudged the wealthy Chinese buying up everything from millions of hectares of prime farming country to the country's most strategic ports, including Melbourne, Newcastle and the country's most northern port of Darwin.

The price of Sydney real estate skyrocketed to become some of the most expensive in the world. There was talk of a law forbidding advertising of property solely in Mandarin.

---

30 Richard Neville in his own words, ABC, 5 September, 2016.

No other country on Earth hocked its most precious assets in the way Australia did.

The wealthy political class shrugged off the resentment, claiming foreign investment was good for the country.

Historically Australia was a proud, vibrant and welcoming country, a once successful immigrant society had been destroyed by diversity and lavish mismanagement. There was always a price to pay for theory over fact. Nobody ever told those most affected that the social engineers deliberately set out to destroy the Australia of old. The descendants of those who built the country were naturally furious, perceiving, rightly or wrongly, massive welfare budgets, job shortages, paralysing public debates over the role of Islam and escalating house prices all to be a result of misguided government policy.

And nobody bothered to ask the indigenous, whose sacred lands they trampled.

The Australian government was almost universally incompetent, and mismanaged absolutely everything. It had mismanaged immigration as well.

Numbers had been at historic highs since John Howard was Prime Minister, finally departing in 2007. It suited the big end of town. They sold more houses, cars, cornflakes and white goods.

In a peculiar collusion between left and right, and a deliberately engineered public confusion of legal migration and humanitarian refugee intake, to even attempt to discuss the subject provoked cries of racism.

Debate was shut down by derision.

> One of the tactics ... is to brand anyone expressing mainstream views as a bigot.
>
> This allows the accuser to claim the high moral ground while smearing his opponent with the sins of racial, gender and sexual discrimination. In Australian politics it is no longer possible to speak truthfully about Left generated issues such as domestic violence, asylum seekers and genderless school programs without experiencing a politically correct bigotry slur...
>
> Inevitably, the people yelling "bigot" are themselves guilty...[31]

Most people just kept their mouths shut or parroted fashionable views

---

31 Slurred into Silence, Mark Latham, *Daily Telegraph*, 7 June, 2016.

they had acquired from the national broadcaster, the Australian Broadcasting Corporation.

The shutting down of healthy public debate made the devolving situation worse.

Even Bob Carr, former premier of NSW and former Foreign Minister, a staunch advocate of multiculturalism throughout his political career, declared that Australia's "third-world style" population growth was far greater than was needed or could be absorbed economically or financially, causing skyrocketing housing costs, increasing urban congestion and was risking the Australian way of life.

> Our population is growing too fast.
>
> It's the result of what I'd describe as a crude, industrial era, force-fed immigration program.
>
> And it's based on a flawed economic model – that is, we need to build up a domestic population. When in fact free trade agreements have opened up the entire world to Australia's north as a market for our products and produce.
>
> We need to rethink this.[32]

The policymakers ignored him.

The slow motion train wreck continued to unfold, freeze frame by freeze frame.

A little social dislocation, a few riots, a little strain in the body politic, a high level of social discontent… the oligarchy cared not, they had their police, their tame media outlets and the useful fools pouring out of the universities to manage discontent.

> Authorities faced with unrest generally have two options: to placate the population with symbolic concessions or fortify their control to minimise the harm it can do their interests. Elites in the West seem to view the second option—fortifying their power—as their better, perhaps only viable course of action to protect their position.[33]

---

32 Bob Carr calls for Australia to take in fewer immigrants, Brendan Trembath, ABC, 16 February, 2016.

33 *No Place to Hide: Edward Snowden, the NSA & The Surveillance State*, Glenn Greenwald, Penguin, 2015.

Alex now saw scenes in Australia which would have been impossible to imagine in his youth. Sniffer dogs patrolling trains, riot police spraying tear gas on protesters a paramilitary police force dressed in full riot gear, brutal repression of dissent, ubiquitous surveillance, flash crowds targeting dissidents, police cruising back blocks in the Outback searching for marijuana plants.

In that uncomfortable lounge room in the Big White House, where the dog Clabear had pride of place, sleeping twenty hours a day while sprawling her large, smelly overweight carcass across the sofa at the same time as guests such as himself perched on old chairs, Alex read Oscar Wilde's *De Profundis* for the first time.

The book was Oscar's last testament, a lyrically sad testament to La Condition Humaine, how we got to this place.

Oscar wrote it in prison, a long paean of wild-crossed love and terrible abnegation, betrayal of himself by himself, ostensibly addressed to his fickle lover Lord Alfred Douglas but written, very obviously, with an eye to history.

The book had been lying around the boot of Alex's old car since the previous year, when he picked it up at a community centre in Lightning Ridge, out there under giant Outback skies, another home for the incurables, jokingly called Australia's largest open-air asylum.

You arrived one terrible day. You never left.

> My tragedy has lasted far too long; its climax is over; its end is mean; and I am quite conscious of the fact that when the end does come I shall return an unwelcome visitant to a world that does not want me; a *revenant*, as the French say, and one whose face is grey with long imprisonment and crooked with pain. Horrible as are the dead when they rise from their tombs, the living who come out from tombs are more horrible still.[34]

It seemed appropriate that there in The Big White House Oscar should come to visit; that house full of ghosts where Peter continued to mourn the death of the great love of his life, Declan.

Peter prattled on about his place in the social whirl, how popular he was when word got around that he was rich, his privileged childhood with nannies and butlers, English boarding schools and summer holidays in

34 *De Profundis*, Oscar Wilde, Letter II, Originally published 1908.

aristocratic country houses. He fussed over the placement of his inherited silverware and sang along to every word of those musicals beloved by the upper strata of rich, ultra-conservative, ultra-Royalist Sydney gay men.

Old Alex remained largely silent. He never told anyone the real story.

Because, of course, there was a backstory to how he came to be there, of unwise liaisons and unwise spending, of dangerous social explorations which had led to him being pursued by mafia and corrupt police and insanely inefficient government security organisations, of having complained uselessly to Interpol about his pursuit.

He kept quiet. None of us are the sum of our histories. We are what we are on this one glorious day, and all too often the past only curdles the present.

> Of all this I am only too conscious. When one has been for eighteen terrible months in a prison cell, one sees things and people as they really are. The sight turns one to stone. Do not think that I would blame any one for my vices. My friends had as little to do with them as I had with theirs. Nature was in this matter a stepmother to all of us. I blame them for not appreciating the man they ruined. As long as my table was red with wine and roses, what did they care? My genius, my life as an artist, my work, and the quiet I needed for it, were nothing to them. I admit I lost my head. I was bewildered, incapable of judgment. I made the one fatal step. And now I sit here on a bench in a prison cell. In all tragedies there is a grotesque element. You know the grotesque element in mine. Do not think I do not blame myself. I curse myself night and day for my folly in allowing something to dominate my life. If there was an echo in these walls, it would cry "Fool" for ever . . . I feel poignant abasement of shame for my friendships.

And now, Alex slept in an attic.

The ever beguiling Lord Douglas, at least as far as Oscar was concerned, is said to have picked up *De Profundis*, this testimony of tragic love by the most celebrated writer of the day, read the first few sentences and thrown it impatiently into a corner.

What need he the love of old men?

Most of Alex's friends were either dead or had moved to the country. As Oscar once put it, there wasn't any difference.

Alex was determined to make his own village, to start anew.

The Big White House was opposite the Carlisle Hotel, on the surface of it one of the only old-fashioned pubs left in an increasingly strictured, shuttered place. There no bartender quoted Responsible Service of Alcohol legislation at any customer who dared to have more than two schooners in an afternoon.

Nor did they refuse to serve shots of tequila, bourbon or whisky, as many bars now did. And nor were people refused service if they looked slightly dishevelled or hung over in the mornings, as happened in so many of the dwindling number of bars left in Sydney, those remnants of freer times.

The Carlisle was one of the few places left in Sydney where the wowsers had not won.

On the blackboard were the words:

> Fill with mingled cream and amber,
> I will drain that glass again.
> Such hilarious visions clamber
> Through the chamber of my brain –
> Quaintest thoughts – queerest fancies
> Come to life and fade away;
> What care I how time advances?
> I am drinking ale today.

The lines were said to have been penned by master of the macabre Edgar Allan Poe while drinking in a tavern in Lowell, Massachusetts and passed on to literary scholar Thomas Mabbott by a barman. While the authenticity of the quote was disputed, it really didn't matter, it was that sort of hotel.

Poe, who struggled with alcohol all his life, died aged forty after being found lying in the gutter outside a polling booth on election day in clothes not his own, delirious, unable to move and in great distress. Theories on the mysterious death of the inventor of the mystery story suggested he was bashed by "ruffians" or was the victim of a voting fraud scheme, where strangers were abducted and forced to vote multiple times. In those days each voter was given a shot of alcohol after voting as a reward, and Poe may well have been suffering from alcoholic poisoning.[35]

That his words should grace the Carlisle more than 160 years after his death was apposite.

---

35 The Still Mysterious Death of Edgar Allan Poe, Natasha Geiling, Smithsonian Institute, 7 October, 2014.

Workers gathered from 4pm to take advantage of Happy Hour. Once they might have cared to exchange their prejudices on all manner of things: the idiocy of politicians, the bastardry of their bosses, the latest piece of bureaucratic inanity or politically correct absurdity. Now they had learned to keep their views to themselves, and talked of little but football, while the rundown poseurs at the other end of the bar sat in self-affirming clutches and exchanged their spiteful, fruitless gossip. Dogs sat on barstools. Crazies muttered.

It was in a sense the archetypal bar:

> We went there for everything we needed. We went there when thirsty, of course, and when hungry, and when dead tired. We went there when happy, to celebrate, and when sad, to sulk. We went there after weddings and funerals, for something to settle our nerves, and always for a shot of courage just before. We went there when we didn't know what we needed, hoping someone might tell us. We went there when looking for love, or sex, or trouble, or for someone who had gone missing, because sooner or later everyone turned up there. Most of all we went there when we needed to be found.
>
> Long before it legally served me, the bar saved me. It restored my faith when I was a boy, tended me as a teenager, and when I was a young man the bar embraced me. While I fear that we're drawn to what abandons us, and to what seems most likely to abandon us, in the end I believe we're defined by what embraces us. Naturally I embraced the bar right back, until one night the bar turned me away, and in that final abandonment the bar saved my life.
>
> There had always been a bar on that corner...[36]

Twenty years earlier, Alex had taken his kids up to the beer garden there each payday for the best cheap feed in the area: large meals, good price, which on a reporter's salary was exactly what he was looking for.

These days meals were an astonishing $27 each and the hotel's restaurant attracted a bourgeois clientele, while the latest raft of idiot laws meant you were no longer able to dine in the beer garden.

---

36 *The Tender Bar*, J.R. Moehringer, Hachette Books, 2006.

With Malcolm Turnbull installed as the new Prime Minister the country was soaring with optimism, and once again everything seemed possible.

He had just written a book subtitled *Workers' Paradise Lost,* and here it was, a country gripped with a wave of confidence and unabashed enthusiasm, the Australia of old.

As long time Fairfax columnist Peter Hartcher wrote in Alex's old alma mater *The Sydney Morning Herald*: "The people leapt to their feet in relief, excitement and anticipation to greet the advent of Malcolm Turnbull, prime minister. It was almost messianic. He was the most popular new prime minister of the past two decades."[37]

The Prime Minister himself famously declared: "There has never been a more exciting time to be an Australian."

An optimistic cry that was quickly turned into a joke: "There has never been a more exciting time to be Malcolm Turnbull."

The cursed weight of responsibility for hundreds of deaths through Australia's involvement in immoral wars, the mask of authority attempting to hide the most blatant of hypocrisies, came to etch themselves hard into Turnbull's once prosperous demeanour.

But for a brief moment the euphoria appeared justified.

The political rhetoric shifted from duty to opportunity.

The country was no longer groaning under the lash of Abbott's rigorous rectitude and puritanical Catholicism, the God of the Early Church, a vengeful, jealous God easily as cruel as that worshipped by Islamic State, the same God, a lash entirely inappropriate for a nation founded by convicts.

Australians were proud of themselves once again. A simple change in terminology, emphasis, personality, and the country changed with it. In a wet, cold summer, as he walked that narrow cross thatch of streets, sun drenched people raised their glasses. Strangers smiled.

It was obvious wherever people gathered: "Oh, that's what a Prime Minister is supposed to look like". The resilient cheerfulness which once defined the Australian character was back, at last.

Support for the Labor opposition fell to wipeout levels.

As Hartcher wrote:

The Turnbull rapture extended from the hard-headed president

37 Through the Looking Glass: Turnbull shrinks as Shorten grows, *Sydney Morning Herald,* 23 April, 2016.

of the Business Council of Australia, Catherine Livingstone:

"Prime Minister," she gushed at the council's annual dinner, "there is a new sense of optimism in this room, and around the country." All the way to the star struck high school student, Aboriginal teenager Matthew McDonald, who was asked to name the highlight of a day spent touring Parliament House: "The Prime Minister pouring m e a cup of tea. Where do you see that happening? I reckon that was awesome."

He had the blessing of enormous public goodwill.[38]

But in those scudding coastal skies storm clouds were already on the horizon.

Turnbull was barely in power five minutes when the next terror attack in Australia came. This time the martyr was 15-year-old Farhad Khalil Mohammad Jabar. On the 2nd of October, 2015, he shouted "Allahu Akbar!" – God is Great – as he shot dead accountant Curtis Cheng, 58, a long-time employee of the NSW Police Department, on the steps of the police state headquarters in Parramatta in Sydney's west.

The new Prime Minister urged Australians to go about their normal day, including celebration of the end of the football season, and to understand that both State and Federal Government and all the nation's agencies were working seamlessly together, with a common determined purpose, to ensure the security of the nation and its people.

We must never forget that our security, safety, indeed our democracy depends on the vigilance, professionalism, and courage of our police and security agencies, who every day are putting their lives and safety on the line to keep us safe. We should live our lives normally, especially on this Grand Final weekend. We should live our lives without fear.

This appears to have been an act of politically motivated violence so at this stage it appears to have been an act of terrorism. It is a shocking crime. It was a cold-blooded murder, targeting the NSW Police Service.

It was doubly shocking because it was perpetrated by a 15-year-

---

38 Ibid.

old boy and it underlines the importance of families, communities, leaders being very aware of whether young people are
becoming radicalised.

And so, today is Grand Final weekend. We go on, we lead our
lives, We are a strong and confident nation.[39]

Through its own rhetoric, the anti-Muslim crusade of former Prime
Minister Tony Abbott – of which Turnbull, a fellow Catholic, had been a
prominent member – and the nation's involvement in America's misadventures in Muslim lands, the government itself had done more to radicalise
the Muslim minority than any other single agent.

Four other men were subsequently arrested for their alleged involvement
in grooming someone prepared to sacrifice his own life for what he perceived
as the greater good. It was Mohammed himself who said that young men
were best suited for acts of martyrdom. It was a religious duty.

In the preceding days police, who had detected additional "chatter", were
ordered to carry a gun at all times, including at their desks.

In the hours before the attack Jabar had attended a local mosque where
he listened to a lecture by Islamist group Hizb ut-Tahrir. The Hizb, who
campaigned tirelessly for a caliphate, were banned in many parts of the
world, including Germany, Russia and Turkey and much of the Islamic
world, but not in the multicultural West, Australia, Britain or America.

> Hizb-ut-Tahrir is an ostensibly non-violent Islamic political
> movement dedicated to the recreation of a global caliphate.
> Although founded in Jordanian-ruled Jerusalem in 1953, it
> has traditionally been strongest in Europe and Central Asia.
> Today, however, it is becoming increasingly popular in the Arab
> world. Hizb-ut-Tahrir works covertly to convince Muslims to
> overthrow their present governments peacefully and establish a
> worldwide caliphate, which will then impose conservative Islam
> over all Muslim majority countries. Once this is accomplished,
> HT hopes that the caliphate will make the whole world Islamic
> through conversion in the first instance and, as a last resort,
> offensive jihads against all non-Muslim states. HT is highly
> organized . . . The group says that it will take power peacefully
> by persuading influential members of the elite to overthrow the

39 Transcript, Doorstop, Prime Minister of Australia Malcolm Turnbull, 3 October, 2016.

government. The organization is illegal in all Arab countries except for Lebanon, Yemen and the UAE where it is tolerated.[40]

Britain's attempts to ban the group all failed.

In recent times the Hizb had held major conferences across America celebrating the coming of the caliphate, including in Washington. In Australia they were referred to as radical or extremist in the mainstream press, but the Grand Mufti Dr Ibrahim Abu Mohamed had appeared in support of them on community television.

"My brother is my brother."

> There's a simple reason governments of all stripes are alarmed by Hizb ut-Tahrir. The radical Islamic transnational political party stridently advocates their overthrow.

> In the place of corrupt Muslim regimes and decadent capitalist governments will rise the caliphate, named for the alliance of states forged after the death of the prophet Mohammed and revered as the purest manifestation of an Islamic state.

The Hizb had been linked directly or indirectly with every terrorist attack in Australia, including teenager Numan Haider outside a police station in Melbourne, and Man Haron Monis in the Lindt Cafe siege in Martin Place, Sydney. No one should ever underestimate how sincere, clever and dangerous Hizb ut-Tahrir are; but for years Australian security forces dismissed the Hizb and other Islamist allied groups as not presenting a threat, dismissing their aims of world domination as being as far-fetched as the Christian notion of the Second Coming of Christ.

Despite repeated political attacks, sensationalist coverage from the tabloid press and not very covert surveillance, in 2016 the Hizb remained extremely active, fulfilling what they believed was their God given role as proselytisers of the faith. They just tended not to use the moniker Hizb ut-Tahrir.

Old Alex first encountered the Hizb as a news reporter back at the turn of the millennium. It had been a Sunday, a slow news day, and somewhat typically the chief of staff, David King, was desperate for a story, any story. Back then, before they came under intense surveillance and media criticism, the Hizb never hid anything. They had put out a press release announcing one of their town hall meetings, and Alex was dispatched to cover the event.

40 Hizb ut-Tahrir's Growing Influence in the Arab World, Terrorism Monitor, Volume 4, Issue, 24.

He never forgot those words, delivered in a powerful mix of English and Arabic: "Ask yourself my brothers, why, why, has Allah been so cruel as to cast you amongst the unbelievers."

It was an epiphany of sorts.

> I first encountered the Hizb in 2002, while working as a news reporter for *The Australian*. I was only vaguely hopeful that we might get a story out of a town hall meeting held by the then obscure group.

> I got more than a story, I got an instant sense of dislocation, that the Australia I knew was not it at all. That all the cosy stories about refugees and new immigrants settling into a welcoming multicultural country were leading straight to hell.

> With pad in hand I sat in that Hizb meeting listening to attacks on Jews, Hindus, Buddhists, Christians, capitalists, communists, socialists, homosexuals and those who dressed immodestly on Australia's beaches.

> That included just about everybody I knew.[41]

Apart from the fact it was their religious duty to overthrow the government, by Australian standards the Hizb lived highly moral lives. They did not smoke, drink or take drugs, they did not steal from their neighbours or sleep around and took good care of their children. They valued higher education, spoke better English than most Anglo-Saxon Australians, and celebrated the academic and intellectual accomplishments of their women.

Fourteen years before he had written:

> In a mixture of English and Arabic, the attentive audience was warned of the dangers of integration and multiculturalism, and Western plots to erode the purity of their belief. They were told to see themselves above all as Muslims and to "dispute the borders we find ourselves living in, and dispute the borders we find ourselves born in". They were told that capitalist countries gain through the oppression of Muslims.

> "Capitalism is a system with no humility, no humanity, no

41 How Tony Abbott Made Australia more dangerous, John Stapleton, *The New Daily*, 7 October, 2015.

compassion," said one speaker. "Comprehensive peace is mere illusion. Brothers and sisters in Islam, there are two different civilisations, two different ideologies ... which will inevitably clash.

This is the final type of conflict we have seen over and over again in history, a military struggle with Islam. Crusades continue until today. The truth will prevail over all other ideologies."

Another speaker said: "We are Muslims first and we live in Australia We must teach our children to live so that when the state is re-established, their loyalty is to the Islamic state."[42]

Way back then, in 2002, even in the previous ten days the group had been making headlines around the world.

Fourteen years on and the group was still making headlines, in Bangladesh, Pakistan, Uzbekistan, Turkey, Britain and America.

In just one example, the group was linked to the killing of twenty people at the upmarket Homey Artisan Bakery in Bangladesh's capital Dakha, including nine Italians and seven Japanese, mostly aid workers. Alex had spent quite some time in Bangladesh during the 1970s, and to this day remembered it fondly for its dense, chaotic crowds and the friendliness of the people. The massacre was notable for its extreme violence and the torture of those killed.

The Hizb were banned in Bangladesh after repeated incitements to regime change and their association with Islamic State became clear. They were a source of inspiration for jihadist attacks across the country, including against bloggers, gay activists and university professors. Detectives described the Hizb as the lead platform for banned militant groups which hoped to establish Islamic rule in Bangladesh.

They were singled out for mention because of their technological expertise and reported links to high-ups in the administration, law enforcement and intelligence agencies, courts, mosques and madrasas.

The group has traditionally claimed to be non-violent and distanced itself from violent Islamist outfits, but has espoused a programme of regime change that is impossible to imagine without violence on a large scale.

---

42 Ibid.

The group was banned on October 22, 2009 but remains active, silently picketing in front of mosques and maintaining a well-managed online presence. [43]

Back in the 1970s foreigners were extremely rare outside the diplomatic enclaves.

If Alex stopped in the street, for instance, to buy something from one of the stalls, he would be surrounded by a crowd growing rapidly into the hundreds.

They would all stare at him silently, moon-eyed, as if he was from Mars.

Finally, someone in the crowd would build up courage, step forward, and ask: "Excuse me sir, do you speak English?" When he replied "Yes", the crowd would relax into smiles.

The second question was almost invariably: "Excuse me sir, what is the name of your father?"

For in that society it was impossible to place someone without knowing who their family was.

Forty years on, foreigners were targets, not honoured guests.

Those killed at the Holey Artisan Bakery failed a religious test: they could not recite verses from the Koran. The infidels were hacked to death with machetes, their blood pooling across the floor. Islamic State released pictures of the cafe interior. The attackers shouted: "Allahu Akbar", God is Great.

ISIS, which claimed responsibility for the attack, issued a statement that nationals from crusader countries were not safe "as long as their aircraft are killing Muslims".

All too much of the world was becoming a no-go zone.

In the Great Southern Land Hizb ut-Tahrir continued to maintain a significant presence.

Former Prime Minister Tony Abbott labelled the group "un-Australian", whatever that meant, and expressed his frustration at being unable to ban them:

> This is an organisation which is very careful to avoid advocating terrorism, but is always making excuses for terrorist organisations and I regard it as un-Australian frankly to stand up there and make excuses for terrorism, to defend terrorism, to blame everyone but the terrorists for their actions.

43 Did Hizb ut-Tahrir enjoy impunity? Dhaka Tribune, 12 June, 2016.

Hizb ut-Tahrir is an organisation with an ideology which justi-fies terrorism and that's why I say it's un-Australian.

It's also un-Islamic, because no respectable Muslim should have these views.[44]

An idiot wind was blowing across the nation. It suited them both.

The Hizb were master propagandists and hit straight back:

Their spokesman Wassim Doureihei, asked by the national broadcaster to condemn the beheadings and brutality of Islamic State, replied:

Why don't you condemn what the Australian Government is doing? Why don't you condemn what the American Govern-ment is doing?

Why don't you condemn the innocent killing of a million lives in Iraq and Afghanistan? Why don't you do that?[45]

The unfortunate thing was, the man had a point.

The Australian public did not know it, because they did not know what their government was doing. The government was involved in what for all intents and purposes might as well have been a secret war. There was no debate, no questioning, none of the street and community protests of the past. One of the consequences of universal surveillance was that demonstra-tions became difficult to organise, people increasingly frightened to speak out. In the end, was it worth losing your livelihood, your kids, your place in the world for a cause which, apart from adding a single voice of protest, you could do nothing about? Instead they snuggled down on the couch and watched "Who Wants to be a Millionaire?". The populace was being driven blindly off a cliff, and no one raised a voice.

As the news site *The New Daily* put it:

If our readers are anything to go by, escapism was the order of the day in 2015.

Who could blame you? With the headlines dominated by terror in Europe and chaos in the Middle East, it's tempting to look the other way.

44 Abbott says Hizb ut-Tahrir is un-Australian and un-Islamic, News, 9 October, 2014.
45 Ibid.

Which could be why our best-read story for 2015 centred around the launch of streaming giant Netflix into Australia, and how much people were resenting the lack of choice in comparison to the US version.[46]

Uthman Badar, a spokesman for the Hizb in Australia, set out the arguments against his group in an opinion piece for *The Guardian*: "Hizb ut-Tahrir nurtures extremism, justifies terrorism and inspires young people to join Isis. Hizb ut-Tahrir is banned in many countries and Australia should follow suit. Hizb ut-Tahrir spreads 'discord and division' with impunity."[47]

These were the claims; seeking to answer them, he argued that no Hizb ut-Tahrir member had ever been prosecuted or convicted for a terrorism-related offence. That was true only in the Australian context.

Hizb ut-Tahrir had operated in Australia for over two decades, legally, without, Badar claimed, contravening a single law. He said that since the Howard era, which ended in 2007 and covered the post 9/11 period when the country went into overdrive passing anti-terror legislation and participating in America's War on Terror, Hizb ut-Tahrir had been investigated by Australia's intelligence and security agencies on multiple occasions. Badar claimed that every investigation produced nothing untoward, or prosecutable.

One of the ironies of a liberal democracy was that you could advocate for its overthrow as much as you liked. That Sharia Law, which the Hizb wished to introduce to Australia, would allow no such apostate divergence of opinion was just another contradiction betwixt and between, on a storm-chopped, twisting sea.

The Hizb's positions on most social issues, including their view that Muslim children should not sing the national anthem in schools, made for easy tabloid headlines. Their ceaseless advocacy for the overthrow of the Australian government and the introduction of a caliphate made for deliberate unease.

Academics acted as their apologists, while the authorities inevitably ruled in their favour.

---

46 *The New Daily* presents our Top Stories for 2015, The New Daily, 31 December, 2015.

47 Hizb ut-Tahrir: is it now an offence to oppose government policy? If so, let it be said plainly, Uthman Badar, *The Guardian*, 23 February, 2015.

In 2005 the Hizb were linked to Britain's first Islamic suicide bombings in London in which 52 were killed and 700 injured. The British Home Office and Pakistan's intelligence agencies investigated the group's links to Shehzad Tanweer, 22, one of the four suicide bombers who targeted the city's public transport system.

Just as it would do a decade later in an Australian context, the Hizb denied any links or connections of individuals to the group or its ideology.

In the wake of the London bombings, then UK Prime Minister Tony Blair was forced to abandon attempts to ban the Hizb on advice from police, intelligence officials and civil libertarians that the group was non-violent – the claim which, as the de facto intellectual wing of the jihad movement, they made for themselves.

The surface claim of non-violence was a twist of logic.

The Hizb advocated the overthrow of the Australian government in favour of an Islamic caliphate and would never stop until their goal was achieved. If this could be done through mass conversions of the populace and without violence, all the better.

Blair's successor David Cameron, demanding to know why the group had not been banned, found himself in the same quandary as Australian politicians, unable to ban the group.

It was all too late.

The oft-made claim by academics that banning the Hizb would simply drive them underground and make radical Islamists more difficult to track was by 2016 all too true; but there were twists even in that truth. The Hizb were highly educated and far more proficient with the rapidly evolving surveillance and counter-surveillance technologies now preoccupying so much spycraft than the average Australian citizen. They might be operating legally, hiding in plain sight, but like icebergs, much could not be seen.

The impact of the intense and pervasive surveillance of entire Muslim communities in America was well documented, and was coming to be increasingly felt in Australia.

The Hizb were one group which did not respond well to government bullying or media harassment. What those haranguing them for failing to adhere to secular ideals did not understand was the Hizb had Allah on their side. Nothing could stop them. Attempt to corral them as much as you liked, they would not be governed. Not here on Earth, not by the infidels.

As far as they were concerned, God Willing, their critics would soon be humbled, swept aside or destroyed as the caliphate and Sharia law were introduced. Allah the All Powerful, All Merciful Lord of All the Worlds, would save the souls of the infidels, or destroy them, as he saw fit.

Another irony in the infernal sea that was now Australian society was that the Hizb were ably assisted by Australia's immigration policies and the plethora of taxpayer-funded refugee councils and government programs aimed at assisting migrants.

In a sense it was all about context.

In the wake of the London bombings and in response to the controversy surrounding the group, in 2005 then Attorney General Phillip Ruddock told the House of Representatives:

> I asked ASIO for advice on whether there were currently grounds in Australia for listing the organisation Hizb ut-Tahrir. ASIO has advised me that at present there is no basis under current legislation for specifying Hizb ut-Tahrir as a terrorist organisation under the Criminal Code. As I understand it, Hizb ut-Tahrir members overseas have called for attacks in the Middle East and Central Asia, but here in Australia it is not known to have—and I use these words deliberately—planned, assisted in or fostered any violent acts, which are the current legislative tests under the Criminal Code for proscription. At this stage the government is not aware of any information that Hizb ut-Tahrir is connected to the London bombings, as has been suggested elsewhere. [48]

Two years later the Labor Premier of NSW Morris Iemma, a first generation Italian and a staunch advocate of multiculturalism whose seat encompassed the Muslim heartland of Lakemba, came out strongly disagreeing with ASIO's assessment.

> This is an organisation that is basically saying that it wants to declare war on Australia, our values and our people.

> That's the big difference and that's why I believe that they are just beyond the pale. Enough is enough, and it's time for the

---

48 Questions Without Notice, Infrastructure Security, Hansard, 11 August, 2005.

Commonwealth to review this organisation's status and take the lead from other countries and ban them.[49]

Western Australia's Attorney General Jim McGinty backed Iemma's call, saying the Hizb were "threatening the very fabric of our community".

The Federal government claimed that the states had the power to ban the group if they so wished. The states said they had gifted their power to ban terrorist groups to the Commonwealth years before.

There the impasse lay.

A place that should have been safe was not safe. Australia, far from being a remote and beautiful hideout from the Apocalypse, was directly in its path.

The Great Southern land was yet to experience its first mass casualty event, but the ground had been well prepared. The drumbeat grew stronger throughout 2016, and a string of news stories conditioned the population to accept just such an attack.

Liberal politicians were notorious for being captives of their bureaucracies.

John Howard knew perfectly well that the Hizb had been banned in many parts of the world, had openly advocated his overthrow and scornfully condemned him and the democratic government he represented at their public meetings in taxpayer-funded town halls.

Prime Minister Howard and Attorney General Phillip Ruddock, echoing their bureaucrats, had both refused to ban the group.

Howard declared:

> There is often a thin line between stupid extravagant language and language which is deliberately designed to incite violence ... or to threaten the security of the country. People can say a lot of ridiculous things and they should be able to say ridiculous things in a democracy without that language constituting violence and extreme incitement to violence.[50]

The only trouble was, the Hizb were not secular. They meant every word they said.

They were not Christians; they were not the People of the Book.

They did not talk about the Second Coming of Christ as if it was some

---

49 Leaders disagree on Muslim ban, Tom Allard, *Sydney Morning Herald*, 29 Jaunary, 2007.

50 Governments row over Muslim group, *Sydney Morning Herald*, 29 January, 2007.

far-off, impossible ancient legend whose literal meaning needed to be interpreted for a modern world. They did not believe the prophecies of a coming Apocalypse were akin to science fiction.

But Australia's secular enlightenment brooked no reality checks.

Indonesian cleric and head of the Hizb in Indonesia, Dr Ismail Yusanto, had no trouble gaining a visa to Australia. He was a regular visitor to the Australian Embassy in Jakarta.

He called on his followers in a gathering at Lakemba to denounce capitalism – and on all military-aged Muslims living outside Sharia states, such as those in Australia, to gain training and join the jihad.

> Once the program is ready it must be implemented as soon as possible. Once successful, the new order would be just the beginning of the new era in the application of Islamic ideology. There is no victory and glory without sacrifice and hard work. No pain no gain.[51]

Those intelligence officers who may have raised alarm bells over the group failed to cut through the prevailing managerial creed of multiculturalism. No individual could be heard through so many overlapping layers of bureaucracy and benighted managers on their own path to secular paradise – a ravishing they had first discovered in the university lecture halls of the 1970s and 80s.

If a single politician listened, such as conservative icon John Howard, it was inevitably for political purpose. A close alliance with America's military synced conveniently with the interests of the ultra-right and Australia's wealthiest individuals and their political friends, while a frightened population constituted a compliant electorate clinging to the certainty of incumbency.

Beginning in 2014 the Australian government ramped up its rhetoric against the group, to no avail. They could not ban them. They could not control them.

> Telling the Muslims of Australia what to think got Abbott precisely nowhere. The Hizb are not some outlying group. They are regularly asked onto campuses by Muslim Student Associations, their meetings are well publicised, and they have the support of the Grand Mufti of Australia.

---

51 Muslim group won't be banned, *Religion News Blog*, 28 January, 2007.

> There needs to be a radical rethink. Many believe it is already too late. Maintained in Islamic schools, in Islamic communities and Islamic prayer halls, the sense of grievance is growing.
>
> The government's mishandling of relations with the Muslim community is only part of the story. The killing of Muslims by Australian bombs is directly inflaming the situation. [52]

For propaganda purposes the ever visible, ever proselytising Hizb made for an easy, convenient media target.

Meanwhile the useful fools would go to their graves convinced they had spent their careers working for the common good.

There was a thrashing, prowling sense of dis-ease and distrust on all sides – a gathering sense of calamity over which no individual had control. It was easier to bury a head in a pillow, pull the doona tighter, narrow one's concerns to a familiar route.

On one assignment Alex covered a Confident Muslim conference, aimed specifically at youth. There were elements, in a sense, of an old-fashioned church group, of taking care of the the next generation.

Outside, during the breaks, there were queues lining up for food, easy conversations, comfortable greetings. People were friendly, ordinary in their dress, their concerns.

These were the terrorists over which the government had cooked up so much alarm? They were no more threatening than the local Presbyterians.

But there the similarities ended.

A former Guantanamo Bay detainee told the conference they were being targeted in an unprecedented way and Australian anti-terrorist laws were even more draconian than those in Britain.

Delivering a videotaped address from London, Moazzam Begg, who was held at Guantanamo from 2002 to 2005 but later awarded compensation by the British government for his imprisonment, said his most powerful memory of the infamous Bay was at sunset, when the American soldiers were obliged to salute their national flag at the same time as the Muslims prayed.

> "Both were saluting the objects of their devotion," he said. "One salutes a flag, the other salutes the creator of the universe."

---

52 How Tony Abbott made Australia more Dangerous, John Stapleton, *The New Daily*, 7 October, 2015

Mr Begg, who was also jailed in 2014 in the UK on charges of training terrorists and providing terrorist funding following a trip to Syria only to have the charges dropped, then asked which was the most sincere of the two groups.

To paraphrase him: Is it the soldiers who were honour bound to defend freedom while imprisoning people without trial, or those who stood firm in the face of great difficulties?

"We know they want to extinguish the light of Allah. These governments are targeting our belief system."[53]

Student associations involved included those from the universities of Sydney, Macquarie, Western Sydney and the University of Technology Sydney. A federally-funded Migrant Resource Centre also made presentations.

Meanwhile the combination of hysteria over Islamophobia and the omnipresent threat of violence meant that it had become impossible to organise a conference or even a debate on political Islam on an Australian campus. The endowment of Islamic chairs of study by oil-rich Gulf States and the building of mosques with Saudi money further inhibited debate.

The most visually and emotionally dramatic moment of the conference came with the re-enactment of a terror raid, accompanied by news footage of police operations.

Lights flashed and sirens screamed as a line of actors dressed in black uniforms blazoned with authentic-looking police insignia, stormed the stage, manhandling a young boy and throwing his middle-aged mother to the floor. The treatment of women during terror raids has been an incendiary issue within the Muslim community.

The scene closed with the woman standing in full burqa on stage.

"I heard the police sirens coming down the street. There was a silence and my heart stopped as I heard the crash at the front door. There were so many of them," she said.

53 You are being targeted, former terror suspects, John Stapleton, *The New Daily*, 7 February, 2016.

"My son is now in solitary confinement, despite being young and with no criminal record. For the Muslims in the Goulburn Supermax there is only the presumption of guilt. No one deserves to be treated in such a way. We must stand up and speak against repressive laws targeting Muslims. We will not accept being made to feel inferior."[54]

Hizb spokesman Wassim Doureihi closed the conference saying he refused to accept the narrative of moderate and extreme Muslims: "Our history is a history of the best of mankind, sent to us from Allah."

He would hear that phrase, or variations of it, all too often in the coming months: "We are the best of men. We are the best of mankind."

It was a claim that justified everything, a duty to purify the Earth and rid it of that malignant spawn, the unbeliever, of sinners such as himself.

Men sat on one side of the hall, women on the other, a Muslim convention which looked odd to Western eyes and which had been the subject of complaints by a female reporter from *The Daily Telegraph*, who determined it was discriminatory.

For Muslims steeped in their own culture it did not appear odd at all. If you asked the women what they thought of being separated from the men, which as an old reporter Alex had done on a number of occasions, they all said they liked it. They thought it was respectful.

The issue of the segregation of men and women became a subject of considerable media commentary, particularly after young News Limited reporter Alison Bevege took the issue to the NSW Civil and Administrative Tribunal.

She began with an opinion piece, notable for its bluntness, in which she wrote:

> For more than a decade governments have replaced the word "Islamist" with "terrorist" to avoid offending the religious or fuelling bigotry against innocent Muslims. It is contemptuous of the public to suggest they aren't smart enough to be told the truth with accurate words – or to guess it without. As a secular state it would not even be our business except the Islamists are here, colonising us.

---

54 Ibid.

Islamists want holy men to dictate what you can eat, what you can wear, and when you will be lashed or stoned to death.

They want any criticism of their political and religious ideology outlawed.

And they are winning.[55]

Bevege concluded with a cry to ban Islamic fascism in Australia, a cry that was never going to be heard.

But it was the issue of gender segregation that most exercised her.

After being told to sit at the back of the room with the women or leave she wrote: "Like Mississippi blacks in the 1950s sent to the back of the bus for the colour of their skin, I was segregated due to my gender."

One of the ironies of Australian multiculturalism was that whenever ethnic groups did adopt elements of their own culture which conflicted with contrary secular creeds such as feminism, including separating men and women in prayer halls, all hell breaks loose.

An appeal to the Administrative Tribunal is a labour intensive and arduous process, but after eighteen months of persistence Bevege won her case.

The Tribunal ruled the organisers broke the law. The Hizb were ordered to make sure everyone in their organisation understood gender segregation was not compulsory and ordered them to put up signs at their venues and in all published promotional material to make this clear. A story in which Bevege celebrated her victory was headlined: "I took on Hizb ut-Tahrir. And I won."

Surely one of the most idiotic headlines ever written.

The Hizb had no intention of complying, would not comply, and there would be no consequence.

As Old Alex sat in the hall that day, he knew there were a couple of government officers in the crowd, although they were not obvious.

One of the women said to the other: "He has no business being here."

He had every right to be there.

This was a democracy, he was a reporter, and he had a moral and professional obligation to observe what was happening in his own country, whether they liked it or not.

---

55 Islamic fascists unveil their hate, Alison Bevege, *The Daily Telegraph*, 14 October, 2014.

After several hours the sign on the lectern making it clear the hall came courtesy of the local council aka the taxpayer was covered up, perhaps because of the presence of a reporter.

There was no need for such sensitivities.

The Hizb were perfectly legal, and would remain so.

Australia's most famous terrorist act to date, the Martin Place siege, was also linked to the Hizb. Perpetrator Man Haron Monis attended numerous Hizb ut-Tahrir rallies and was reported to have strong links with the group's hierarchy, including its leader Australian leader Ismail al-Wahwah. The two were snapped together at a rally in front of the Egyptian consulate in Surry Hills.

> "He spent two hours talking to (Hizb ut-Tahrir) people at the rally," said a source who attended the demonstration.

> "As if they knew each other really well."

> Hizb ut-Tahrir is a hard line Islamic political party that calls for a caliphate run on Sharia law.

> Their flag – the shahada written in white on a black background – is the same one used by Monis.[56]

Whatever you wanted to say, a mantling cloak of ignorance, those who had eyes but could not see, a conniving circumstance had already led to tragedy in the Martin Place siege. The perpetrator Man Haron Monis, out on bail, had been under the nose of the authorities since he arrived in Australia in 1996 and could hardly have done more to bring attention to himself, including sending offensive letters to the grieving families of soldiers killed in Afghanistan. Those families were told by the authorities that it was all bold talk, and Monis presented no actual danger. In the months that would follow, numerous stories of police mismanagement in the handling of the Lindt Café siege emerged.

The truth would always out, this time through the arduous and lengthy process of a coronial inquest. Even to an Australian public inured to tales of government incompetence, however, the spate of revelations of flaws in the police handling of the siege, including critical communications failures

---

56 Martin Place terrorist Man Haron Monis's links with extremist group Hizb ut-Tahrir revealed, *Daily Telegraph*, 1 February, 2015.

between officers, broken equipment and a damaged negotiation truck, were remarkable.

Cafe manager Tori Johnson was the first to die in the siege. Even though police could see he was being forced to kneel and snipers had a clear line of shot to take out the assassin Man Haron Monis, news of developments failed to reach commanders.

At one point during the inquest the forward commander, whose name had been suppressed, a common tactic in the Australian judicial system, described the operation as a "high stakes game" and refused to apologise to the families of the deceased for his choice of words.

Rosie Connellan, mother of Tori Johnson, stormed out of the inquest shouting: "You're an absolute disgrace."[57]

Thomas Zinn, Tori's partner, said:

> How sad for our country that our law enforcement is betraying their own system under oath in the court of law and nobody seems to be able to do anything about it. They are trying to cover up as much as they can. The loss of memory, unawareness and confusion among them is mind-boggling: one would not think they could work for the police or carry guns if this was a true reflection of their state of mind. Everybody in the court-room knows that some of the police's evidence is orchestrated and the witnesses previously admitted that they aligned their accounts prior to the hearings.[58]

The whole thing smelled of a botched security operation; but if the Martin Place siege did turn out to be a stuff-up by security agencies such as the Australian Security Intelligence Organisation, publication of such detail under a new raft of laws would be illegal. The public's right to know had been trashed in the name of freedom.

The same inquest which exposed multiple layers of incompetence by the police would never reveal the same about ASIO:

> A directions hearing in Sydney . . . heard the role that Austra-lia's spy agency ASIO played during the siege may never be publicly known.

---

57 Lindt Cafe siege: Tori Johnson's mother labels police commander 'absolute disgrace', Patrick Begley, *The Sydney Morning Herald*, 19 July, 2016.

58 Tori's partner speaks out: Siege chiefs' cover-up betraying their own system, Sam Buck-ingham-Jones, *The Australian*, 29 July, 2016.

ASIO officers gave evidence about what contact they had with gunman Man Haron Monis prior to the siege in lengthy closed court hearings last year.

The agency also tendered documents and evidence explaining what, if any, surveillance the former Iranian refugee had been under.

Counsel assisting the inquest Jeremy Gormly SC told the hearing it was important that the ASIO segment of the inquest be conducted outside "the public eye". Mr Gormly told the inquest it was his expectation that the coroner would deliver a restricted report of his findings and recommendations relating to ASIO.[59]

Those restricted findings would only be made available to federal Attorney-General George Brandis, the Inspector-General of Intelligence and Security, Margaret Stone, and ASIO.

The new Prime Minister played to the gallery as a progressive, but did nothing to fix the body of oppressive legislation his party had passed since coming to government only three years before, including restrictions on the reporting of what critics labelled a parallel secret police force and a direct threat to democracy, the Australian Security Intelligence Organisation, ASIO.

Certainly it was not under dispute that Monis, who frequently complained about being under surveillance and the stresses it was causing him, had been on an ASIO watch list, and later dropped off. NSW Police were reportedly surprised to discover agency officers in attendance at some sessions of the inquest.

A national security hotline received 18 warnings about gunman Man Haron Monis in the days before the deadly Sydney siege, an inquest has heard.

The Australian Security Intelligence Organisation and the NSW Police decided he was not a threat.[60]

---

59 Sydney siege inquest: ASIO's role may never be publicly revealed, ABC, Jessica Kidd, 8 September, 2016.

60 ASIO received warnings on Monis days before Sydney siege, inquest told, Patrick Begley, *The Sydney Morning Herald*, 18 November, 2015.

Hizb leader al-Wahwah, with whom Monis was so well associated, was not just a religious leader but an outspoken critic of the democracy that allowed him to speak so freely. Two months before the Martin Place siege he told a rally:

> They send their troops to Iraq to bomb Iraq to spread democracy. We will send our troops to Australia, to France to Germany. We believe the world deserves another world order. We are ready to sacrifice everything for our concept.[61]

A shift in the debate over Islamic State took place. As a number of commentators were now observing, for many years the failure by the West to understand the religious nature of Islamic State led to massive loss of life, treasure and moral standing, all of it done in society-wide blind spots, the public ignorance engineered by government.

The West had roped itself further and further into a trap which, ironically, Islamic State and its ideological, theological and administrative predecessor al-Qaeda had explicated in full.

One of the peculiarities of the morass in which the West became entangled was that their enemy had broadcast their intentions in multiple arenas.

Precursor and later both ally and competitor to Islamic State, al-Qaeda laid out the seven stages of their plan in 2005. By 2016 the world was entering the sixth stage. Al-Qaeda military commander Saif al-Adel explained the phases to ultimate victory to Jordanian journalist Fouad Hussein as follows:

1. The Awakening. To last from 2000 to 2003, essentially from the fall of the Twin Towers to the fall of Baghdad. . The aim of the attacks of 9/11 was to provoke the US into declaring war on the Islamic world and thereby awakening Muslims. The first phase was judged by the strategists and masterminds behind al-Qaida as very successful. The battle field was opened up and the Americans and their allies became a closer and easier target. It came to pass.

2. Opening Eyes. Between 2003 and 2006. The jihadists to develop into a network. The aim was to make the West aware of the Islamic community and for the organisation to

---

61 Martin Place terrorist Man Haron Monis's links with extremist group Hizb ut-Tahrir revealed, *Daily Telegraph*, 1 February, 2015.

develop into a movement. Iraq was to become the centre for all global operations, with an army set up there and bases established in other Arabic states. It came to pass.

3. Arising and Standing Up. From 2007 to 2010. Al Qaeda prophesied that there would be a focus on Syria, while fighting cadres were already preparing in Iraq. Attacks on Turkey and Israel were predicted. It came to pass. By 2016 Turkey had seen a series of jihadist attacks, including at its airport, and had become a major transit route for Islamic State fighters. Turkey was frequently accused by of profiteering from oil and weapons trade with Islamic State, at the same time as playing a key role as a part of NATO and the so-called War on Terror. Following a military coup, its' streets were full of the cry: Allahu Akbar, God is Great.

4. Between 2010 and 2013, al-Qaida aimed to bring about the collapse of the hated Arabic governments. They believed the creeping loss of the regimes' power would lead to a steady growth in strength. A decade on from the original prophecies, the governments of Libya and Yemen had collapsed, becoming so-called "breeding grounds" for jihadists. Tranches of territory had already been declared part of the caliphate. Syria could hardly have been more unstable. More than a million Muslim refugees flooded into Europe in a single year. One refugee shouted at the television cameras: "You cannot stop us. God has sent us."

5. This would be the point at which an Islamic state, or caliphate, could be declared. The plan was that by this time, between 2013 and 2016, Western influence in the Islamic world will be so reduced that resistance will not be feared. Jihadists hoped that by then the Islamic state would be able to bring about a new world order. In 2016 nation states were under attack across the globe. Traditional democracies were failing The heirs to the al-Qaeda doctrines, Islamic State, had become the biggest story on Earth.

6. From 2016 onwards there would be a period of total confrontation. As soon as the caliphate had been declared

the Islamic army would instigate the fight between the believers and the non-believers. leading to The Final Battle.

7. Definitive Victory. This final stage is described as "definitive victory." Because the rest of the world had been so beaten down by the one-and-a-half billion Muslims the caliphate would undoubtedly succeed. This phase would be completed by 2020.[62]

2016: the prophets of jihad were right on schedule.

As a major player and supporter of America's conflicts in the Middle East, Australia had been sucker-punched into an escalating conflict, at the cost of billions of dollars. In the suppression of dissent within their own borders, their own once freedom-loving society was actively destroyed.

The declaration of a War on Terror, a never-ending war, allowed for all the wartime conditions, including the shutting down of freedom of speech. Amongst the cognoscenti the rhetoric shifted once again.

Increasingly the question was asked: "What is it that the West has that is worth saving?"

The War on Terror had become a War on the People. The hard won freedoms of modern democracies were abandoned. Western governments became in a twinkling just as repressive, just as invasive of privacy, just as inclined to hide their maladministration behind cloaks of authoritarianism, to prosecute immoral wars and to hunt down dissenters within their own midst, just as dishonest in their intentions, and as totalitarian, as the world's worst regimes.

Michel Houellebecq published his political novel *Submission* in 2015, presaging the rise to power of the Muslim Brotherhood in France. His dystopian novel, set in 2022, was predictably dismissed as Islamophobic, as were so many attempts by independent thinkers to debate the social transformations of the early millennial period.

Associate Professor in Political Science at the University of Queensland David Martin Jones wrote:

> The liberal dread of being labelled Islamophobic, a penchant for tolerating the intolerant, combined with the fear of provoking

---

62 The Seven Phases of the Base, Bill Roggio, *Long War Journal*, 15 August, 2005. Paraphrased and expanded.

violence, has effectively silenced intelligent debate about the rise of political Islam. The post-Iraq utopian Left, comprising trans-national networks of NGOs, sympathetic academics, radical pacifists, indigenous peoples and environmental activists, seeks to overthrow the neo-liberal empire. Those committed to this anti-capitalist worldview now lead hundreds of activist groups and NGOs, conduct seminars and receive support from Western governments and institutions, enjoy various despots as their cheerleaders, are woven into the workings of the UN and the EU...[63]

The chattering classes had become a din, drowning out all but their own voices. They could not hear those they so effectively drowned:

The novel's protagonist, Francois, an alienated Sorbonne professor, observes that mainstream political parties had created "a chasm between the people and those who claimed to speak for them, the politicians and journalists. The latter, "who had lived and prospered under a given social system", could not "imagine the point of view of those who feel it offers them nothing, and who can contemplate its destruction without any particular dismay". In this context, the political system "might suddenly explode".[64]

But in the end the silenced would speak.

In Australia, as everywhere else in the West, there was a dramatic rise in anti-immigration and anti-Islamic movements. The government security forces, Alex suspected, paid more attention to them than they did to those campaigning for the introduction of sharia law.

The ceaseless official celebration of diversity – ethnic, cultural, reli-gious, sexual – was leading straight to a quagmire. Despite the many tens of billions Western governments had spent on multicultural propaganda, refugee programs, housing, education, welfare, and, ultimately, vast sums quelling and monitoring those who felt they were the losers in the social and demographic transformations being implemented by government, there was increasing discontent and disbelief.

---

63 The Illiberal Left and the Resistable Rise of Political Islam, David Martin Jones, *Quadrant*, July-August, 2016.

64 Ibid.

The public finally began to understand that the price they would pay for the march of the progressives was the destruction of their own heritage and their own culture.

The security agencies were closely monitoring dissidents, but just who was tailgating who in 2016 became a moot point. They were facing societal collapse. All that was keeping it together, all the government knew how to do, was to reach for the nearest instrument: fear.

The West had walked blindly into a trap, the outlines of which, ironically, had already been clearly drawn.

The Australian public remained entirely ignorant of the extreme danger into which their government had led them.

The break in the international commentariat's understanding of the religious nature of Islamic State came with the work of that superbly gifted journalist Graeme Wood, published in *The Atlantic*. As he stated in his ground-breaking piece "What ISIS Really Wants", it was vitally important to understand Islamic State in order to defeat it – an understanding so far absent within military, intelligence and political circles.

> Our ignorance of the Islamic State is in some ways understandable: It is a hermit kingdom; few have gone there and returned. Baghdadi has spoken on camera only once. But his address, and the Islamic State's countless other propaganda videos and encyclicals, are online, and the caliphate's supporters have toiled mightily to make their project knowable. We can gather that their state rejects peace as a matter of principle; that it hungers for genocide; that its religious views make it constitutionally incapable of certain types of change, even if that change might ensure its survival; and that it considers itself a harbinger of— and headline player in—the imminent end of the world.[65]

A failure to understand the enemy was at the core of the West's failure.

It was a failure to which the Australian public had been all too readily signed up by their politicians; a failure ultimately costing the Australian taxpayer billions of dollars at the same time as it brought threat and fear into their daily lives.

There is a temptation to rehearse this observation—that jihad-

---

65 What ISIS Really Wants, Graeme Wood, *The Atlantic*, March, 2015.

ists are modern secular people, with modern political concerns, wearing medieval religious disguise—and make it fit the Islamic State. In fact, much of what the group does looks nonsensical except in light of a sincere, carefully considered commitment to returning civilization to a seventh-century legal environment, and ultimately to bringing about the apocalypse.

The reality is that the Islamic State is Islamic. Very Islamic. Yes, it has attracted psychopaths and adventure seekers, drawn largely from the disaffected populations of the Middle East and Europe. But the religion preached by its most ardent followers derives from coherent and even learned interpretations of Islam.

Following takfiri doctrine, the Islamic State is committed to purifying the world by killing vast numbers of people.[66]

Old Alex watched a video of a woman caught in the street with her face only partially covered. She was forced to kneel on the ground. Young men took pictures of her on their smartphones. A preacher, with long hair and black robes, swaying back and forth as if demonically, medievally possessed, talked over her, warning the crowd against any defiance of Allah's will.

Then the preacher took a pistol and shot the woman in the head, her blood pooling in the street.

Allah the Most Merciful.

Her shooting went straight up online, there for her children to see. Australia's white bread politicians urged racial and religious tolerance; yet at the same time were an active part of the jeering mob condemning anyone who dared to ask the questions: "How did we get here? Why are we at war?"

The rhetoric partitioned off Islamic State in the public imagination as nothing but a few crude barbarians running around in the desert sands beheading people. It fooled the populace into thinking that IS was easily defeated, their own nationalism noble and their money well spent; that even in going about their lives, in "the best country in the world", they were striking a blow for freedom.

It was a sad, bumbling delusion.

The aridity of Islamic State's vision and the brutality of its practice meant the group contained within itself the seeds of its own destruction. But the

---

66 Ibid.

more they were bombed, the more they metastasised, and the greater grew the drift to extreme fundamentalism across the Muslim world, fuelled by a profound sense of injustice and persecution. It was an immolation of common sense as the martyrs walked through flames on the path to an apocalypse, fuelled by the deaths of thousands of mujahedeen, their women, their children – felled by the blind excesses and self-interest of the American military.

> Virtually every major decision and law promulgated by the Islamic State adheres to what it calls, in its press and pronounce-ments, and on its billboards, license plates, stationery, and coins, "the Prophetic methodology," which means following the prophecy and example of Muhammad, in punctilious detail. Muslims can reject the Islamic State; nearly all do. But pretending that it isn't actually a religious, millenarian group, with theology that must be understood to be combated, has already led the United States to underestimate it and back foolish schemes to counter it. We'll need to get acquainted with the Islamic State's intellectual genealogy if we are to react in a way that will not strengthen it, but instead help it self-immolate in its own excessive zeal.[67]

In the wake of Wood's seminal piece, and in the same month as a 15-year-old martyred himself at the Parramatta police headquarters and killed a police worker, another ground breaking piece of work, *ISIS Apocalypse*, was launched to international acclaim.

Written by one of the world's leading scholars on militant Islam William McCants, it began by setting the scene in mid-2014 when Islamic State marched across Iraq and conquered the country's second largest city Mosul.

> Mass executions, enslaved women and crucifixions soon followed, parading across cable news and Twitter. The danse macabre didn't stop there. Black flags rose, and government buildings were painted the same sombre shade. The Islamic State's leaders proclaimed the establishment of God's kingdom on earth, called the caliphate. Prophecy was fulfilled, they said, and Judgement Day approached.[68]

67 Ibid.
68 ISIS Apocalypse, William McCants, St Martin's Press, 2015.

The suggestions that Islamic State was an errant strain of Islam which could, in essence, be easily eradicated in order to make the homeland safe, were plainly false. As McCants wrote, the new caliphate was expansive and flush with weapons and billions in cash.

The caliph Ibrahim al-Baghdadi, a formerly obscure Iraqi religious scholar who had spent time in one of America's notoriously brutal Iraq prisons, took up arms after the 2003 American invasion.

Baghdadi had been a confidante of the Americans, who used him to sort out difficulties within the prison system.

Iraqi jihadists had networked inside the prisons in a way it would have been impossible for them to do outside.

There had rarely been a better example of the Law of Unintended Consequences.

By 2016 Baghdadi's followers inside the caliphate numbered in the tens of thousands. Thousands more applauded him in Europe and the Middle East. The group threatened to topple American allies in the Middle East, destabilise world energy markets, foment revolution abroad, and launch attacks across Europe and the United States.

That there were mass casualty events coming to Australia seemed almost a certainty.

> Questions flew. How had the Islamic State conquered so much land? Why was it so brutal? Why would such a murderous group claim to do God's bidding and fulfil prophecy? Did it really have anything to do with Islam, the world's second largest religion? And what threat did it pose to the international community?

> Readers who want more than sound-bite answers to these questions face a daunting challenge. Much of the Islamic State's propaganda is in Arabic and cloaked in medieval theological language that confuses Arabic-speaking Muslims, much less English-speaking non-Muslims. Making sense of it all would require a guide proficient in Islamic theology and history, modern jihadism, clandestine bureaucracies, and Arabic.

> That's what I am...[69]

McCants went to the heart of the ancient prophecies defining the present day.

---

69 Ibid.

The West had not just severely underestimated Islamic State from the beginning, they had failed to recognise the religious nature of the conflict; and thereby the motivations and actions not just of Islamic State but of their own politicians, those Western politicians who believed they were doing God's work by re-engaging in a crusader war, by spending billions of dollars on a war on the other side of the Earth.

There was a profound lack of understanding. This was a war all about God, and the gross over-simplifications of the West's propaganda had dumbed down the populations whose taxes paid for it. In Australia all they ever got from former Prime Minister Tony Abbott, the staunch Roman Catholic who re-engaged the country with Iraq, was "death cult" rhetoric. And from the new Prime Minister Malcolm Turnbull a terrible silence or obtuse rationalisations on an abstract terror threat; the end result being the people did not understand, and did not act as if, their nation was at war.

In that cold wet spring in Sydney, as Alex struggled to stay warm, events were already beginning to slide towards cataclysm. President Barack Obama authorised the first sustained deployment of special forces to Syria, reversing a long-standing refusal to put US boots on the ground. For over a year, the US had led a 65-member coalition that had conducted air strikes against more than 13,000 Islamic State targets in Iraq and Syria. Traditionally, at least since the Vietnam War, America's lack of concern for "collateral damage", that is civilian deaths, had been a major point of contention.

A year later, the results could clearly be seen, as Aleppo became a living hell, hundreds of children were killed, and every day more bombs rained down on a ruined city and a deeply frightened population. And Australia was in there all the way.

Even most educated Australians were unaware their country was actively involved in dropping bombs on Iraq and Syria.

In Turnbull's first full month of office Australian aircrew flew 78 sorties across Iraq, a total of 570 hours. There were 34 bomb drops, on the mujahedeen, killing warriors, women, children. The public were never told. Any attempt by journalists to discover the truth, exactly who and how many people Australian bombs were killing, was met with bureaucratic obfuscation or referral to the Americans. Australia had, it would seem, no foreign policy of its own, except obeisance to the Americans, a policy many of the country's leading strategists increasingly questioned.

As critics of the West's involvement in the Middle East repeatedly pointed out, you cannot bomb an idea.

In November, Turnbull was responsible for dropping another 73 bombs off 540 flying hours, higher than any month during the reign of his war-hungry predecessor. How many Muslims were killed by the then record number of Australian bombs was not known.

The government released no information on the targets, no estimates on the civilian and military deaths. One could safely assume they ran into the hundreds, even thousands.

The Australian public did not know, and would not be told.

In the crudest of terms, Turnbull was responsible for killing Muslims on the other side of the world. There would be consequence. And he knew it.

In December Turnbull dropped even more bombs, 81 on Iraq and 21 on Syria.

The nightly scenes of burnt and bleeding children as both countries collapsed should have been enough to haunt anybody's conscience.

But there Australia was, in the thick of it.

Military campaigners, even with their drones and high-tech weapons and massive smart bombs, were using largely traditional tactics against an enemy they could not defeat, not with bombs, not with guns, not with money, certainly not with the cowardice of air strikes.

As the man most directly responsible for Australia's killing of Muslim fighters on the other side of the world, the blood of the martyrs was already congealing around Turnbull, whether he liked it or not.

It wasn't long into his tenure before the Prime Minister's appearance and disposition, that of a wealthy, successful, chipper, buoyant, well fed Eastern suburbs success story, changed – his demeanour became more authoritarian, his face more sinister, more Mussolini-like, starkly lined, and his glib reiterations of government policy to the Australian public more patently false.

It was all leading straight to the pit.

Men pursued power, and power destroyed them.

As the world's most famous whistle-blower Edward Snowden put it, we had gone from the elected and the electors to the rulers and the ruled.

Contempt for his subjects oozed from Turnbull's every pore.

Malcolm would have been far happier sticking to the cocktail circuit.

If there had been any credible alternative, in a desecrated political landscape, the country might have been better off.

As it was, Australians copped the jovial lie; the faux stories cooked up by administrators, crafted into elegant speeches.

Of real debate, there was absolutely none.

Australia's obeisance to America's foreign policy had been backfiring at least since the Vietnam War, and here they were, the nation's political elite, dragging the country through yet another morass. Every bomb, every death made the situation worse.

There was no winning hearts and minds.

There was no winning, full stop.

Upon the Hour. The Final Battle.

Old Alex grew up in a fundamentalist Christian household, where the family had been preparing for the end times and his childhood dreams were filled with the chants of the damned as they queued to face their Lord; the far-off, refracted beat of the Rolling Stones a sure sign of the end times.

Now, in a new millennium, his country was fighting an enemy prepared to die in the scorching sands of Iraq and Syria in the name of God. While from afar, in their expansive Sydney mansions, those who made the orders acted as if nothing was happening.

They dared not tell the Australian public the truth.

Nor listen to their own dreams, as the souls of the dead began their haunting.

> Jihadists of all stripes, not just Islamic State followers, have been stirred by the promise of fighting in the final battles preceding the Day of Judgement. "If you think all these mujahedeen come from all over the world to fight Assad, you are mistaken," said a jihadist fighting in Aleppo. "They are all here as promised by the Prophet. This is the war he promised—it is the Grand Battle." Another fighter in Syria believed the same. "We have here mujahedeen from Russia, America and the Philippines, China, Belgium, Germany, Sudan, India and Yemen and other places. They are here because this (is) what the Prophet said and promised, the Grand Battle is happening. God "chose the best of people to come", to Sham (the Levant), asserted Abu Muthanna, a Yemeni from Britain. "You see where the muhajirin," he said, using the Arabic word for "emigrants". "This is the biggest evidence they have that they are upon the haqq," or truth.[70]

---

70 Ibid.

The mujahedeen achieved martyrdom courtesy of Western bombs; Islamic State perpetrated and filmed the goriest and most graphic ritual killings ever disseminated on the web, gifting ever more and more souls to the heavens. Millions worshipped, and the disturbance grew. Many more would join them.

Old Alex was just beginning to spend time at the Big White House. Poofter Palace, the locals called it.

Still drained from the previous book, devoid of purpose, his head running every which way, he sat in that damp, over-watered back garden in Newtown.

Or he sought company in the Carlisle opposite, attempting to find a winsome twist in community life.

He had lost his tribe and was looking for a new one. Some days he churned out news stories for a quid, and at the end of the day just wanted to relax, like everybody else. Some days he just wanted to get lost, to escape his own head. Most of all, he wanted his own village.

The ever status-conscious Old Opera Diva Peter, with whose life he so oddly collided, in an attempt to explain Alex's distracted presence, told everyone at the pub he was a genius. It was entirely unhelpful. He wanted to blend in. Instead the genius talk, although not of his own making, got him promptly labelled a wanker. This was Australia. Nobody liked someone who thought they were better, or smarter, than everybody else.

Besides the obvious, if he was such a fucking genius, why was he driving around in a beaten-up old car and sleeping in an attic?

As he had experienced repeatedly during his working life, the only journalism the average punter understood was television. At scene after tragic scene, the neighbours and inevitable eyewitnesses would always put themselves forward for the TV crews, something to tell their mates, they were on Channel Seven, Nine, Ten.

As for newspapers, they never read them and were proud to tell you so. An agitated man on a tight deadline with a reporter's pad in hand asking too many questions simply did not make sense. But a television camera did.

These days Old Alex was on his own. There was no accompanying photographer on assignment to smooth out local ructions, to put on a funny face behind his back and make the subjects laugh as he fired questions and scribbled away in his mix of Pitman's, speed writing and personal hieroglyphics.

Once the photographer convinced the targets of their working class bona fides – that Alex was a bit eccentric, that was all – they would inevitably walk off with the story, and the subjects got their tale about the blokes from the big city paper.

He no longer worked for a multibillion dollar media giant, and had neither the regular income, cache or infamy that went with being a reporter on a daily newspaper.

The sky above was a sticky, disturbed prelude to winter, while below the citizens asked no questions, had no eyes to see, no ears to hear. If they were not being attacked from behind, they were being attacked from above.

This was a place where nothing could be more unfashionable than talk of conflicting visions of God or clashing state creeds. Or whether excessive migration was disrupting the social fabric, creating housing and employment crises and turning the nation's once proud story into a modern-day Tower of Babel.

There was no-one he could talk to about the last book or the next; far less how crimped Australian conversation had become; the collapse of quality journalism, the rise of government-controlled media and the march of a group-think tertiary educated elites into the professions.

Everyone had their view – most often, at least in that part of town, acquired via the national broadcaster. They could tell themselves they were progressives, their friends would nod in agreement and they slept peacefully at night. They were good people.

If their views were out of sync with the prevailing fashions, or with the Australian Broadcasting Commission, most had learnt it was easier to say nothing at all for fear of being labelled misogynist, racist, sexist, ignorant, uncaring.

> So the Jews gathered around Him and demanded, "How long will You keep us in suspense? If You are the Christ, tell us plainly."

> "I already told you," Jesus replied, "but you did not believe. The works I do in My Father's name testify on My behalf. But because you are not My sheep, you refuse to believe.

> At this, the Jews again picked up stones to stone Him. But Jesus answered, "I have shown you many good works from the Father. For which of these do you stone Me?"

"We are not stoning You for any good work," said the Jews, "but for blasphemy, because You, who are a man, declare Yourself to be God."

Jesus replied, "Is it not written in your Law: 'I have said you are gods'?[71]

These Gods sat on their barstools along the length of the old fashioned bar, wreathed their prejudices ever closer to themselves and talked of little else but football. In truth, they were not welcoming. They did not heed Muhammad's admonition: be kind to the traveller, courteous to the stranger.

Islamic State were not the only ones who believed they were key agents in a coming Apocalypse.

There were many fundamentalist Christians who also believed humanity was marching towards the Final Battle, that the Apocalypse was upon the world, the Day of Judgement nigh.

Almost all faiths held doomsday visions of the end of civilisation, from the grand epoch-spanning projections of the Hindus to the poisoning of the sacred lands which heralded a different apocalypse.

Old Alex still did his Buddhist exercises sporadically, those he had picked up and adapted from the Falun Gong while doing yet another story, in the old graveyard or wherever it felt right, trying to calm his spirit, its jumping fear.

A staff reporter, he was commissioned to do the story on the Falun Gong more than a decade before. "You're never going to run it, Murdoch has too much money invested in China," he replied. To which he was assured their independent editorial line meant they had no such concerns.

He spent a month sitting in parks meditating and listening to the Falun Gong, clocking up a considerable amount of overtime in the process.

Founded in 1992, the practice rapidly attracted millions of followers around the world, including across Australia.

More than anything, the Falun Gong, or Falun Dafa as they were also known, familiar in the West as groups of Chinese performing tai-chi-like exercises in parks, believed that these were The End of Days, to quote the title of a book about them.

They believed their exercises and their practices, developed over thou-

71 John 10: 22-34, The Berean Bible.

sands of years by the highest of spiritual masters in the remote monasteries of the Himalayas, provided a fast track to enlightenment. They were being made available at this time to the ordinary person, here at the "end of days", because the world now faced a final apocalyptic fall.

Falun Gong was banned in China in 1999 and their followers persecuted. There was history.

Another millenarian cult known as the White Lotus overthrew the Chinese government of the day a thousand years before.

Even the most sympathetic of journalists covering the Falun Dafa story around the globe remarked on their wild cosmology.

Plants had souls. You could be reincarnated into a rock. Multidimensional universes were a given. There were multiple heavens, for Christians, for Muslims, heavens filled with millions of the faithful and heavens filled with only a few enlightened souls, from all parts of the galaxy.

While there was much that was wise, sometimes the teachings appeared just plain hallucinatory.

But Alex quickly noticed that the exercises did have a profound effect, throwing him, in a sense, into a hyper-real world. He had been extremely stressed at the time, and if nothing else, after the month he spent pursuing the story he felt healthier, more organised, more coherent in the head, somehow more peaceful.

Sure enough, although a fair bit of time, effort and money had gone into it, the paper, just as Alex predicated, never ran the story.

It sat in an electronic filing system, "the hold basket" as it was known, for a year; and would occasionally emerge and he would be relayed the instructions, "make it more critical".

After all, they were a cult; and here we were being nice to a cult. They were no more a cult, no more fantastical, than the monotheistic faiths, Christianity, Islam and Judaism, or the others, Hinduism, Buddhism, the Sikhs, Jains and many others.

Alex never did toughen up the story in the way demanded; and it slid into another uncelebrated, wasteful, hypocritical media moment.

As farfetched as it seemed, Falun Gong always maintained that advanced spiritual beings appeared and disappeared around their practice sites, and that their own advanced practitioners possessed the ability for precognition, prophecy, healing, even the ability to walk through walls.

Failing to comply with his own forecast that the Falun Gong were about to become a major world religion, in 2016 there were few attendees in the parks; and those who still gathered seemed like pale imitations of those who had gone before.

Perhaps, Alex conjectured, the discipline's most powerful beings, sensing the coming apocalypse, simply moved on to a different plane, vanished to safety.

In that year Alex spent some time with Christians, and they, too, were captured by the conviction that the End of Days was nigh, the Apocalypse upon the world.

He had read the Koran by the burning gates in Varanasi in India, and read, if not every word, much of the Bible, particularly, as an old fan of apocalyptic imagery, Revelations. An urgent redemption. He had been to the holiest place of the Sikhs, Hemkund in the Himalayas. And he had been to what was once claimed as the largest mosque in the world, in Lahore in northern Pakistan, watching as thousands of men bowed in worship, with snow-capped peaks in the far distance and the pink stone giving off a kind of shimmering, as the heat itself sucked away at the souls of the faithful.

To those captured by Christian symbology a Holy War, long touted by various fundamentalist Christian sects as beginning in the Middle East, looked as if it had arrived.

The religious imagery of the Four Horsemen of the Apocalypse seemed, for those inclined towards millennial cults, to be coming true: false religion led to war led to famine led to pestilence.

The white horse, false religion, Christianity, Islam, idol worshippers, consumerism, liberalism, globalism, celebrity gossip, democracy, immorality, take your pick. A new era of Twitter feeds and short-term memory loss, of fads and waves of group-think, swept around and through what passed for the culture and disappeared as quickly as they came. The centre could not hold.

> And I saw when the Lamb opened one of the seals, and I heard, as it were the noise of thunder, one of the four beasts saying, Come and see. And I saw, and behold a white horse: and he that sat on him had a bow; and a crown was given unto him: and he went forth conquering and to conquer.[72]

72 Revelations 6:1-2. King James Version.

The red horse, war, was no mystery; the high-tech bombers killing inno-cents, the plumes of smoke, the Islamic Warriors waving flags proclaiming God is great, Mohammad is his Messenger, the fears of random beheadings of ordinary Australians, the soldiers hunkered in their barracks:

> And when he had opened the second seal, I heard the second beast say, Come and see. And there went out another horse that was red; and power was given to him that sat thereon to take peace from the earth, and that they should kill one another: and there was given unto him a great sword.[73]

In a more prosaic land, where an unconfined panic, a baleful disturbance, was beginning to seep through city streets, the Parramatta terror attack on police headquarters was garnering maximum media coverage.

It played into the hands both of those who wished to sow dissent, and those who wished to expand the power of the state.

Head of Hizb ut-Tahrir in Australia Ismail Al-Wahwah was obliged to attend police headquarters for questioning.

Al-Wahwah refused to reveal the subject of the Friday's lecture to waiting media. If true to form, it concentrated on the perfidy of the West, the perse-cution of Muslims both in Australia and around the world, urged the bene-fits of a sacrifice to an Islamic life and paid reverential tribute to Almighty Allah, Lord of all the Worlds.

Ismail had previously made a joke of Australia's much argued racial vilifi-cation laws when he called Jews the most evil creatures of Allah and declared the embers of jihad would continue to burn:

> Moral corruption is linked to the Jews. Prostitution in the world began with the Israelites. Usury and gambling began with the Israelites. Killing began with the Israelites … They will pay with blood for blood, with tears for tears, and with destruction for destruction.[74]

The comments received worldwide attention when they were translated by MEMRI, the Middle East Media Research Institute, which ran a contro-versial, well-resourced site based in Washington where it was possible to get all the latest beheading videos and which had survived repeated calls for it to be banned as a jihad site.

---

73 Revelations 6: 3-4. King James Version.

74 Dismay over failure to charge al-Wahah, *The Australian Jewish News*, 3 September, 2015.

It was widely used by commentators and researchers alike as providing an insight into many of the latest developments in the global jihad movement.

MEMRI survived thanks to America's freedom of speech laws. It had tax exemption status as an educational institution.

Any teenager could access it.

After killing the police accountant, 15-year-old Jabar, in black Islamic dress and shouting in Arabic "God is Great", paced up and down outside the police headquarters, aiming at other targets.

He was shot dead by one of three special constables returning fire.

Jabar, an Iranian-born boy of Iraqi Kurdish background, was a pleasant looking kid in Year 10 at Arthur Phillip High School. The school was named after the first governor of the state of NSW and the founder of the city of Sydney.

In the cold clutter of the inner city Old Alex looked at a thin, bright, personable, dark eyed girl with short blonde hair working behind the bar at the Courthouse Hotel. "You will die young," he thought.

He passed an anorexic, angular-faced, stick-thin woman with large black eyes, an ice addict who had been living upstairs in the Carlisle. "You will die young," he thought.

He looked at a wasted junkie, a young man he knew survived from stealing, and thought: "You will die young."

But whether he would have thought the same if he had looked at Jabar, he very much doubted.

The killing heightened tensions and threw up a wall of debate, dumbed down to questions of Islamophobia. The great story of Australian democracy was unravelling at high speed.

Columnist Andrew Bolt, invariably labelled by his many critics as arch-conservative, wrote:

> They treat us like fools. Police and politicians are telling untruths about what inspired Farhad Jabar to kill.
>
> Those untruths are meant to build trust with Muslim Australians, which we need. But everyone else will wonder: "What other lies are we being told?"[75]

Protesters waved placards such as "Immigration is the Elephant in the

---

75 Police and politicians lying, Andrew Bolt, *Herald Sun*, 7 October, 2015.

Room", "Say No to Sharia", "Child Brides Australia Says No" and "It's a Foreign Invasion."

In their naivety, they thought the authorities would think much like them, would rush to their defence, support their courage for standing up for an Old Australia.

They thought they were simply being patriots.

They did not know what lay before them, did not understand what had happened to the government which once represented them. Just as in days of old, they instinctively rose up to fight the invaders of their lands. It was a matter of honour and of principle.

But this was an invasion, an influx of foreigners, managed by government and supported by billions of dollars of propaganda, backed by vast bureaucratic edifices.

The problem was: the propaganda had stopped working.

Instantly their phones were monitored, every detail of their lives picked over. And in an oft-used tactic, the authorities would try to quell them into silence by making their surveillance more than obvious.

The country became a land of whispering campaigns, of dog whistling to the Muslims, to the Christians, to the lunar right and the doctrinaire left.

Everyone thought they heard the whistle, everyone thought they knew the truth; in reality a chimera, a shimmering, contested field of competing ideologies.

ASIO warned of the potential for violence at anti-Muslim demonstrations.

> The increased participation and activities of Australian-based anti-Islam groups, fuelled by a steady stream of violent jihad videos, was being used as evidence that Islam was not compatible with Australian values or the Australian way of life.

> "Reclaim Australia rallies will continue to be held throughout the next financial year and, due to their potential for violence, will remain of concern," ASIO's Annual Report said.

> "While anti-Islam numbers increased, there was a concurrent increase in counter protests on platforms of social inclusion, anti-racism and anti-fascism."[76]

---

76 Terrorism Threats Worse than Ever Report, *The New Daily*, 20 October, 2015.

In that Big White House in Sydney's inner city, the Home for the Incurables, Alex began settling into what he briefly thought might be a home, or at least a bolt-hole. There was, he thought for a time, a ready set of friends at the hotel opposite. The Old Opera Diva knew everybody and, as the saying went, could talk the leg off an iron monkey. There was always a party to go to, a group of friends to meet up with, a new restaurant.

At the Carlisle, any attempt to discuss the vexed issue of Islam in Australia would have been howled down as racist in that inner city milieu, and Old Alex barely ever mentioned the book he had just written, although it had consumed much of the previous year.

He began once more taking on journalistic assignments; and terrorism was a subject impossible to ignore. The stories were a ready break from the prolonged and often lonely difficulties of writing books, and besides, his business badly needed the cash flow. Along with that, it kept his hand in. He learnt a lot just by the act of doing.

One of the first was a story on the country's lead spy agency, the Australian Security Intelligence Organisation (ASIO). It was the only one of Australia's bank of intelligence agencies besides the Inspector General of Intelligence and Security which was required by law to produce an annual report to parliament, and the only one even vaguely known to the Australian public.

With the government gifting billions of dollars of additional funding to a bank of secretive national security agencies, ostensibly for the war on terror but with considerable resources being used for domestic spying, ASIO was seen by its critics as a powerful, dysfunctional, discredited and dangerous secret police force which was a direct threat to the nation's democracy.

ASIO had been founded in secrecy by military operatives in the 1940s, its very existence only acknowledged to the general public in 1977. Its military origins and military mindset jelled perfectly with the increasingly autocratic mindset of present day governments.

Back in the early 1970s, one of reforming Prime Minister Gough Whitlam's first items of business was to order that his Ministers be neither investigated nor harassed by the Agency, an extraordinary edict for a country's leader to be obliged to issue.

A few years later there was considerable speculation, and considerable evidence, that the agency had already played a significant role in overthrowing Whitlam's democratically elected, left-leaning government.

The unalloyed good which ASIO was supposed to represent was a myth peddled by its political apologists on both sides of the house.

ASIO's penchant for secrecy was in itself a stand-alone joke.

Back in the 1980s Old Alex had made Column Eight, the immensely popular column of gossip and quirky news which ran on the front page of *The Sydney Morning Herald* for decades. That was in the days when there really were eight columns of print across the nation's most respected broadsheet.

Back then the paper was regularly listed as one of the Top 20 newspapers in the world, and to get a job there and enter its hallowed portals had been like entering the Sistine Chapel.

Now it was tabloid in format and tabloid in content, cursed with decades of chronic mismanagement and hapless strategic thinking, plummeting profits and more recently talk that it was about to become digital only, with the final print editions scheduled for early in the new year.

The collapse of serious media was a hobbyhorse for Old Alex, a recurring theme which reflected the deterioration of national debate and had serious ramifications for the country as a whole; but he digressed.

Back then, in the course of his duties as a relatively junior and enthusiastic, energised reporter, he discovered that not even the media public relations officer would reveal her name, she alone, in the government's steadily growing army of soothsayers.

It would have been easy enough to come up with a *nom de plume* or a cover story, security personnel made up names every day of the week. But not the spin doctor herself.

Not much had changed over the decades.

ASIO staff introduced themselves at conferences only by their first names, while claiming they worked for the Attorney General's Department.

> Such a plethora of agencies, each jealously guarding its secrets, inevitably leads to overlap and duplication, along with rivalry, suspicion, information hoarding and turf wars. There are myriad anecdotes to this effect. A participant at a recent conference attended by representatives of various agencies in Sydney tells how delegates sniggered when an ASIO staffer told the gathering, "you can't write my name down, so if anyone's written my name down would you please pass the piece of paper up to the front of the room."

The speaker following him announced "my name's [withheld] and you can write my name down and for fuck's sake don't hand the piece of paper up to the front." This second speaker was reportedly furious, having learnt that ASIO had kept important new research data to itself, and went on: "This is supposed to be an adult working environment but as you can see it's not. They lie to us continuously, and I don't know why they do it, but it makes our job impossible."[77]

Australian taxpayers had no way of knowing whether their money was being well spent or not. They were forced to accept the word of their elected representatives, that Australia had the best security agencies in the world. To a disengaged populace, their politicians had less and less credibility; but on this matter they had no choice but to believe – there were almost no other sources of information.

What was most striking about the country's descent into totalitarianism was that the future had already been forecast, certainly at the so-called Tables of Knowledge, the collections of the wise and not so wise who took up daily residence at hotels, watering holes, cafes and meeting places around the country. Everyone from "tradies", builders, electricians, plasterers, construction workers, many of whom were far more astute than politicians and bureaucrats ever gave them credit for, to ragged, subsiding alcoholics in poor health, drinking and smoking too much in the nation's public bars, all had lamented Australia's drift towards some state the other side of communism, where personal freedom had all but disappeared.

The nation's more independent-minded cognoscenti reached the same conclusions. Half a dozen years before, one of the country's best journalists Sally Neighbour wrote: "The extraordinary growth of Australia's intelligence behemoth has occurred in the absence of any vigorous public debate. Questioning of the fact is routinely muted by the bipartisan consensus that national security must be protected, seemingly at any cost."[78]

Neighbour went on to quote barrister and civil rights activist Greg Barns:

From a policy perspective, the difficulty of assessing whether these agencies are performing is that agencies such as ASIO

77 Hidden Agendas: Our intelligence services, Sally Neighbour, *The Monthly*, November, 2010.

78 Ibid.

are unaccountable – you never know what they're doing and we're not entitled to know, and it makes it very difficult for the community to make an assessment. What government is going to cut back money for the security agencies? Then it'll leak out: 'sources say government risks terror attack'. So they've got them over a barrel.[79]

At the time the new headquarters of the troubled Australian Security Intelligence Organisation was just rising from a piece of land the size of three city blocks, located beside Lake Burley Griffin in Canberra, costed at a staggering $585 million.

ASIO's grandiose new headquarters are a monument to an intelligence complex on which Australia now spends around $1.4 billion per annum, out of a total national security budget of about $4 billion. According to the Australian Defence Almanac 2010–2011 published by the Australian Strategic Policy Institute (ASPI), ASIO's slice of that pie has risen 535% since 2001. Its twin, the foreign spy agency the Australian Secret Intelligence Service (ASIS), has enjoyed a budget increase of 344%, while analysis agency the Office of National Assessments (ONA) has had a 443% bonus.[80]

Those numbers would increase yet further in the years to come, while the building itself reinforced ASIO's powerful image. The building was aligned uncannily, not just in sightlines, but in cost, weight and physical presence, with Parliament House itself.

Forty years on from Whitlam's demise, and a conservative government was gifting ASIO and other agencies in Australia's clandestine intelligence community yet more funds, while at the same time passing legislation which added to their already substantial powers.

ASIO sought, for example, the power to detain people for seven days without charge and without so much as a judicial warrant.

Secretive, unaccountable and to its critics operating as a parallel police force, for some ASIO was the last organisation which should be granted yet more powers.

Those thus jailed would no doubt be further detained if they revealed what went on during those seven days.

---

79 Ibid.

80 Ibid.

Law Council of Australia President Arthur Moses said:

> We're talking here about persons being detained in custody and deprived of their liberty. That takes it to an entirely different level.

> Western democracies have always taken the position that we do not in effect have a situation where a politician can give that authority ... Usually people have the protection of a judicial officer ... In my view it's unprecedented.[81]

In an opinion piece, *Sydney Morning Herald* columnist Tim Dick wrote:

> Australia's top spy thinks ASIO shouldn't have to bother convincing a judge to lock someone up for interrogation, someone who isn't doing or plotting anything bad but might know someone who is.

> ASIO can already ask to have someone detained if it thinks he knows something about a terrorism offence. That it now has the nerve to seek to dispense with judicial oversight shows the state of liberty in Australia today . . . the fragility of the liberal democratic project.

> Australians are not nearly as conscientious as they ought to be about protecting liberties.

> But every time we erode a protection, we erode a little more of the freedom we're supposedly so eager to protect.[82]

At the same time as ASIO was being gifted yet more funds and more power, it was being made even more unaccountable, including having its officers exempted from being sued for illegal conduct. The Agency was wreathing itself in protective legislation it had itself helped to draft.

America maverick shock jock Alex Jones was close to the truth: "Australian Senate Kills Civil Liberties with Draconian New Anti-Terror Law in Orwellian Orgy of Baseless Fear-Mongering."

Former Chairman of the National Crime Authority, barrister Peter Faris,

---

81 ASIO asks for detention powers without warrant from judge, David Wroe, *The Sydney Morning Herald*, 22 August, 2016.

82 Erosion of Liberty a Slippery Slope, Tim Dick, *The Sydney Morning Herald*, 29 August, 20166.

put it thus: "It's all bullshit. A lot of security related evidence is completely overrated. My experience with secret organisations is not only do they use it to cover up material that's sensitive, but they use it to cover up all material including errors they've made. There is no transparency or accountability, and that's my concern."[83]

ASIO might be the only one of the security agencies required by law to submit an annual report to parliament, but even then an entire section of the report was redacted.

Exactly what was in that section Old Alex would dearly have liked to know.

In a time far, far away, if he was that determined he would have found a way, and worked out with the company lawyer how best to publish.

Now the laws were so stringent, the state so powerful, that both the journalist and the whistleblower faced jail, their trials conducted in secrecy.

Even so, what was on the public record was enough to indicate an agency in serious trouble.

Alex did two stories off the Annual Report, the first essentially the same one that other journalists had done.

In the report ASIO head Duncan Lewis repeatedly emphasised that terrorism from Islamic extremists was now the number one security threat facing Australia.

It was the exact message their paymasters wished to project.

Cynics might have suggested that an inflated terror threat meant ever increasing funding; while a frightened populace would accept almost any abrogation of their freedoms.

Lewis claimed six terrorist plots were disrupted and two terrorist attacks, the Martin Place and Endeavour Hills attacks in Sydney and Melbourne, occurred during the period covered by the report.

However, the "crude lone-actor attacks", so-called "lone wolf" attacks which had so far characterised terror incidents in Australia and attracted so much media attention, were far from the only threat. Lewis said no-one should leap to the conclusion that small-scale modes of terrorism had replaced the threat of larger scale and more organised attacks. There had been ongoing growth in the numbers attracted to violent extremism, and active encouragement from overseas for attacks to be conducted in Australia.

83 Ibid.

More than ever, violent extremist groups and individuals see Australia as a legitimate target for a terrorist attack.

The principal terrorist threat to Australia, Australians and Australian interests continues to come from those who adhere to a violent extremist ideology.

This ideology is associated with a range of groups that share the single ultimate objective of driving 'apostates' and non-Muslims from Muslim lands and establishing an Islamic state ruled in accordance with their deviant interpretation of Islam.

All share the view that Western countries, including Australia, are enemies of Islam and that terrorist attacks against the citizens and interests of those countries are not only legitimate but also obligatory.[84]

The second story Alex found in ASIO's Annual Report to parliament was not picked up by any other journalist. No normal reporter in those stressed times read anything beyond the press release, and at best the Executive Summary and the Conclusion.

In an industry on its bare bones, with rapidly dwindling staff numbers and each journalist expected to churn out multiple stories every day, there simply wasn't time.

The report warned, albeit in the fabric rather than the dot points, that enormous damage could be done to Australia's security as a result of malicious insiders.

The warnings came after the Edward Snowden and Bradley Manning cases exposed huge flaws in the conduct of US intelligence, including universal surveillance.

A similar release in Australia of the case files of Islamic jihad sympathisers, for example, would have a devastating effect on Australia's security operations.

The report stated that a major threat to the country's national interest was the risk posed by self-motivated individuals exploiting their privileged access to information to make unauthorised disclosures of classified or privileged information. The harm these individuals could cause had been

84 Terrorism threat 'worse than ever': report, John Stapleton, *The New Daily*, 20 October, 2015.

greatly increased by modern information technology, which allowed large amounts of information to be aggregated, copied and easily distributed to a wide audience.

> Malicious insiders are trusted employees and contractors who deliberately and wilfully breach their duty to maintain the security of privileged information, techniques, technology, assets or premises.

> ASIO has identified vulnerabilities and significant weaknesses associated with current Australian personnel security arrangements, in terms of both the current practice and the ability to respond effectively to emerging issues.

> This creates an unacceptable level of risk for government. As a result of these vulnerabilities, the secure conduct of government business cannot be assured.[85]

To repeat: The secure conduct of government business could not be assured.

Yet the same government continued to throw billions of dollars into opaque, unaccountable security networks.

Terrorism expert Professor Clive Williams of the Australian National University said there was an increased emphasis on the role of managers in the security management of staff under their control.

> Despite the security vetting process, which is hugely backlogged, the reality is that most security problems come from vetted insiders who for various reasons have become disenchanted or disaffected, often mid-career.

> Managers are now expected to know all about their staff and their problems. Security access reviews should be conducted periodically, but the reality is that most agencies struggle to do the reviews on time.[86]

Professor Williams said Manning and Snowden may not be Australian, but they were very damaging cases on everyone's mind within the intelli-

---

85 The internal threat that has ASIO worried, John Stapleton, *The New Daily*, 4 November, 2015.

86 Ibid.

gence community: "They have had a significant impact on our intelligence and security operations because of the way we are interconnected with the US and the other members of Five Eyes."

It was one of the great puzzles of Australian governance, a question Alex had frequently asked himself: why did Australia slavishly follow America into wars which were so clearly counterproductive for the countries in the firing line, and equally raised conflicts and tensions at home?

The explanation lay not just in the hundreds of military contracts which Australia had with America, but with the so-called Five Eyes agreement.

This was an intelligence alliance between Australia, Canada, New Zealand, the United Kingdom and the United States.

Australia had traditionally spied on its own citizens at higher levels than its Western counterparts, and enthusiastically embraced the sharing of technology and information which the arrangement offered.

And it all came back, that trail full of potholes and diversions, highways and byways lined with the bodies of the crucified and filled with Servants of God, with fundamentalist Christians and fundamentalist Muslims all worshiping the same Abrahamic God from the early years of their faiths, to whistleblowers.

Edward Snowden, even better known that year after the release of the Oliver Stone movie Snowden, joined the US intelligence fight for what he saw as freedom in Iraq, and for a better world.

> What Snowden unearthed was not deceptive US conduct in some far-flung corner of the world; he stumbled across a war against the American people: a surveillance state where no one could have a private life. It was the ultimate betrayal of what he believed he was working for: a more just world, where tyrants were brought to account. What he discovered was deception, lying and cheating on a grand scale, all carried out by the US government. But it wasn't just the US government that was culpable. It had supplicant supporters.[87]

As senior journalist Andrew Fowler wrote in *The War on Journalism: Media Moguls, Whistle-blowers and the Price of Freedom*, these nations, including Australia, were not just complicit; there was also a very high social cost.

---

87 *The War on Journalism: Media Moguls, Whistle-blowers and the Price of Freedom*, Andrew Fowler, Random House, 2015.

Though the United States provides a large amount of the technical hardware the other four countries do their own spying too, much of it on behalf of the NSA. It's their way of paying back the United States for access to its global spy network. But there is a bigger price the United States charges: obedience to its foreign policy.[88]

Snowden argued that the Five Eyes partnerships were organised so authorities in each country could insulate their political leaders from the backlash when it became public how grievously they were violating the privacy of their citizens. Too late.

Alex's ASIO article was accompanied by a photograph of demonstrators waving placards saying: "We the People Oppose the Surveillance State", "Stop Mass Spying" and "Thank You Edward Snowden!"

If there was one person on Earth Alex had become fascinated by during his own journey of discovery, apart from Julian Assange, it was the hyper-intelligent Edward Snowden.

Whether he was hero or devil depended on your point of view: whether you were a government with secrets to hold, or a seeker after truth, a believer in the trappings and abuse of power, or someone who longed for a world where it was impossible to lie.

As a journalist, Old Alex opted for hero.

By exposing the true extent of mass surveillance, Snowden's leaks allowed for a profound re-evaluation of the surveillance state and abuses by the American military and intelligence services. Socially and politically, his work was of major significance.

Intercept, arguably in 2016 the world's single most cutting edge journalistic outlet, published more than fifty stories based on the 1200 documents Snowden had released to date.

Material exposed included images from hacked drone feeds, and information on PRISM, the program which vacuums up hundreds of millions of internet communications every day from the people the National Security Agency targets. Another program, Upstream, gathers communications while they are travelling through the cables of the internet, including voice and text.

Yet another program exposed by Snowden, Boundless Informant, was

88 Ibid.

a data mining tool which detailed and mapped by country the extensive volume of information the NSA was collecting from computer and phone networks.

As a result of Snowden's work consumers were aware that Google, Apple, Microsoft, Yahoo and Skype were all selling information on their customers to the US government.

Amongst the many "cracker yarns", as in journalistic parlance great stories were once known, Snowden revealed that the US's National Security Agency used electronic surveillance, rather than human intelligence, to target people in its assassination programs.

A far cry from its rhetoric of precision terror targeting, and rather than confirming a target's identity through informants on the ground, the CIA and the US military was simply targeting a SIM card, which could easily be being used by friends, family or children.

There was no doubt innocent people were being killed in the program.

The scandalous stories of America's military actions kept on rolling out; and all the while Australia remained the most loyal of allies.

While Snowden's revelations helped to curb, at least for a time, some of NSA's more excessive, and arguably illegal, levels of surveillance, Australia marched in the exact opposite direction.

Snowden was extremely critical of Australia's intelligence services, which he said were much more unrestrained than those in the United States: "We have seen intelligence services in Australia become more aggressive. We have seen the Australian Government pass new laws, indiscriminate dragnet surveillance laws."[89]

Australia's metadata laws, which were introduced under the pretence of fighting terror, turned every smartphone into a "snitch" device.

Privacy, the very thing the Australian government had so effectively and determinedly destroyed, was, Snowden told his Australian audience, the foundation right from which all others followed.

Privacy is the right to the self.

What's the point of freedom of speech if you don't have the space to think about what it is you want to say?

---

89 Edward Snowden wants you to give a damn about privacy, Jo Lauder, ABC Triple J Hack, 23 May, 2016.

What is the point of freedom of religion if you simply inherit a religion from someone else but did not decide it for yourself, if you didn't have the space to decide what the truth of the universe really is for you.

These programs were never really about terrorism. Terrorism is the justification for these programs.

These programs are about economic espionage, diplomatic advantage.[90]

Snowden was particularly critical of the conduct of the Australian Federal Police, which had abrogated its duty to democracy by allowing itself to be used by politicians to hunt down whistleblowers, including sources on stories about asylum seekers and the National Broadband network.

Is it the role of the AFP to be uncovering the private sources of parliamentarians, of journalists that are revealing issues about scandals, about waste fraud and abuse, about information about abuses of government authority or just revealing matters of public importance?"

For everyone in the room right now that has a cell phone on them, the government knows you are in this room. No matter who you are, no matter what you're doing, no matter how innocent your life may be, you're being watched.

They know who you talk to the most, they know when you talk to them, they know when you're awake, they know when you're sleeping, they know when you're working, they know how you get to work, they know where you go shopping.[91]

Snowden's virtual tour of Australia via video-link from his exile in Moscow was foreshortened after corporate boycotts; money, power, government, self-interest, in the Great Southern Land they ran together in a steaming cauldron.

Except that this was the day after, and there was nothing left but a stinking, distasteful mess.

The place of Snowden in history was assured.

---

90 Ibid.

91 Ibid.

The place of the Australian politicians who had betrayed the best interests of the citizens of their own country most assuredly was not.

In the end it became a choice not of whether or not to be surveilled, but to hope like hell that those thus tasked were good of heart, healthy of intellect, sound of mind.

It rarely proved the case.

By this stage, Alex had heard too much.

"'Alpha male' cop culture exposes AFP women to rape, bullying", "Sex harassment rife within AFP", "AFP needs champions at the top to reform toxic culture", so thundered the headlines after a report into gender issues within the Australian Federal Police.

He could assure anyone who cared to listen that from his own impressions, from what he overheard and was meant to hear, the boofhead culture was not confined to targeting women.

The technology was having a savage affect not just on those surveyed, but on those doing the surveying, turning them, as Schneier wrote, into predators.

Just as humans themselves were infinitely malleable, so, in the end, were the structures they built vulnerable to those cursed with lack of conscience, with maliciousness, malevolence, greed, cruelty and grievance.

Spies begat spies. Surveillance begat surveillance. In the end, nobody could trust anybody. And in secretive and essentially unaccountable organisations like ASIO, with no proper reporting trails to elected representatives or to the public, the circularity of process became disastrous.

Who were all these people, spying on each other, spying on the populace?

The business of intelligence became as much about negotiating to the jurisdictional disputes of competing agencies as it did about investigating those who were a genuine threat to national security.

ASIO and the AFP would have gladly ushered him off the mortal coil. Let us lead you to the Garden of Infinite Delights. Paradise. While all the time another even more clandestine and far more adroitly managed agency was secretly trying to enlist him.

Truth, as always in those cursed days, was stranger than fiction. In her review of Canberra barrister Pamela Burton's book *Foreign Affair*, Vice-President of Australians for War Power Reform Alison Broinowski, wrote:

The capital is "Kafka country" . . . where ASIO "has regularly ruined people's careers for no better reason than having a Communist in the family". Feminists in ASIO, says an ASIO man, are "likely to blow the whistle if someone nicks some paper clips and a biro", and they are worse than terrorists to have around. Canberra is "a shadowy town. Spy city, that's what it's become". How do the spooks decide what is secret? "It's secret if we say so". And ASIO always wins: "the bigger the stuff-ups, the greater is the need for more personnel to cover them up". "If a brave prime minister says, 'No more money', a terrorist act will occur, accompanied by the head spook's words 'I told you so'." [92]

It truly was the case: The Enemy Within.

Those who did not tow the party line were frozen out of their jobs, or became, in an increasingly turbulent world, targeted and discredited by the government they themselves served. In the Brave New World of the 21st Century, there was no room for lack of conformity, much less freedom.

ASIO: The Enemy Within, written by Michael Tubbs, an activist turned barrister who spent much of his career representing clients with grievances against the agency, was a combative book thrown into the mix of the failing reputations of the agencies.

Old Alex, who in his inflamed imagination had been hearing far too many things in reverberating walls, came across it by accident and seized upon it with delight.

The by 2016 elderly Tubbs had been a left-wing activist in his youth who became incensed after accessing his own 1500-page file.

He later became a barrister specialising in representing people whose lives had been damaged by ASIO and were attempting to seek redress through the court system.

Tubbs argued that the Australian Intelligence Security Organisation had no place in Australia's democracy and should be abolished. Since its formation by military officers in 1949, its very existence hidden from the public until the 1970s, it had acted as a partisan political secret police force, ridden roughshod over civil liberties and engaged in illegal activities, all with the aim of creating and managing a docile public. It had succeeded. The once

---

92 Book Review: *A Foreign Affair*, by Pamela Burton, Alison Broinowski, *Sydney Morning Herald*, 27 May, 2016.

politically and socially engaged population could barely name their own political leaders, and cared less. They hated them or dismissed them, as serfs once dismissed the pampered, pompous antics of their overlords, gossip all they knew or wanted to know.

In his foreword, retired Macquarie University Senior Lecturer in Law Gil Boehringer questioned how it had all come to be, how they had got away with it. We could sum up a major lesson of history by those two fundamental words the radical journalist and social critic I. F. Stone enjoined us to never forget: "Governments lie."

> Australian people will demand the end of secret policing. Why? Because it has been used against their interests, even their country. It is a rare thing that the target of secret police have the opportunity to turn the tables and shine some light on the hidden, ambiguous world of the clandestine institutions which we are continuously told operate to protect our society and our country.
>
> Tubbs links the specifities of secret policing here to the general transformation of Australian state and civil society over the last 50 years. Not surprisingly, in the wake of the social impact of pressures to restructure Australia which built up in the 1980s and especially the 1990s, and the coincidence of the 'war on terrorism' since 2001, there has been an intensification of secret policing and surveillance. Indeed, we could say that a surveillance culture has crept up on us.[93]

They were optimistic words. The Australian public might demand the end to secret policing if they knew anything about it. But they did not.

Many people attempting to speak the truth took great personal risk. In the course of Old Alex's lifetime, striking a blow for freedom of expression against powerful vested interests had become a high risk enterprise. Tubbs wrote that we all like the idea of freedom. We like to think we are free – and the freer we feel, the better we think of our society. But freedom was illusory, the public hoodwinked. For hundreds of years, by convention, Parliament had a hands-off approach to our freedom. It could be easily measured to a large extent by what common law fundamental individual rights applied throughout society.

---

93 *ASIO: The Enemy Within*, Michael Tubbs, Boolarong Press, 2014.

In a psychological context, two basic things make us feel safe and secure – one deals with our material needs, and the other our mental state. Our basic psychological requirement is the peaceful enjoyment of our life – the knowledge and peace of mind that comes from feeling that we are free, safe and secure in our home and community. I contend that this feeling only exists if we are imbued with the knowledge that we have certain fundamental rights as free citizens, exercisable against ordinary abuse – even abuse by the government in its many manifestations. But feeling free and being free are not always the same thing.

No sooner had the Cold War withered away than our government imposed its rhetorical 'war on terrorism', and with it, its attack on our freedoms and rights.

Today, even if we might still think we have guaranteed basic rights and freedoms, we do not! They are all gone.[94]

The country was a democracy in name only.

That's the way it felt. That's the way it was.

Tubbs was utterly scathing of a rogue institution which was not just secretive but almost entirely unaccountable, and of the generations of politicians on both left and right who not just let it happen, but failed to warn the public. Political leaders had surreptitiously created an atmosphere of fear within society, and increased the power and reach of ASIO until it effectively became a huge national network of secret political police that spied on political parties, unions, community organisations and individuals.

The terror narrative so beloved by conservative politicians and so ably prosecuted by Murdoch's newspapers in Australia, hand in glove with the government, had allowed for a massive extension of state power.

ASIO . . . is a right wing political organisation, and part of a still growing fifth column criminal conspiracy against the political freedoms and rights we consider sacrosanct. The conspiracy was started many decades ago by fearful right wing vested interests worried at the influence, directly after World War II, of the political ideas and values of the centre and left with and across

94 Ibid.

the broad political movement. It was a conspiracy against the public and its democratic processes, rights and freedoms.

As the years roll on, many more laws have been passed which both individually and synergistically lessen the exercise of our individual free will.

At first, every conceivable thing in public life was gradually regulated, so that only in our private lives could we generally feel free. Today, even that freedom has been taken away.[95]

In his own restless dreams, fearful he may have become the subject of jurisdictional disputes between the agencies, Alex heard the phrase repeated time and again: "They are dangerously incompetent. They are putting the future of the nation at risk."

He could guess, of course, which agency was being referred to.

The arrogance of government grew at the same time as politicians grew weaker, a financially battered media stuck to a narrow band of stories reflecting the fashionable concerns of journalists or of the government, not of the public, and the populace as a whole grew increasingly disaffected.

The collapse in quality journalism wrought by the internet, a barrage of laws restricting freedom of speech and a shifting journalistic culture, along with the conduct of media moguls, most particularly Rupert Murdoch, occurred in a kind of deathly dalliance.

As Fowler recorded, the primary role of journalism in disclosing inconvenient truths and acting as a counterweight to the excesses of executive government had all but been abandoned. In wartime, newspapers nearly always toed the government line by not reporting sensitive information that might be against what is generally known as the national interest.

Now engaged in Orwell's perpetual war, the media having abdicated its traditional, respected role as critical observer and become, instead, a servant of governments and corporations, the profession stank of defeat.

Having devolved to become little more than entertainment or propaganda, an instrument of government and big business, in failing to confront the growing list of misdemeanours of the Iraq and Syrian Wars, as just one example of the many ills facing the country, journalism itself was paying a high price in loss of readership and credibility.

---

95 Ibid.

"Multiculturalism has utterly failed," "ban Hizb ut-Tahrir now" and "Bulldoze these Mosques" read posters from the Freedom Party in protests following the Parramatta shooting. On the other side were banners from the Socialist Alternative: "Stand with Muslims Against Racism".

Here in the heartland of "the most successful multicultural society in the world" Alex had first heard the Hizb's critique of multiculturalism fourteen years before: "If you believe in everything you believe in nothing."

Speaking to reporters after Friday prayers, Chairman of the mosque Neil el-Kadomi said Muslims "should not abuse the privilege you are Australian, which is very important. Get out. We do not need scumbags in the community."

He rejected suggestions the mosque was a breeding ground for extremism.

"I'm not hiding anything. You see in the mosque, there's not guns in it," he said. "We reject terrorism."[96]

The Grand Mufti of Australia Dr Ibrahim Abu Mohamed refused to call the Parramatta shooting an act of terror and snubbed the new Prime Minister, instead sending a representative to a meeting called in the wake of the Parramatta shooting.

And why shouldn't he snub the most powerful man in the land? The Mufti had previously made it very clear he was not going to play puppet or cooperate with the government's messaging.

The good Muslims of Australia answered not to a political leader but to Allah himself. They did not need to be told how to conduct themselves by the unbelievers.

Turnbull's bombs were raining down on Iraq, that week as every other week, killing Muslim men, women and children. Who was the greater criminal?

Turnbull knew full well there would be a price to pay, that virtually every last Muslim in the country disliked him for it.

Dr Mohamed had previously appeared in Islamic broadcasts with Hizb ut-Tahrir, the same group linked to every terrorist death in Australia.

Instead of meeting with the Prime Minister, Dr Mohamed attended a meeting in Bankstown, one of the hearts of Sydney's Muslim West and the old seat of former Labor Prime Minister Paul Keating, one of the staunchest advocates of multiculturalism and high immigration rates.

The group rejected attempts to apportion blame by association and raised

96 'We do not need scumbags': Mosque leader, SBS, 9 October, 2015.

concerns about "message of hate and threats of violence" against Australians of Muslim faith.

Dr Mohamed said violent religious extremism was a rare but serious issue threatening the entire Australian community.

"Sadly, a very, very small number of Australians of Muslim faith have chosen this path," he told reporters through an interpreter.

In the days following the Parramatta shooting there was the usual plethora of white bread politicians declaring Islam to be a religion of peace, the jihadis an aberration, and urging against racism of any kind.

In the next edition of the Islamic State glossy magazine *Dabiq*, titled Just Terror, echoing exactly the early Christians' "Just War", the Foreword praised the Parramatta shooter:

> On this occasion, we will not forget to commend the martyred "lone" knights of the Khilāfah who struck out against the kāfir and apostate enemies near them. These brave men were not content with merely hearing news about jihād battles. They did not use the obstacles laid down by the kuffār on the path to hijrah as an excuse to abandon jihād against the enemies. They did not use a younger age or lack of training as an excuse to be mere bystanders. They sacrificed their souls in the noblest of deeds in pursuit of Allah's pleasure. We consider them such, and Allah is their judge. Amongst these brave knights of tawhīd and jihād was fifteen-year-old Farhad Khalil Mohammad Jabar, who on "2 October 2015" struck the crusaders of Australia and killed one of their personnel.[97]

The same magazine recorded the words of Islamic State's caliph Abu Bakr al-Baghdadi:

> By Allah, we will take revenge! By Allah, we will take revenge! Soon, by Allah's permission, a day will come when the Muslim will walk everywhere as a master, having honour, being revered, with his head raised high, and his dignity preserved. Anyone who dares to offend him will be disciplined, and any hand that reaches out to harm him will be cut off. So let the world know that we are living today in a new era. Whoever was heedless must now be alert. Whoever was sleeping must now awaken.

The Muslims today have a loud, thundering statement, and possess heavy boots. They have a statement that will cause the world to hear and understand the meaning of terrorism.[98]

There were flames inside and out.

The escalating and highly strategic attacks making headlines around the world were acting as an ever-expanding instruction manual.

Even before summer arrived, winter was coming to the Great Southern Land.

Then he was commissioned to do a story on the escalating deadliness of Islamic State's lone wolf attacks.

Senior lecturer in National Security and International Relations at Curtin University and a former senior officer with the Australian Federal Police Dr Mark Briskey told him there were now researchers worldwide looking at the phenomenon of massacres by lone actors. There could well be mass shootings in Australia.

Part of the way to fight against the phenomenon was to decrease the appeal of both Islamic State and other terror groups, and the appeal of far right groups which had now developed a political architecture across Europe, and indeed across Australia.

The events were triggered by the development of a critical mass, depending on the individual's psychosocial makeup and the political situation. While the ideologically driven groups claimed credit, the individual sought glory.

The lone wolf attacks are going to continue so long as people can connect themselves.

Lone wolf actors all say this is a revenge for something that the West has done. They reach a decisive moment where they can no longer host hate blogs or participate in demonstrations or bashings.

A decisive moment is reached where they must act on what they have only previously thought.

It is unfortunately a tragic and evil game changer.[99]

98 Ibid.
99 Lone wolf massacres are on the rise, experts warn, John Stapleton, *The New Daily*, 17 June, 2016.

The more polarised a society, the more likely an incident.

In response to the Parramatta shooting, Turnbull claimed Australia was a world leader in countering violent extremism.

> It is not compulsory to live in Australia, if you find Australian values are, you know, unpalatable, then there's a big wide world out there and people have got freedom of movement. Not all extremist talk – intolerant, hateful speech – not all of it leads to violence. But it's where all violence begins. And we have to call it out. We have to call out the language, the examples of disrespect, the language of hatred wherever it is practised.[100]

Decades of enlightened rhetoric on tolerance, diversity, anti-racism and multiculturalism, and Old Alex had never seen the country more polarised.

Associate Professor of Sociology at Victoria University Ramon Spaaij told him that rather than being members of Islamic State, many of the recent killers had been inspired by them: "One really strong common trait is moral righteousness, a worldview divided into good and evil, and a strong sense of being on the right side of history. They are trying to destroy an enemy that is encroaching on society."[101]

As always the official line was anti-media; the instinctive bureaucratic response of Just Say No promoting acquiescence to the official line.

The Australian Federal Police issued a statement to the ABC's Media Watch program:

> Emotive headlines and the use of simplistic news grabs can help extremists amplify their deliberate strategy to incite fear and hate.

> Extremism and terrorism is real and affects us all, and the media plays a pivotal role in providing information that influences public opinion, therefore it is incumbent on the media to exercise responsible judgement on the news it publishes.[102]

Dr Michael Jetter of the University of Western Australia also waded into the

---

100 Prime Minister Malcolm Turnbull appeals to all Australians to show mutual respect, Anna Henderson, ABC, 10 October, 2015.

101 Lone wolf massacres are on the rise, experts warn, John Stapleton, *The New Daily*, 17 June, 2016.

102 Episode 37, Media Watch, ABC, 12 October, 2015. The AFP, which has a long history of hostility towards the media, did not respond to a request for a copy of the original.

extremely vexed issue of how both Western media and the Islamic State were feeding off each other: "The more coverage you give to terrorist attacks, the more terrorist attacks you see ... The way these guys operate is that they stage some kind of attack and then they get the press for free... Normally if you wanted to get that kind of attention, you'd have to buy advertising space."[103]

Each strategically placed attack, the beheading of journalists, the bombing of airports and nightclubs, the extremely well-choreographed snuff movies, with their high production values, the pictures of injured and screaming children injured or killed by Allied bombs, all were escalating towards a confrontation.

The seeds of chaos could not have been sowed more artfully.

In a mere two years Islamic State had become the biggest story on Earth, terrified the socks off half the world, inspired millions worldwide and cost the intelligence, security and military apparatus of the West many tens of billions of dollars.

They could not have achieved the same effect with the combined advertising budgets of Coca Cola, Nike and McDonalds.

The West was being weakened, exactly on schedule.

Intertwined with the amplifying effects of media coverage was the internet. The same technology which had once promised the greatest liberation of intellect and democratisation of knowledge in history allowed Western democracies to become Surveillance States, seemingly overnight.

And also greatly empowered the jihadists.

Islamic State flooded the internet and thereby the world with choreographed violence.

Two years before its incarnation, very few people had ever seen a snuff movie. Now hundreds of millions of people had seen people being beheaded, stoned to death, crucified in village squares, dragged behind cars, drowned cages, blown up, stabbed, tortured, burned alive, hacked to death, lined up in rows and shot by children.

All of it was being filmed, and beamed out on the internet. If anything was to cut through the blather of a drowned world, the media-saturated 21st Century, it was ultraviolence.

Crucifixions, beheadings, the hearts of rape victims cut out and

---

103 Ibid.

placed upon their chests, mass executions, homosexuals being pushed from high buildings, severed heads impaled on railings or brandished by grinning "jihadist" children—who have latterly taken to shooting prisoners in the head themselves— these gruesome images of brutal violence are carefully packaged and distributed via Islamic State's media department. As each new atrocity outdoes the last, front-page headlines across the world's media are guaranteed.[104]

Far from being an undisciplined orgy of sadism, ISIS terror was a systematically applied policy that followed ideas put forward in jihadist literature, notably in an online tract, *The Management of Savagery.* The aim was to wear down an effeminate enemy.

The media in which Old Alex had spent much of his working life acted both to conceal and reveal, to diminish and promote. It concealed the bombings of the Western allies and the many people they killed and injured, it simplified and codified the conflict into a battle between good and evil with the West on the side of good, it hid the mayhem their policies had fomented and transformed the enemy into a cardboard monster justifiably slaughtered; and at the same time it sent the exact message Islamic State wanted to send, across borders, into millions of lounge rooms, across hundreds of millions of devices.

Be afraid, be very afraid. Believe. Or die. The choice is yours.

But even without the amplifying effect of the media coverage being given to the unprecedented wave of massacres, these were surface storms across a disturbance being entrenched ever deeper into a malevolent fabric.

There was no stopping the cyclone that had been unleashed.

The devil peered through peepholes. A spiritual stain spread across the heavens. One attack was simply a prelude to another. And there really was No Place to Hide.

---

104 Islamic State: The Digital Caliphate, Abdul Bari Atwan, University of California Press, 2015.

DOG WHISTLING IN AMNESIA

A PLACE in the world. A crack in time. An awful dread and a magnificent resonance. The Big White House. The Home for the Incurables. In that October, a damp cold spring in the Great Southern Land, Christmas came early.

After a year running to stand still in a faltering economy, their hearts lifted with a new Prime Minister, worn out by the predecessor's constant exhortations to God, everybody just wanted to relax, to go back to the people they once were.

Swamped in the peculiar claustrophobia of that backyard, Old Alex dreamt of other places, other times, other projects, grander futures and grander pasts. He had intended travelling to Nepal the coming year to write a book called *Buddha's Birthplace*. It did not come to pass.

"You must heal yourself, no one else can, no one else should," read one of the placards posted around Buddha's birthplace, Lumbini in Nepal, where he had spent several months not so long before.

Of all the sayings of the Buddha, that one meant the most to him.

In a place where the electricity only worked for two hours a day, where the surrounding villages were entirely pre-industrial, and where the local shops could not change the equivalent of a five dollar note, he found a kind of peace after the terrors of Bangkok, the haunting menace of the Russian and Thai mafia bar owners he had so unwisely stirred.

Some things in life can neither be repaired nor revisited; and one thing was for certain, he would never again write about the bars of Bangkok.

At the time Buddha's Birthplace felt like the only safe refuge on Earth.

"You die for sure," was the most common threat he heard in Thailand, The Land of Hungry Ghosts.

It began, that terrible pursuit, in the fetid heat of Bangkok. He learnt, all too well, the meaning of the Thai word "tahm peet": mistake.

Everything crashed; fire streaks across battle-scarred ground; the place from whence we would never be the same again, the City of Black-Eyed Angels.

He had loved the chaos of the Bangkok streets, the intricacies of the culture, the beauty of the music, even the choking traffic.

His favourite lines on the city once known as the Venice of the East came from Thai author S.P. Somtow's short story "The Last Time I Died in Venice":

> He beckoned to me in the dying sun.
>
> Venice? What a joke. The Venice of the East. Some antediluvian travel brochures still call it that, but most of the canals were filled in before I was born, and now a skein of highways and overpasses covers the city like a threadworn yarmulke. Instead of the vaporetto, there's fleets of neon-colored taxis; if you fancy a gondola, hop on the back of a brimstone-belching motor-cycle taxi and weave like a maniac through harrowing streets. Here you don't sit sipping a cappuccino on the Lido, gazing at the hazy sea, but instead, sit nursing that self-same cappuccino, perched on the eighth floor of an endless shopping mall, staring, glazed, at the consuming throng.[105]

But even then other visions kept breaking through in recurring dreams: flying over the infinite, an ocean inky black, the black beyond dark matter and oil spills, the only light the faintest sliver of a moon in a starless sky. This was the dream that kept recurring and he didn't know why – black on black, uncanny, beautiful in all its inexplicable mystery and power, the vast sea, a distant shore, a profound absence.

It was the empty shells of high rise buildings next to the freeways that most clearly exemplified the Bangkok of his imagination: full of an evoca-

105 The Last Time I Died in Venice, in the collection Dragon's Fin Soup, S.P. Somtow, Asia Books, 2002.

tive sense of something that had already passed, of the mystery of lives carried out in crowded places, lithe forms, the sunny smile of a pretty girl, the companionship of men, of a history never written. He admired their crumbling forms in the cool of the pink air-conditioned taxis of the present, a master of the universe, able to afford a taxi fare in one of the world's most quixotic cities, the decay of those abandoned buildings a perfect rejoinder to the soaring condominiums in the middle distance; and the skyscrapers spiking the horizon.

Until everything turned bad, he had been perfectly at home in that most charlatan of cities. Tahm Peet. Mistake.

Everyone made mistakes, particularly there. He had been mad, mad with it, the stupid regret.

Sometimes the images of that broken, magnificent city still swirled through him in that dank back yard and were gone; as he listened to the endless, targeted derision of the Watchers on the Watch.

Back in Lumbini, on Nepal's magnificent Terai, life was about simplicity.

He listened and watched elaborate Buddhist ceremonies, all of which, so profoundly, were swept away at their completion.

He lived on the traditional Nepalese dish of rice and vegetables known as Dal Bhat, consumed once a day, and came to love the local saying, which went: "Dal Bhat power, 24 hour."

In a vendetta beyond imagining, his mafia pursuers followed him even there; but could not strike, not on hallowed ground. Contract, contract, assassinate, assassinate. As cruel, callow, vengeful and prideful of their own power as they could be, even gangsters and their corrupt government cohorts were superstitious.

As was his wont, he went to Lumbini on a whim, and was rather surprised to discover it was not a pilgrim-infested village high in the mountains, its paths lined with sadhus and devotees, as he had imagined from past trips through the Himalayas, but was located on the flat plains near the Indian border, that impossibly beautiful area known as the Terai. These were the same plains which stretched across the subcontinent to the Arabian Sea and the Bay of Bengal.

Each day he would explore the area known as Buddha Park, a multi-country project akin to the great cathedrals of Europe. It would take centuries and generations to complete, but was magnificent already.

He would walk through the enclosed UNESCO World Heritage site covering the centuries of accreted temples built on the reported site of Buddha's birth; would explore the gardens, say a prayer at the local temple, and walk, always walk.

He was struggling to make sense of what had happened to him, what was to be vanquished or retained.

He spent much of his days with the local rickshaw drivers, who, he slowly discovered, were mostly Maoists who had fought in recent uprisings. Many of the large houses of the bourgeoisie dotted across the plains were in ruins. The drivers were friendly, kind, invited him to their homes. The Nepalese are a fundamentally traditional people; if one of the rickshaw drivers had less than seven children they would be ribbed for being a poor husband.

These same men could mobilise in an instant, had their own gendarmes and generals, were essentially a hidden army.

Buddha might have ascended, but some of his disciples were still there, or so it felt. The local people had been worshipping in the same area across a two and a half thousand year span, and the spirits of that place had heard their daily woes, their sicknesses, gratitude for the blessings of their children or grief over unfortunate deaths, trepidation or delight at coming marriages or unfortunate loves, their wishes for good luck or success in their school exams, a longing for peace within their own souls, even for enlightenment; there amidst the pre-industrial villages and the swarms of children playing beneath the ancient mango trees.

"You're an interesting case," one of them said to Alex one day, laughing, these spirits of place were always laughing. "Different."

"You knew the Buddha?" he asked.

"Yes. I was one of his disciples."

"Where is he now?"

"He doesn't exist as a singular personality anymore. He's in the heavens. We're still here. We like it here."

Just as he did, he liked it here, this astonishing Earth.

"The world is so beautiful," Buddha is alleged to have said on his deathbed.

It felt, at least for a time, as if one of Buddha's disciples, recognising that he needed help, came with him after he left, returning first to Bangkok and then to the mysterious southern land of his birth.

Although he had obviously heard about it all from the tourists, the disciple, who had been on the flat plains of the Terai for more than two and a half thousand years, was astonished, most of all, by air travel, as together they looked down upon the clouds. "How is this possible? It's so beautiful."

And then Old Alex was back in Sydney, that place where he had so avidly declared he did not want to be. And along came Peter, the Aging Opera Diva. If there was one thing Alex had spent his life avoiding it was upper crust gay men and their musicals, their collections of Barbara Streisand records and Bette Davis movies, their adoration of Joan Crawford – but there it was, forbearance at the fore.

One thing the two of them had in common: they both wanted to make a home.

There were cosy dinners and a barbeque or two in the backyard. They watched the whole of Downton Abbey, from beginning to end. His children, now young adults, came to visit.

An aspiring writer – or at least that was the cover story, he was too intelligent to be just one thing – came to dinner with his girlfriend Joy one evening.

Glen was a little chubbier than perhaps he should have been, blonde, a flashing cheerfulness with a quick, insightful wit, struggling, sometimes, with everything that tumbled through his head. Alex took to him instantly; could tell, when the shields weren't up, what he was thinking. Lively of mind, there was a sackful of artfulness but none of the malevolence he sensed in so many others.

Once, in one of those previous incarnations of youth, Glen had, or claimed to have been, a teenage tout on the Kings Cross strip of nightclubs, brothels and strip joints; precocious, physically appealing in a floppy-dog love-everyone trust-no-one way, generous of spirit if not of body, you can have me if you're very, very lucky, and spend lots of money, maybe, maybe. He was very good at sweet-talking punters into the strip joints.

Older, already from a different era, nostalgic for lost beauty, Alex could swear he had noticed him years before on his odd surveillance trips through one of the country's only red light districts; clairvoyant, charismatic in a street sense, in a land where conformity had become the norm.

Alex assumed that Glen had been caught in a compromising situation, one of the agencies had noticed his precocious talents, particularly with computers, and recruited him. Alex would have hired him in an instant. The truth, which he was never going to hear, didn't matter, Alex liked him and that was that. Whatever stories Glen told the mundanes on shift, Alex knew the truth. In this clandestine, crystalline world saturated with dishonesty, this Kafka country, there were few points of commonality or rapport left. He had not wanted to be here, this time, this place, and he took what friendship he could.

"Do you believe in empaths?" Glen asked over dinner that evening.

"Is it even possible?" his girlfriend asked.

"Sure," Alex replied. "The full potential of the human brain is rarely explored. A military trained empath is in and out of your head in a second, an untrained one senses images, emotions, intent, loud thoughts, but that is all. They can cause a lot of problems. They leak all over the place. They are often troubled individuals. They have difficulty making sense of everything around them. They don't understand their condition. They don't understand why nobody else hears what they hear."

As if by way of explanation.

As if, in the accelerating crisis by which they were now gripped any of these gifts would be enough to save them.

There were always multiple betrayals. "Nothing is as it seems." The thought kept thrashing through his tired washing machine brain. These were the fantastical times. There was even a website, he discovered, Help for Empaths.

The conversation flowed on, as if nothing had happened, the question of empaths quickly disappearing as Peter regaled the table with tales of his youth, of rich boyfriends, fabulous social sets and operatic triumphs in London and New York, in a time far, far away.

Later, in the garden, Glen, having twigged to and been puzzled by the level of harassment he was experiencing, knowing just how off-tap and off-target the intelligence agencies could be, said: "They don't have to harass you to harass you."

It was the break in the traffic, a key to understanding what had happened which he long hoped for, in those years when he had became increasingly depressed, relentlessly pursued. Most of his life he had been complimented for, and made a living from, his ability to write. Now, mixed uncomfortably with the aging process, his profession and his passion had become a malevolent impasse. They thought intimidation would work; it usually did.

To Glen, Old Alex would be forever grateful. Someone had stood up for common decency, taken the sting out of the assault. Or perhaps it was just another false trail, designed to elicit trust. Whatever the motive, in a sense it saved him.

Glen introduced him to the concept of "seahorsing" which, in another sick, contemptible black joke by the agencies, he dishonestly and disrespectfully claimed to mean the deliberate orchestration, the ceaseless cries of the harpies: "One day that man will kill himself. A broken man. A tragic figure. His back against the wall. For him it's five minutes to midnight. God, did you see that body? If he thinks he's got something interesting to say about Australia, he's sadly deluded. He should have retired a long time ago. He was quite a top notch reporter in his day. How old is he now? He was handsome in his day, a good looking man, hard to believe now. Prone to conspiracy theories. He could never help himself, straight to the pub."

He had heard it all, a lot of it more brutal, more personal than he cared to recount.

"That's happened to me," Old Alex said, recognising explicitly many of the techniques Glen was recounting.

"They're called Psyops, or Psychological Operations. There's a whole theory behind it. Look it up. There's plenty of material around. You become conditioned. They can trigger a fright-flight response just by a sound. And if the person has had any problems, say with a particular drug, they will find themselves suddenly being offered it wherever they go."

Came the spiel about targeted individuals, synchronicity, mimicking, gossiping, the treacherous undermining or destruction of the reputation or credibility of those who dared to go against the government line, the many many things that didn't make sense and made the targeted individual doubt their own sanity.

Alex asked: "And so, the person is so disturbed, so disoriented, he thinks he's going mad, and either retreats or commits suicide?"

"Precisely."

"Why don't they just kill the person in question?"

"Because that would look suspicious."

Once he asked a rare friend among the Watchers on the Watch a similar question; why don't they just do the deed? The only answer he ever got was: "They've tried. You're a hard man to kill."

"So if the person does the job for them, kills himself or overdoses on drugs or has a heart attack, all the more convenient?" he asked Glen.

"Quite."

"And if the person cracks or does something stupid? Goes and gets completely smashed?"

"That's when they pounce."

Distressed and depressed, and for a seeming eternity unable to understand what was happening and blaming himself for his own disturbed state of mind, this was a world stranger, more debased and more basely motivated than even he could have imagined.

Old Alex had been the victim of a Psyop operation, of that he had absolutely no doubt.

He had to admit there had been moments of erratic, inappropriate behaviour, human frailty, as if longing for the corporeal. Well, ballyhoo, he wasn't dropping bombs on innocents, he wasn't misleading the Australian public.

The point of the obsession with his own surveillance was not self pity, although he certainly at times felt entirely bewildered, but that if it could happen to him, it could happen to anyone.

Glen was the first person he had ever been able to talk to about any of it. Broach the subject and you sounded certifiable. That was the point.

> The biggest cost is liberty, and the risk is real enough that people across political ideologies are objecting to the sheer invasiveness and pervasiveness of the surveillance system. This is wrong. We should be free to talk to our friends, or send a text message to a family member, or read a book or article, without having to worry about how it would look to the government: our government today, our government in five or ten years, or some other government. We shouldn't have to worry about how our actions might be interpreted or misinterpreted, or how they could be used against us. We should not be subject to surveillance that is essentially indefinite.[106]

Long-term surveillance had an eroding effect on the individual, and an equally destructive impact on the society at large. It had certainly eroded him. It had gone on for years. There on that cloistered plane, in the cluttered backyard and rooms of the Large White House, he knew he was displaying signs of long term stress. He would have done anything to escape, but had no way of knowing how.

---

106 US Supreme Court Justice Sonia Sotomayor quoted in *Data and Goliath: The Hidden Battles to Collect Your Data and Control Your World*, Bruce Schneier, W.W. Norton & Co, 2015.

Instead he had been thrashing pointlessly; ever more broken-hearted as he was defeated each time he struggled to rise from the bottom of an aquarium filled with liquid lead.

That was why Glen came to be so important to him – a simple hand, extended, for whatever motive, to a brother in arms.

It was in that same backyard, through the same source, that for the first time he came across the concept of predatory gang stalking – also known as vigilante or cause stalking and often funded by government. Of that, too, he had firsthand experience, although for a long time he simply had no idea what was happening to him – how it was even possible or what technology was being utilised.

Much of it sounded completely insane, as it was meant to.

> Predatory Gangstalking is a criminal phenomenon referring to a group of loosely affiliated people who, in an organised and systematic manner, relentlessly invade all areas of an individual's life on a continuing basis, as part of their lifestyle. While each individual gangstalker does his or her small part, what defines Predatory Gangstalking is the collective intent to do harm.[107]

Could it have just been paranoia, something he had never previously suffered from? Decades of reporting, diminished to boxing at shadows? Impossible to prove, but in a networked society without borders, where the rights of the individual had been totally eroded and the surveillance state was all pervasive, why was it not possible that this was the next step in the evolution of an increasingly totalitarian world. One of the purposes was to elicit fear. Psyops. He had certainly, at times, become very frightened.

> The purpose of these gang-stalking activities is not just to unnerve the target and make them look foolish or even crazy in public, or to frustrate or intimidate them, or to punish them for some perceived misdeed. The deeper purpose is to coerce them into conforming, to force them to silently accept what is going on, and to break their will and draw them into taking part in this system of control. Anyone around the target will be

---

107 R.B. Ross, quoted in various publications including Gang-Stalking and Mind Control: The Destruction of of Society through Community Spying Networks, Anthony Ferwood, Lulu Publishing, 2015.

clueless as to what the target is experiencing, and the target will appear to be delusional should he or she mention anything to anybody. The sense of isolation that often results, due to a lack of anywhere to turn for help, is meant to break down the target and force his or her silent submission. [108]

Oddly enough, at exactly the same time a spate of books exploring the phenomenon began appear, mostly written by targeted individuals: They included: *The Perfect Crime: Organised or Group Gang Stalking, Coherent Madness: Effective Defence Against Covert Warfare, How To Deal With and Defeat Gang Stalkers, Tortured in America: The Life of a Targeted Individual, Gang Stalking: The Threat to Humanity and My Life Changed Forever: The Years I have lost as a Target of Organised Stalking.*

> It is in the end the stuff of nightmares and what has been called dark prophecy or conspiracy theory is actually ancient agenda in its final stages of being played out.

> On a personal level, participating in any form of gangstalking is not only insane but utterly immoral, and spiritually and criminally corrupt. If you care, choose never to participate, inform the target (carefully/secretly), make a united stand with friends and neighbours not to participate and log all the evidence you can – take down all information you can. Be smart, technology and the capabilities of those that have orchestrated these world terrors are immense.[109]

Fortunately, in a rapidly devolving situation, there were bigger fish to fry rather than spending his time wondering about whispering campaigns and how or why group of people with nothing better to do with their lives, government-funded or not, acted the way they did. They were all leaves in a bigger storm, about to be hit by lightning.

Alex had once, a long, naive time ago, thought people were basically well-intentioned. As they gathered in their hundreds to watch women in cages burn, delighted in throwing gays off buildings or stoning them to death, as they crucified unbelievers in village squares; or on the other side of the equation as they rained down bombs from the sky, leaving hundreds of

---

108 Ibid.
109 Supplied.

thousands either dead or maimed for life, leaving countless thousands of children fatherless, and told lie after lie after lie to justify their actions, he had changed his mind.

Sometimes he watched in the footage as the doomed embraced their captors. Their death was Allah's will.

As for his own interminable surveillance and the harassment he had endured, he asked Glen, there in that dripping backyard lit with tea-candles: "What sort of people would do that to someone else? Low dogs?"

"There is usually a motive. People need to believe that something is true."

"Does it happen in Australia?" he asked, and the answer came in the affirmative.

"ASIO, AFP?"

The response was a shrug; for one to know and the other to find out.

"If you try to talk to anyone about it they will think you are mad. That's the point. There is no privacy."

"From the bathroom to the bedroom."

To the backyard.

That he knew all too well. He had been listening to their vicious, vacuous, redneck comments for years. One could only pray for a glimmer of intelligence amongst the lot of them. Kindness, compassion, understanding, you could only dream.

The state was eating itself, viciously rounding on its own citizens; a kind of cannibalism of its own soul, pursuing outliers, the outsiders, "the creatives" as the marketers at work used to like to call the journalists. The country's best assets destroyed, at the same time as well-fed academics prattled on about "social capital".

In the days that followed, the words rang in his ears: "Assisted Suicide. Our Taxes at Work. We're from the government and we're here to help you."

But mostly the words "Assisted Suicide". And he would shout at no one in particular: "Low dogs. Low dogs." At the whole treacly, malevolent mess – a cauldron of malicious, mean-spirited bastards.

Sometimes, with feeble narratives running every which way, daily journalism to bash out, a business to get on top of, a certain grizzly short-circuited thought disorder filled his head while excitable anguish jumped from his skin like static electricity.

Or was it simply putrid desire, a commonplace longing which would not be filled by any random acts of kindness? "I want to see you again; I want to live with you."

A desire to live in the flesh, so brief in the passing, filed through the dank, overheated air.

Some days were just psychotic breaks.

Once there had been that expression, the nobility of man.

Perhaps the Biblical prophecy was true, in the End Times there would be no natural feeling; people dry-eyed after massacres, ready to face the television cameras.

Volcanoes of jihad were erupting into the splintering black, tearing through the fabric.

> O soldiers of the Islamic State, continue to harvest the soldiers.
> Erupt volcanoes of jihad everywhere.
> Dismember them. Snatch them as groups and individuals.
> Light the Earth with fire.[110]

Brooding in that damp backyard, Old Alex wondered why, in shadows of shuddering fear, with history on the turn and apocalyptic imagery everywhere, destiny had dealt him in and he had dealt himself out. Perhaps that was not it at all, perhaps he was simply suffering the consequences of being hunted to the edge of extinction. The purveyors of surveillance knew the severe psychological and physiological impacts their predatory behaviour had on the targeted individuals. Government operatives had abrogated any and all duty of care. There was no choice but to dive into the ordinary. Heal yourself, the Buddha said, but to heal yourself while being constantly watched, that was difficult.

In the wider world all 224 on board, including 17 children, were killed when a Russian A321 bound for St Petersburg crashed into the Sinai desert.

A security officer at the scene of the crash said:

> The plane split into two, a small part on the tail end that burned
> and a larger part that crashed into a rock. We have extracted at
> least 100 bodies and the rest are still inside. We are hearing a lot
> of telephones ringing, most likely belonging to the victims, and
> security forces are collecting them and putting them into a bag.[111]

---

110 ISIS Leader al-Baghdadi: 'Erupt Volcanoes of Jihad', NBC News, 13 November, 2014.

111 Russian plane crash: Flight 7K8268 crashes Egypt's Sinai Peninsula, *Sydney Morning Herald*, 1 November, 2015.

Sinai was the scene of an insurgency by militants close to Islamic State, who had killed hundreds of Egyptian soldiers and police and attacked Western targets.

Russian authorities initially dismissed claims of responsibility by Islamic State. In the end there was no doubt.

ISIS celebrated the deaths in its official propaganda, while an affiliated group put out a statement on Twitter: "The fighters of the Islamic State were able to down a Russian plane over Sinai province that was carrying over 220 Russian crusaders. They were all killed, thanks be to God."[112]

On his first day in office the new Prime Minister Malcolm Turnbull declared: "We need an open government... that recognises that there is an enormous sum of wisdom both within our colleagues in this building and, of course, further afield."[113]

Worse than complete deception, on Turnbull's watch the public could not have been treated with greater contempt; and the legal apparatus arrayed against journalists and whistle-blowers went from draconian to totalitarian.

In the three short years of the Abbott/Turnbull government freedom of speech had gone backwards. There had been backflips and backward steps targeting journalists in all the major democracies but Australian politicians, with much to hide, had excelled, actions which were already having a ruinous impact on the country's democracy.

Journalists going anywhere near the subject of national security or the operation of the country's intelligence services faced the threat of jail on multiple fronts.

The level of legislation was a kind of dark Alice in Wonderland dystopia: difficult to believe, difficult to digest. Could this really have been a freedom-loving country only a few short years before?

In the Australia of 2016 governments regarded journalists in the same way as terrorists, as a direct threat to their power. Under new legislation reporters such as Alex were labelled "persons of interest". To adopt the once honoured role of social observer had been criminalised by the most lunar-right and most dishonest government Australia had ever seen.

Respect for truth and the public's right to information are funda-

112 Ibid.

113 Criminalising the Truth: Suppressing the Right to Know, The Report into the State of Press Freedom in Australia in 2016, MEAA, 2016.

mental principles of journalism. Journalists describe society to itself. They convey information, ideas and opinions, a privileged role. They search, disclose, record, question, entertain, suggest and remember. They inform citizens and animate democracy. They give a practical form to freedom of expression.[114]

As Alex knew all too well from his own experience, Australian taxpayer dollars were being wasted to survey, harass, bully and intimidate journalists and dissidents.

The dumbing down of the media, the click-driven dive to the bottom, the government's secretive, asinine pursuits, all of it was crippling public discourse. It suited the powers that be to have a dumbed down populace, and pivotal to the deliberate creation of ignorance was the destruction of a free press.

The human brain could be an infinitely complex thing, the reason why so much human endeavour was soaring and why the species had attracted so much attention from the gods, these vessels for the soul; but equally, as Orwell wrote, men were infinitely malleable.

In a trice of history, in their millions, they were moulded into slaves.

Journalism was once an admired profession, one he had been more than proud to join.

Now journalists were viewed as enemies of the state; and the religious thugs who had seized the strings of power and were so actively destroying a once liberal laissez faire country were shielded from account.

Intelligence officers could no longer be charged with illegal activity, meaning thousands of Australians were entirely exempt from the laws of the country, and could target and harass whoever their bosses chose, with impunity. Listening, optical surveillance and tracking devices no longer needed so much as a warrant. The identification of an officer or a so-called SIO, a Secret Intelligence Operation, even inadvertently, could lead to ten years imprisonment. The definition of what constituted an SIO was in the hands of the agencies.

With billions in extra funds, justified by the War on Terror, Australia was building itself an entirely unaccountable secret police force.

Australia was in a league of its own.

The suppression of normal journalistic investigation had been more rabid

114 MEAA Journalist Code of Ethics.

in Australia than even Britain or the US, which both saw major assaults on press freedom.

> The flurry of anti-terror legislation introduced in Australia over the past decade has led to an erosion of freedoms and protections. But increasingly, safeguards were being removed from Australia's surveillance and law enforcement laws at the same time that surveillance and law enforcement powers are being increased. In short, Australia's legal framework was subject to increased susceptibility that these powers could be misused due to lack of independent oversight.

> It criminalises legitimate journalist reporting of matters in the public interest. It overturns the public's right to know. It persecutes and prosecutes whistleblowers and journalists who are dealing with whistleblowers. It imposes ludicrous penalties of up to 10 years' jail on journalists. It imposes outrageous surveillance on journalists and the computer networks of their media employers. It treats every Australian as a threat and denies their rights of access to information and freedom of expression.[115]

Influential bodies including the Committee to Protect Journalists and the Columbia Journalism Review condemned the hostility of Barack Obama's administration as the worst in the nation's history.

President Obama aggressively campaigned on a pledge to bring in the most transparent administration ever. He did the exact opposite, mounting an unprecedented campaign against whistle-blowers, combined with aggressive surveillance of journalists and introducing to his administration intense hostility towards the normal processes of news gathering, thereby shielding the government from accountability.

> In the Obama administration's Washington, government officials are increasingly afraid to talk to the press. Those suspected of discussing with reporters anything that the government has classified as secret are subject to investigation, including lie-detector tests and scrutiny of their telephone and email records. An "Insider Threat Program" being implemented in every government department requires all federal employees to help

---

115 Going After Whistleblowers, Going After Journalism, MEAA, 2015.

prevent unauthorized disclosures of information by monitoring the behaviour of their colleagues.[116]

Instead of using normal news channels, the Obama administration used its own social media, videos and websites to provide the public with government-generated information about its activities.

They must have been giving lessons – as Australian politicians implemented the same strategies.

Their tactics were compounded by the taxpayer-funded Australian Broadcasting Corporation, purportedly independent but nothing of the kind. With no profit motive, and despite their constant cries of poverty significantly resourced, the ABC held an ever-increasing grip on the dissemination of news across radio, television and the internet. For large swathes of the population they were the only source of news or analysis.

Very occasionally uncomfortable for politicians, it was never uncomfortable for bureaucrats or the judiciaries, the unaccountable wings of Australian democracy. The failure of elected representatives to check their excesses and multiple incompetencies, enabled by a compliant media, was a significant factor in the failure of Australian democracy.

The national broadcaster's coverage had devolved into little more than regurgitation of government media releases or a mouthpiece for politicians.

The national debates were the politicians' debates. The Tables of Knowledge were never going to get a look in.

The autocratic impulses of government and the shutting down of public discourse was enhanced by the collapse of quality journalism as newspapers struggled to cope with the internet age, meaning more and more of their stories originated from government or corporate press releases rather than independent inquiry.

In the debacle of Australian's collapsing democracy, failure was further sickened by collusion between government and corporate media, nowhere better exemplified than in the ongoing war in Iraq:

> Though all of Murdoch's newspapers and media outlets had championed the war, without exception, giving the lie to the oft-repeated assertion by Murdoch that his editors make up their own minds, it was in Australia that some of the most unques-

---

116 The Obama Administration and the Press, Committee to Protect Journalists, 10 October, 2013.

tioning support for the war came. Those who stood in the way became victims of a powerful alliance between Murdoch newspapers and the federal government.[117]

The Iraq War was the first war in history to be built entirely on disinformation planted in the media. Murdoch and the Australian government, particularly its politicians, played a significant and nefarious role; and the country was still paying the price. In 2016, they thought they could get away with it all over again.

Australia, and America, ignored far more reliable intelligence that Iraq posed no security threat to any other country, its so-called Weapons of Mass Destruction program was fragmented and self-contained; that there was no evidence of cooperation between Iraq and al-Qaeda; and that embarking on a war would create a humanitarian disaster.

Then Prime Minister John Howard, who led the country into the war, was awarded an honorary doctorate in the Great Hall of the University of Sydney, over the protest of academics. It was here he had graduated in Law in 1961, and built many of the powerful associations which were to serve him, if not the country, very well indeed.

Outside the ceremony protesters waved placards reading "Howard War Criminal" and "One Million Dead".

News Corp Australia titles accounted for 59% of the daily newspaper market, with sales of 17.3 million papers a week, making it Australia's most influential newspaper publisher by a considerable margin.[118]

There were always close relationships between the editors at News Limited and the administration. From his strategically placed desk, an eyrie on the third floor, under fluorescent lights and directly outside the Editor-in-Chief's office at News Limited headquarters with views down the central atrium of the building, for years Old Alex had watched the politicians with their begging caps come and go.

You scratch mine and I'll scratch yours.

Murdoch was only ever going to run with an expose that suited his purposes; and thus, the politicians hoped, their interests and influence would be preserved.

---

117 *The War on Journalism*, Andrew Fowler, Random House, 2015.
118 FactCheck: Does Murdoch own 70% of newspapers in Australia, The Conversation, 8 August, 2013.

Alex, as a lowly general reporter, seemingly powerless in that over-lit place, longed for a world where it was impossible to lie. In the tribal, polarised media landscape of left and right, exemplified by the entwining interests of corporate and government Australia, lay no truth at all.

"My time in jail," he often thought during his fifteen years at News. As it turned out, upon leaving all he did was enter a wider prison, the panopticon.

If he had not experienced his own savage levels of invasive harassment and sustained abuse Alex would never have believed the lengths to which the Australian authorities would go to silence journalists.

Leaks from Edward Snowden showed not only that America's National Security Agency, the NSA, was illegally monitoring and collecting billions of communications worldwide; but also that in the mother country, which some Australians still thought of the United Kingdom as, Britain's chief intelligence agency GCHQ actively hacked journalists and news organisations, literally classifying them on the same threat level as terrorists: "Having investigative journalists on that level undermines the idea of 'free speech' and 'freedom of the press', both removed when the GCHQ actively hacked and surveyed different news organisations at length."[119]

Journalist and researcher Sarah Harrison, who was involved in the Snowden case, decried the attacks on freedom of speech and freedom of the press:

> Today instead of meaning "to ensure the stability of a nation for its people", national security is a catchphrase rolled out by governments to justify their own illegalities, whether that be invading another country or spying on their own citizens. This act – it is now crystal clear – is being consciously and strategically deployed to threaten journalists. It has become a tool for securing the darkness behind which our government can construct a brand new, 21st-century Big Brother.
>
> This erosion of basic human civil rights is a slippery slope. If the government can get away with spying on us – not just in collusion with, but at the behest of, the US – then what checks and balances are left for us to fall back on?[120]

119 British Intelligence Agency GCHQ lists investigative journalists as 'terrorists', David Curry, ITPROPORTAL, 20 January, 2015.

120 Britain is treating journalists as terrorists – believe me, I know, Sarah Harrison, *The Guardian*, 15 March, 2014.

In Australia it was all trending the wrong way.

Sometimes he heard his pursuers in the strangest of places, in places where no man should be followed. He felt as if the word ASIO was bleeding out of damp driven walls; and so they were both led ever further into a diabolical dance, the pursuers and the pursued, the predator and the target.

Lead them out onto the ice, watch them drown. Or in the old journalistic parlance: "Let them hang themselves."

Snowden discovered deception, lying and cheating by Australia's closest ally America. The National Security Agency was conducting massive surveillance operations without the knowledge of, and against the best interests of, the broader public.

> The NSA was spying on everyone on Earth. Every detail scooped up from emails, phone calls and social media archived forever, providing a huge searchable database on every individual on the planet. The NSA shared the load with its sister organisations in other English-speaking countries. They had built massive complexes around the globe where the colossal volumes of data could be stored and analysed – in Canada, the United Kingdom, New Zealand and Australia, where a former sheep farm near the nation's capital, Canberra, had become home to mega-computers in buildings the size of aircraft hangars: on the southern wing of the NSA's vast digital archive.[121]

Australia was not just complicit, it was an active participant.

Classified US National Security maps leaked by Snowden revealed the four Australian facilities involved in the US surveillance of telecommunications and internet traffic worldwide. They were the US Australian Joint Defence Facility at Pine Gap near Alice Springs, which was also being used as a front-line weapons facility directing drones to carry out extrajudicial killings on behalf of America, and three Australian Signals Directorate facilities: the Shoal Bay Receiving Station near Darwin, the Australian Defence Satellite Communications Facility at Geraldton and the naval communications station HMAS Harman outside Canberra.[122]

---

121 *The War on Journalism: Media Moguls, Whistle-blowers and the Price of Freedom*, Andrew Fowler, Random House, 2015.

122 Snowden reveals Australia's links to US spy web, Philip Doring, *The Sydney Morning Herald*, 8 July, 2013.

The data thus collected could be searched in milliseconds by any agent with the appropriate level of security clearance anywhere in the world using a program called XKeyscore. The program permitted the user to monitor anyone's email and online searches in real time.

Snowden's magnificent achievement was to alert the world to the fact that everybody had lost their privacy, and if they wanted to regain it there would have to be a long hard struggle.

> They also knew that anyone who tried to hold intelligence organisations and government to account, like investigative journalists, would have to outmanoeuvre the very systems the surveillance state had put in place to defend itself from exposure. It was going to be a deadly game of hide-and-seek, where journalists would be hunted like criminals.[123]

It always does to ask the simplest of questions: how did we get here?

Spooked: The Truth about Intelligence in Australia, a book which was later to take on a particular significance in Alex's own life, provided some of the answers.

In the wake of the 11th of September 2001 attacks against the Twin Towers, Australia became an extremely active combatant in the war on terror, particularly in the field of legislation.

There was a remarkable burst of law making, with the country's legislative performance eclipsing the relatively paltry performances of the UK, US and Canada, not only in the extent of these efforts in inhibiting the liberties and rights of every Australian, but in their sheer quantity. Dozens of pieces of legislation were passed.

Turnbull would soon be following his predecessors, introducing yet more terrorlaws – a legal and political charade cloaking incompetence and failure with an air of busyness.

As security specialist Dr Mark Rix wrote in *Spooked*, misuse and abuse of information, inscrutable but far-reaching information classification procedures and downright obfuscation had all become key weapons in the counterterrorism arsenal of a democratically elected government. He suggested that instead of a war on terror the legislation created a war on openness and accountability, such were the curbs on transparency and public disclosure.

---

123 Ibid.

The secrecy surrounding information, national security information, security, national security, international relations and law enforcement interests is baffling, all-pervasive and largely impenetrable. Successive Australian governments have successfully added to this secrecy and impenetrability. It is far less clear whether this has helped to make Australians more secure from the threat of terrorism. It is clear, however, that it has left them more vulnerable to the secret, clandestine and sometimes illegal activities of ASIO, which, surrounded in secrecy, founded on sloppy, all encompassing and unfathomable legislation, is subject to few if any requirements for openness, transparency and accountability. In the end, this can only lead to one conclusion: there really is no security in secrecy.[124]

Ultimately there would be no reason for attack, because there was nothing left to defend. Australia was becoming a totalitarian society by stealth, no better than the societies it was morally bankrupt enough to bomb.

Whether the general populace knew it or not, the pursuit of journalists and whistle-blowers and the progressive dumbing down of newspapers, radio and television ultimately was having a terrible effect on the society at large, and thereby on themselves.

The shutting down of whistle-blowers, freedom of expression and the public's right to know would become one of the worst legacies of the Abbott/Turnbull era.

In the report "Criminalising the Truth: Suppressing the Right to Know", journalist's union Chief Executive Paul Murphy wrote that Australia had gone from being a bastion of press freedom to a country that criminalised legitimate public interest journalism. As a result democracy was being destroyed – all in the name of terror, national security, the public good; but in reality so the government could avoid embarrassing scrutiny.

Our Parliament has ruled that journalism is a crime. In recent years it has passed laws that can imprison journalists for up to 10 years for simply doing their job. New national security laws have focussed not only on fighting terrorism but also silencing voices, punishing truth-tellers, suppressing the public's right to

---

124 *Spooked: The truth about intelligence in Australia*, Edited by Daniel Baldino, University of NSW Press, 2013.

know and criminalising journalism. Government has been so determined to inoculate itself from embarrassment that it has developed a battery of laws to punish and imprison those who expose the truth, whether they are whistle-blowers or journalists.

In order to further persecute and prosecute whistle-blowers, the government has now equipped itself with the two-year mandatory metadata retention laws, and the Journalist Information Warrants that accompany them. Journalists' telecommunications data can be secretly accessed by 21 government agencies. All this because government is embarrassed: not because a news story is wrong but because it's true and everyone knows it. So press freedom and the public's right to know are being trampled on in a mockery of open and transparent government.[125]

The laws were being blatantly abused to suppress dissent, as Alex knew all too well from the attempts to discredit and intimidate him.

The universal monitoring of journalists' phones had rapidly destroyed any independence of investigation, turning journalism into anodyne entertainment or government propaganda. It was no longer possible for any government worker to simply make a phone call to a journalist and blow the whistle on corruption or malfeasance within their own wing of government. That call, whether made from an office phone, home phone or with the increasingly universal use of voice detection software, from a public telephone, could be immediately traced. No phone was safe. The old trick of borrowing someone else's phone or going down to the local phone box no longer worked.

Those who possessed the resources and the technical ability to beat the system were almost always those with the most malevolent intent.

The only way someone wishing to inform on government waste or maladministration could safely contact a journalist was to use private messaging applications, and even then, with so much contradictory information flying around it was almost impossible for the layperson to determine which messaging systems were the most secure.

As was easy to discover online, Islamic State liked the mobile app Telegram and had issued a warning against WhatsApp; perhaps they knew something.

125 Criminalising the Truth: Suppressing the Right to Know, MEAA, 2016.

Old Alex was commissioned to write a story about it, and then decided to download the app himself. Just in case.

> For once the advertising logo is correct. The headline grabbing mobile app Telegram promotes itself as a "new era of messaging". It uses military grade encryption to ensure the privacy of communications. That it is one of the most popular programmes for jihadists and Islamic State supporters is for some beside the point. You might as well criticise the mujahedeen for driving cars.
>
> For others it is entirely the point.
>
> A new era of encryption products has created a nightmare for security agencies worldwide.[126]

Critics called Telegram the command and control centre of terrorism. In recent months ISIS had claimed responsibility for the Paris massacre, the shooting down of a Russian airliner and other attacks, all on Telegram, as well as using it as a major propaganda tool.

> A terror plot can be hatched without leaving a whisper in cyberspace. Messages can be set up to self-destruct within a second, while end-to-end encryption combined with the use of a Virtual Private Network, which scatters IP addresses around the globe, ensures that the user cannot be traced and the communications cannot be decoded.
>
> So confident is Telegram that its messaging cannot be decrypted, last year it began offering a $US300,000 reward for anyone who could do so. The prize remains unclaimed.[127]

Old Alex grew up in an era when it was enormously impolite to read other people's messages or letters, where communiqués would sit unopened for days or even weeks before they were opened by the intended party.

In the Australia of 2016 such common decency was a quaint, fantastical notion. Now encrypted phones, voice distortion software and virtual private networks were all becoming part of an increasingly complex game.

---

126 Telegram App, written for *The New Daily*, available on the website The Journalism of John Stapleton.

127 Ibid.

He hadn't wandered into writing about terror for any other reason than that it was the most obvious story around.

He hadn't wanted to fall foul of the government, to come under surveillance and harassment, to learn about and thereby expose the conduct of those who spent their time pursuing and attempting to destroy other people's lives.

The level of surveillance and suppression that was now a defined part of government apparatus had been in its infancy during much of his working life; one of which he had been barely cognisant and towards which he had been entirely dismissive.

Even though, with crowded newsrooms his place of work for decades, he was used to operating in the open, Old Alex became increasingly disturbed by the level of intrusion.

It was no false scare.

Snowden and WikiLeaks revelations, made in the public interest, exposed widespread illegal activity by intelligence agencies and other arms of government. The revelations also exposed thousands of breaches of privacy rules and misuse of private information. Journalism played a crucial role in making the public aware of what governments had been doing in the name of the people.[128]

Alex wished he had a tech-head to advise him. The closest he ever came to was Glen, who made it clear he had no intention of providing the service.

He heard Glen saying one day, "I'm going to stop lying to him." But he never did. Under surveillance from their own bosses, he knew intelligence officers could not reach out and explain that they, too, thought the entire operation against him had been a disaster.

And so Alex just ploughed on… sick of it all, and particularly sick of the rank hypocrisy of the nation's leaders.

Some Australian politicians, including former Prime Minister Kevin Rudd, mouthed weasel words about freedom of information and protecting whistle-blowers. They meant not a word of it. Rudd had been one of the worst purveyors of surveillance the country had ever known.

That was until Tony Abbott came along. In introducing to parliament the greatest assaults on freedom of expression and journalistic practice the country had ever seen, Abbott declared: "I believe that Australian police and

---

128 Going After Whisteblowers, Going After Journalism, MEAA, 2015.

security agencies operate in a fair and reasonable and responsible manner. And this is an unprecedented additional level of protection for journalists and I'm pleased that we are able to offer it."[129]

In the Australian context, "Orwellian" became a feeble term.

Recent tranches of legislation even included a charge of "recklessness": a term in sloppy, hastily drafted legislation which, in the hands of any capable lawyer, could mean virtually anything. Conviction would turn entirely on the biases of judges, who had their own nests to feather.

Shutting down scrutiny of multibillion-dollar defence contracts was just one of the reasons for the cloaks of secrecy. The malfeasance so characteristic of so many government departments and agencies and spreading through to the judicial system had to be hidden from the public at all cost. Just try and get the travel budgets of High Court and Family Court judges, a subject of particular interest to Old Alex, and see how far you got. They were spending public money hand-over-fist on their five-star world junkets, and should be made accountable, but most certainly were not.

At the same time as he was introducing his full frontal assault on democratic government, journalism and the public's right to know, at a speech dedicating the War Correspondents Memorial in Canberra Prime Minister Malcolm Turnbull declared:

> Let me deal with the greatest role of ... all journalists, and that is to stand up to the powerful – to hold up the truth to power ... Our democracy depends not just on the politicians, not just on the judges, it depends on the armed services defending our freedoms but it depends vitally on a free press; on a free and courageous press; on free and courageous correspondents who are not cowed by governments and big vested interests.

> It takes courage for any journalist, for any correspondent, to stand up to big businesses, to vested interests, to governments and never more so in a time of war, when all of the arguments of patriotism can be levelled, inveighed against a journalist who seeks to tell the truth.

> We are one of the oldest democracies in the world. Our democ-

---

129 Prime Minister Tony Abbott, joint press conference, Parliament House, 18 March, 2015.

racy depends on many men and women, on many institutions ...
but none is more important than a free and courageous press.[130]

The cliché "breathtaking hypocrisy" didn't even begin to encompass the
perfidy of it all.

Ross Coulthart was one of the last investigative journalists in Australia, a
plier of an ancient trade.

Alex had been stuck on general news for decades, what was dismissively
known as "ambulance chasing" or "human-interest" stories.

The legions of political reporters whacking their bylines across government
press releases had higher status than journalists writing stories about people
rather than policy. There was no respect for reporters in any case, and certainly
no respect for specialist generalists, which is what he was, someone who could
write about anything at a moment's notice, in the degraded journalistic culture
of Murdoch's News Limited where he had worked for so long.

But Alex had always been an admirer of Coulthart, who he was friendly
with decades before, when they had both been earnest young journalists on
The Sydney Morning Herald thinking they could change the world, leave it
a better place. Alex had thought the path lay through providing a voice for
the voiceless. Ross thought it was through exposing the misconduct of the
powerful. They were both right.

In the sadly diminished times they now found themselves in, Ross had
become Australia's most outspoken journalistic critic of government legislation restricting reporting.

On his own journey of discovery, Alex went to interview Ross in one of
those noisy Sunday cafes full of well-maintained children and prosperous
parents, those who had benefited from stable relationships and Sydney's
property boom. Some of what Ross had to say confirmed his worst fears,
some he was hearing for the first time, such as software that automatically
scanned the communications of journalists every five minutes. For the
government apparatus could only survive in secrecy, and any journalist
was a threat. If the truth would out, the malcontents in the jungle would
revolt, in the society they had the nerve to call a community, where no
community lay.

---

130 Tribute to War Correspondents, Prime Minister of Australia's website, 23 September,
2015.

Since 9/11 the national security laws which were brought in to ideally protect the public against terrorism have been increasingly used to suppress dissent, to hinder media scrutiny of issues that have nothing to do with terrorism or national security. The scale of surveillance and the number of intercepts is mind boggling. There are thousands of requests made every year by a score of government agencies, without warrant. It is not sanctioned by a judge, not effectively oversighted by anyone. Politicians have remained silent because they are scared about it and it suits their purposes.[131]

In an address to the Press Freedom Dinner, run by the Walkley Foundation which ran Australia's most prestigious journalism awards, Coulthart recalled the early days:

When I first came to Australia 30 years ago, there was a huge public outcry against the proposed Australia Card – essentially a national photo ID card. Those concerns now seem very tame compared to the threat posed today by metadata surveillance and other spy laws. And that's especially a worry if you're a journalist.[132]

After considerable public outcry, then Prime Minister Bob Hawke, who had been barracking for an Australia Card, backed down.

Australians did not want to be followed, identified by government agencies, become one of the government's targets. It was in their colonial DNA – they wanted to be free.

Decades before, Alex himself had done front page stories on the damaging impact the Australia Card might have.

As always with government intervention, the Law of Unintended Consequence was in full play.

Back then, thirty years before, there were travelling bands of fruit pickers on the so-called harvest trail: apples in summer in the Adelaide Hills, asparagus in autumn at Koo Wee Rup south of Melbourne, cherries in winter in Tasmania, tomatoes in spring at Bundaberg 360 kilometres north of Brisbane. Each travelling band had mapped out their own harvest trails to suit

---

131 Interview by author with Ross Coulthart, 12 June, 2016.
132 Transcript of Press Freedom Dinner 2015, sponsored by the Walkley Foundation. Supplied.

themselves and the seasons. They all had their favourite places, favourite farmers. If they were not treated well, they did not come back.

The travelling bands lived the gypsy life. It was hard work, they were knockabout families, they had no permanent home and they liked it that way. With virtually zero exception, they were paid in cash and were also on welfare benefits.

They believed that an Australia Card would put an end to their lifestyle and their double-dipping.

The system worked. The farmers had their seasonal labour. The workers made enough money to make the backbreaking work and the itinerant lifestyle worth their while.

They all said the negatives would outweigh the positives if they couldn't also collect the dole, which helped cover costs and the times between employment as they travelled between farms and regions.

A Whistler-style picture propelled the story onto the front page on Saturday, the paper's biggest-selling issue.

But in the end the government got its way through another door and with the increasing expansion of state control, a way of life which had endured for generations was extinguished. True to their word, the pickers stayed home and collected welfare cheques.

Farmers remained chronically short of seasonal labour to the present day, and many fruit growing operations became unviable. Fruit withered on the trees; entire orchards were ploughed into the ground. Government sponsored schemes to encourage backpackers to go fruit picking were deeply flawed and regarded as hopeless by farmers, who had to teach each new batch of uninterested backpackers how to pick an apple.

And so another part of Australian life and tradition was destroyed by bureaucratic over-reach, all for the sake of an entirely counterproductive tax grab.

Fast forward thirty years, and the level of state surveillance the working man's hero Bob Hawke tried to introduce looked positively benign.

Coulthart told the Press Freedom Dinner the country was seeing the revenge of national security nerds, who had nothing but contempt for journalistic scrutiny of their operations.

> What we're seeing is the revenge of the national security nerds,
> who seem to have nothing but contempt for journalistic scru-

tiny of what they do, and the evidence suggests Government's wrapping itself in the flag with questionable claims of national security to try to shut down often legitimate journalistic investigation of Government wrongdoing.

What the Government doesn't seem to realise is that sooner or later truth will out anyway. It's easier now to steal entire databases and to leak those rather than to go public as a whistleblower. I suspect Government bullying with laws like this may actually prompt sources to lay low but to instead recklessly leak data as with Chelsea Manning's drop of an entire diplomatic cables database to WikiLeaks or Edward Snowden's equally massive digital download of secrets from the National Security Agency. Even the most highly secure data can be breached by folly...which is why every Australian should be asking why in heaven's name we are trusting our Government with massively increased powers to store our metadata.[133]

Coulthart, with his impeccable contacts, was talking to everyone from the Prime Minister to drug traffickers via encryption apps.

Determined to shut down any transparency, the government was trying to close even this tiny and extremely technical window of communication between journalists and informants. Under Turnbull, anti-encryption legislation had been passed into law which made the teaching of encryption illegal, and was so loosely worded it potentially outlawed not just the use of encryption apps on smartphone. s, but even the phones themselves. Even email.

It was yet another piece of world-beating overreach. Legal, academic and cryptographic experts all warned that almost anyone could be caught up in the web of the new laws, and face a ten year jail term as a result.

At that point, everything Alex knew about encryption could have been written on the back of a postage stamp.

Stories equalled money; and with Glen living opposite, albeit for a short time, he encountered him on most days. Alex quizzed him for ideas – and he suggested the idea of the government crackdown on encryption.

His own kids would say: "It's so simple even old people like you can understand it, Dad. Just Google it."

But he just couldn't get his head around it.

---

133 Ibid.

All he knew was that the technology was now so complex he could not escape it, the key-logging on his computer, the following of every word he wrote, the absurd levels of surveillance. And all he could do was to be mischievous, to hope he laid a trail that would blow up in their faces. Over-surveillance produced its own pitfalls; they could be spun any yarn, decoys and IEDs laid along their path, and ultimately be hoist on their own petard, as the saying went.

He just wanted them to get the message: bugger off.

How could you even form new relationships when your every bumbling move was monitored and ridiculed?

If only he could sue for damages. As it was he lacked the technical ability to escape, or the power to eradicate the past.

At one point, while travelling through Asia, he went without a phone for six months; unable to escape the clutches of the so-called "snitch device", unwilling to be constantly tracked, to have every word and every communication recorded. Instead he chose to make no phone calls at all.

For a journalist, even one taking a break from daily reporting, it was far from ideal.

In the end they resorted to other tactics to follow him. There was no escape, only surrender, on long walks and short, in slums, on planes, in humble homes and high-lord mansions. The shuffling anonymity which had once served him so well served him no longer.

He gave up. Surveillance was a rabbit hole that could consume amateurs such as himself trying to evade it; and the technology bit both ways. One man was drowned out amongst the voices of millions; one man could access the world. They could be crucified by their own incompetence in the same measure as the target could be intimidated. Drown yourself in data, and it became impossible to know what was important. Survey someone constantly, and all you got was information on how someone behaved under constant surveillance.

Sitting in that damp, cluttered, over-watered backyard, with the mosquito breeder aka water feature beginning to go regularly on the blink, he and Glen cooked up the encryption story.

The news site he had begun doing assignments for liked the idea, and away he went.

The innocuous-sounding Defence Trade Controls Act was a

bloated and poorly drafted piece of catch-all legislation which imposed enormous compliance burdens, includes in its many categories encryption, the process of encoding a message so that it can be sent privately.

As many of the industries and professions involved are government-funded, the burden falls largely on the taxpayers.

No estimates on the cost of the compliance have been made available.

Once the preserve of spies and governments, encryption has now become an essential part of modern life, used to safeguard everything from medical records to online banking.[134]

The legislation covered almost everything to do with international interaction, publications, conferences, teaching, research, correspondence and informal scientific exchanges, editing and peer review, commercial consulting, foreign nationals, patented information, sanctions, travelling and working overseas and records management.

Renowned international lawyer Geoffrey Robertson told him the Defence Trade Controls Act was "so sloppily drafted that it is a real threat to academic research which has no sensible connection to military technology. There should, at the very least, be an exemption from criminal penalty for those who are engaged in legitimate education or research exchanges."

For Alex it was just more evidence, if any was needed, of the bizarre levels of ineptitude Australian governance had reached, the iron grip of bureaucratic thinking over common sense.

Ross Schulman, Senior Counsel for the Open Technology Institute in the US, told him there was not much that could be done to stop the use of encryption because so much of the products were either open source, or produced by companies not within the jurisdiction of the various concerned governments.

Legal mandates are bad policy for privacy, commercial, and cyber security reasons, and are often times simply unenforceable.

They are our digital homes, and people are seeking to protect

---

134 Malcolm Turnbull's doublespeak on encryption, John Stapleton, *The New Daily*, 25 November, 2015.

these devices in the same way we all seek to protect our physical homes.[135]

Old Alex had neither a physical nor digital home – dwelling only briefly in places over which he had no control and in which he was grotesquely over-observed. Hunted, pursued, fed up, he never stayed in one place very long.

President of the Law Institute of Victoria Katie Miller told him the bill was so obscure that not even a lawyer of her longstanding experience could understand it:

> This Act is highly technical and broad in its reach. It potentially affects significant parts of our economy and community, including individuals who are using encryption for legitimate uses. It is imperative that the Government communicate the changes and clarify whether the amendments are intended to extend to commonly used encryption and, if not, amend the Act as a matter of urgency.

Dr Daniel Mathews, a lecturer in mathematics at Monash University, described the laws as vast overreach, an outrageous attack on academic freedom – and for the lay person, an assault on the right to privacy.

> It is so uncertain. It scares a lot of researchers to go overseas where there is not such uncertainty and potential risk of running foul of the law. It is hard to imagine the government coming after your smartphone, but the definitions are extremely broad. It is not clear at all.
>
> A lot of teaching at university is streamed online through overseas campuses. If a researcher is talking about encryption for everyday purposes, do they really need an export license to teach it in that class?[136]

In that story, as with so many others, there was no sense emanating from government, no defence, no response, no justification. The Government no longer felt any need to justify itself to mere journalists, those gateways to the broader public they allegedly served.

---

135 Notes for Malcolm Turnbull's doublespeak on encryption, John Stapleton, *The New Daily*, 25 November, 2015.

136 Ibid.

Experts from around the world joined in condemning the laws, with the International Association for Cryptologic Research organising a petition, signed by an impressive swag of world experts.

The country with the audacity to market itself as an "innovation nation" was happy to dive headlong into monitoring every last single aspect of every citizen's life – never mind the cost or the damage to the society at large.

Decades of cowardly, lazy and incompetent politicians and years of grasping political turmoil had allowed vast bureaucracies to spread ever wider, and what would have once seemed so extreme became commonplace – even laws which could be used to ban smartphones.

There was no singular or intelligent voice at the top of the pile. Instead the nation was hostage to bureaucrats whose natural instinct was to protect their positions and expand their powers.

It was no wonder the country was crumbling, death by a thousand cuts. The unwieldy machinery of government continued undisturbed by universal criticism of its actions. It never responded to anything anymore. It did not have to.

For an aspiring writer Glen showed remarkably little interest in the technicalities of actually writing the story. Perhaps he was distracted by the investigation into the ice dealers at the Carlisle opposite, where he was briefly staying, or the parallel investigation into police conduct towards local Greens Member Jenny Leong.

Now thereby hung a tale, and a very revealing one at that.

Following her call to end harassment of ordinary citizens by police using tazers and sniffer dogs, her Facebook page was hit with a slew of racist and sexist comments – coming, as it would turn out, from the police themselves.

Legislation allowing police to harass the hapless, harmless folk who might be carrying the odd joint, was another totalitarian gift from that great friend of the people, former Premier Bob Carr, who would declare outright he had spent a lifetime serving his Party (the Labor Party) – a cry worthy of any communist apparatchik.

He never once said he spent a lifetime serving the people.

The war on drugs had failed – and was now feeding directly into the dire situation the country faced. For decades politicians ignored the advice of experts that the laws, by making drugs appear like forbidden fruit and driving up the price to such highly profitable levels, were empowering both criminals and corrupt police – in other words, all the wrong people.

Of commonsense there was none.

With no accountability, vast amounts of the national security budget were taken up with agents playing cops and robbers with drug dealers – while creating fertile ground for corruption.

That the situation got progressively worse, harming not just the country as a whole but criminalising swathes of the population for no purpose, appeared at least in the official version of events to be beside the point.

Ironically, perhaps, at around the same time Ms Leong was being harassed, Alex was commissioned to do a story headlined "The war on drugs has failed".

All the warnings by the nation's experts that the laws were counterproductive had been ignored.

Old Alex had written about drug policy for decades and could see for himself that all the calls for commonsense by the nation's academics in the field had been ignored; and Australia was now facing the consequences. The country was in the grip of an entirely avoidable ice epidemic, the trade was being run by ethnic gangs and a significant slice of the profits from the multibillion dollar industry were being directed straight into jihad networks, the outcome of decades of failed policy.

> The failure of successive government to accept the advice of policy experts has led to a booming drug trade, according to experts. The trade is apparently so profitable the Australian Crime Commission admitted this year that hundreds of millions of dollars are now being funnelled by crime gangs out of Australia to fund terrorist groups such as Islamic State.[137]

You reaped what you sowed.

Ignorance is bliss. Well, not necessarily. In ignorance lay unbridled fear – and consequence.

Decades earlier, he had come to the attention of the authorities when he wrote a prominently displayed story on former Prime Minister Bob Hawke's $100 million Drug Offensive, which was launched with great fanfare and accompanied by a flood of television and print advertisements.

The story demonstrated that the government ignored its own compila-

---

137 The war on drugs has failed, say experts, John Stapleton, *The New Daily*, 13 November, 2015.

tion of research from around the world that such campaigns did not work, arousing rather than dampening interest and defining margins towards which people were drawn. The Hawke Government was prepared to put electoral gain before the welfare of the public. It was not a story that went down well with the powers that then were.

Decades on, and former Commissioner of the Australian Federal Police Mick Palmer told Alex that taxpayers were not getting value for money out of extensive drug operations: "Seeing this as simply a law enforcement issue has proven a failed exercise. It hasn't worked, never worked and has no chance of working."

Commissioner Palmer said it was difficult to get political traction for drug law reform because being "tough on drugs" was an easy message to deliver: "In my experience it is hard to get politicians even to enter the debate."

All the warnings over the decades that the harsh-on-crime drug laws beloved by politicians were clearly counterproductive, gifting extensive and intrusive powers to police which were easily abused, had been ignored. The case of the harassment of Jenny Leong demonstrated just how badly police could act at even the slightest threat to their power.

Even by their own low standards the behaviour of the NSW Police Force towards Ms Leong was extraordinary, exhibiting all the worst aspects of animalistic, pack behaviour.

On March 17, Ms Leong introduced a bill to the NSW lower house aimed at ending the use of drug detection dogs in public spaces without a warrant.

A day later, her Newtown office, just down the road from where Old Alex was staying, published a photograph on her official Facebook page condemning the actions of two police officers seen patrolling a Sydney train with tasers and sniffer dogs. The post said: "This kind of harassment and intimidation is exactly what the Greens' bill is aiming to stop."

Ms Leong said she had always anticipated a "lively" and "robust" political debate about the policy and bill. But what followed was an avalanche of criticism about the train post, swelled by a wave of unrelated, sexist and racially driven abuse – some of which was posted, shared, liked and applauded by police officers via their private Facebook pages.

> As Ms Leong's shocked staff worked to have the lewd posts taken down, they continued to be fanned across Facebook – with the aid of police involvement.

As the MP's own Facebook page continued to be deluged by offensive material, police employees publicly celebrated the abuse – and contributed to it with other derogatory memes carrying her image. "Ha! Top Shelf!" said one officer based at Cabramatta who added: "Now people are posting screenshots of it back on her page!"

Another, at Sydney LAC, wrote: "She is still copping a smashing – love it!" He later added: "I haven't been banned yet and she is still getting it both barrels."[138]

Leong's father was called a "swamp monkey". A city-based detective posted a modified image of the Greens MP's Facebook profile picture and suggested: "One condom could have prevented this from happening."

All of this was being conducted at taxpayer's expense.

Soon enough Old Alex would find out for himself just how poorly behaved the Newtown police were.

Meanwhile the crackdown on Australia's freedoms was reaching bizarre new levels.

Journalist with *Guardian Australia* Paul Farrell found that the Australian Federal Police, who were pursuing his sources on reports into the government's asylum seeker regime and Australian incursions into Indonesian waters, had exhaustively accessed his metadata.

Australia's treatment of asylum seekers was one of those hot button social justice issues whipped up by media and taxpayer-funded refugee lobby groups which galvanised sections of the Australian community either for or against, as much as Australians could be galvanised about anything anymore.

Journalists were prohibited from speaking to the asylum seekers themselves, actions which would have humanised those the government sought to demonise.

As a result all the talk of the abuses of refugees in offshore detention camps, a particular obsession of government-operated media, became a dog whistle to the opposite tranche of public opinion: that foreigners were a threat and the government's tough-on-borders approach was working.

The AFP was empowered to investigate and prosecute leaks to Farrell

---

138 NSW Police Officers caught trolling Greens MP Jenny Leong on Facebook with racist and sexist posts, Eamonn Duff, *Sydney Morning Herald*, 10 April, 2016.

under Section 70 of the Crimes Act, which criminalised the "unauthorised disclosure" of information by a Commonwealth officer.

That was, any information. The release of any material whatsoever, even if not classified and readily available from other sources, now opened up the threat of prosecution.

Any government officer who, no matter how clearly appalling the evidence in front of them might be over maladministration, criminal activity and wastage of taxpayer funds and whose conscience mandated they contact a journalist to make the information public, could be jailed.

The truth was the government's greatest enemy.

Farrell had been through a typically murky, elaborate, expensive and time-consuming process in order to get the information he sought, procedures beyond the ken or resources of any ordinary citizen. The admission from the AFP that it had accessed his phone and email records came in a complaint to the Privacy Commission.

> The Australian Federal Police has admitted that it sought access to my metadata in pursuit of my sources. In a submission to the Privacy Commissioner, it revealed it had sought "subscriber checks" and other forms of email checks relating to me as part of one of its investigations.

> What's most extraordinary is that it was entirely lawful for the AFP to access my phone and email records. And that's a real problem for journalists and their sources in Australia.

> It's become a sadly normal reality that journalists' sources can be targeted in Australia in an effort to hunt down whistle-blowers.

> And almost always it's about politics. It's not about national security. It's about stopping embarrassing leaks that tell uncomfortable truths about power in Australia.[139]

The government may have portrayed the introduction of its tranches of new national security legislation as a fight against terrorism, but let slip that it was more motivated by fear of Snowden-like leaks.

Snowden had worked closely with journalists to reveal that US govern-

---

139 Australia's attacks on journalists are about politics, not national security, Paul Farrell, Criminalising the Truth, MEAA The State of Press Freedom in Australia 2016.

ment officials routinely and deliberately broke the law. Snowden declared he was willing to sacrifice all because he could not in all conscience allow the American authorities to "destroy privacy, internet freedom and basic liberties for people around the world with this massive surveillance machine they are secretly building".

The Australian Government wanted no such repeat in the Antipodes. Politicians ignored vitally important concerns about press freedom, prepared to damage the country as a whole in order to protect themselves.

Snowden, convinced his own life was in danger, believed the threat extended to any journalists who dealt with him. He later wrote: "The US intelligence community will certainly kill you if they think you are the single point of failure that could stop this disclosure and them the sole owner of this information."[140]

Were the Australian authorities prepared to kill to protect their own interests?

Old Alex thought: "Almost certainly so."

They were certainly prepared to target and attempt to destroy any journalist who got in their way; that much he already knew for certain.

> Public interest journalism relies on whistle-blowers, the confidential sources that provide crucial information to journalists – sometimes placing them at great risk.
>
> If the identity of whistleblowers can be revealed then that has a chilling effect on public interest journalism; sources needing anonymity cannot rely on their contact with a journalist being kept secret. When that happens, we all lose.
>
> If you are going after whistleblowers, you are going after journalists.[141]

When an event was organised to mark the 30th anniversary of Freedom of Information laws in Australia, not one government minister attended or made any contribution.

Legislation to entirely exempt parliamentary departments from the Freedom of Information Act was rushed through parliament, even though

---

140 *The War on Journalism*, Andrew Fowler, Random House, 2015.
141 Going after Whistleblowers, Going after Journalism, MEAA, 2015.

this was contrary to submissions from those departments. The government stopped responding to key reports from the Information Commissioner. It ignored a suggestion that ministerial appointment diaries be published on the web. Australia did not join the International Open Government Partnership formed in September 2011, which now had 64 member countries.

When Malcolm Turnbull's party first came to government under Tony Abbott it announced the abolition of the Office of the Information Commissioner in its first budget. When its efforts were blocked in the Senate, it promptly defunded the OIC.[142]

This was a government extremely uncomfortable with scrutiny. What did they have to hide? A very great deal.

Because the procedures for Freedom of Information applications had become so expensive and complicated, and public servants so obstructionist, increasingly any challenge to the official narrative was the purlieu of giant media organisations, the only bodies that had the required resources.

The taxpayer-funded Australian Broadcasting Commission, which dominated almost all debate across the country, only challenged the status quo in a warbling confine of soft left concerns and identity politics, which in any case suited the powers that be, mopping up as it did the normal social justice and fair-go instincts of the Australian populace. Let them get in a self-righteous lather over gay marriage aka marriage equality, or the fate of refugees aka asylum seekers, or climate change aka global warming; meanwhile we're going to screw you.

On the opposite end of the spectrum, exposures were confined to those that suited corporate interests.

The War on Journalism, to reference Andrew Fowler's recent book, had a profound impact on the psyche of the country. The lack of questioning, the lack of spirit, was everywhere you looked: the dispirited gaze of a window cleaner, the earnest but orthodox debates of youth, the drivel that emerged from the car radio. Beyond the gutless front pages and the servility of a defeated population, it also impacted, in a technical sense, on the practice of journalism itself – particularly on those most noble and isolated souls, whistle-blowers, whose brave acts were often lost on modern-day journalists and news editors gripped with their own populist notions of what constituted news. The dive to the bottom, to the lowest common denominator, was in capable hands.

---

142 Media Got Complacent, in Criminalising the Truth, Laurie Oakes, MEAA, 2016.

Long ago, in a different life, Alex had been on friendly terms with Jean Lennane, founder of Whistle-blowers Australia. She was a fearlessly uncompromising and highly intelligent woman who could not abide the groupthink that was taking over the country. While reflecting her own professional concerns as a psychiatrist, Dr Lennane had been a powerful force for common sense; and in the Australia of the 2010s there was more than one type of mob rule, epitomised by the thuggish behaviour of the so-called "thought police" and lack of respect for the opinions of ordinary workers, the Tables of Knowledge.

"I won't back down," written by Tom Petty and famously covered by Johnny Cash, could have been her theme song: "You can stand me up at the gates of hell / But I won't back down."

During his research, Alex began to wonder what had happened to her and searched the internet, only to discover, sadly, that Jean had passed away in 2014.

She had survived long enough to enter a barely recognisable world where whistle-blowers were for all intents and purposes extinct. And with their extinction came the death of investigative journalism, for in the world without privacy which the Australian authorities had created, no whistle-blower could approach a journalist without being detected. Even if communication could be made with the use of elaborate and highly technical means of subterfuge and encryption, sledgehammer legislation would likely see the perpetrator in jail. An act of courage made in the public interest to expose corruption and abuse in office brought down the full weight of the state on often lonely individuals. The thugs had won, and these gangs were funded by the taxpayer.

An unfettered government was a dishonest government, and in the Australia of the new millennium nobody trusted the overlords.

A distrust of government also meant a distrust of the government's wars.

There was a price to pay.

If you had to abrogate personal freedoms and create a compliant, unquestioning, docile population in order to get away with your programs, the price was too high.

If you had to introduce sledgehammer legislation to quash legitimate public interest journalism, jail whistle-blowers and manufacture an anodyne level of public discourse, then the price was too high. For media, both new and old, was one of the primary vehicles through which a productive, inquiring, independent-minded people were born.

Jean was one of the very few professionals who spoke out about the outlandish abuse of psychiatric reports within the judiciary, in particularly within the Family Court, the NSW Department of Community Services, and within children's courts around the country. It was no accident that these organisations, all with dire reputations, had at the core of their corruption the same idiosyncratic psychiatric practices. The truth was nowhere to be found.

The last post on the Whistle-blowers Australia website, a tribute to Jean Lennane, declared that these were dangerous times for whistle-blowers, those who stood with them and the 'fair go' society that Australians once so loved.

> Solid information is becoming very hard to come by and it is likely to become even harder . . . These laws have little or nothing to do with maintaining the security of our borders and everything to do with frightening good people into silence in the face of human suffering and tragedy. More than ever before we need people of goodwill . . . to stand firm with those who come forward in the public's interest to put what is right ahead of rampant political self-interest.

> We may need to see many more of us pushing back with rallies and social media like the 'je suis Charlie' campaigns with 'je suis refugee' # tags, flags and banners flying from every corner of our nation before our political representatives get the message of not in our name, you don't, when you try to stop good people exercising their ethical and professional responsibilities to speak out ...[143]

The tribute post to Lennane referenced the end results of Australia's laws, including its morally, ethically and militarily indefensible involvement in Iraq. In darkness and in secrecy evil blooms; and bloom it had.

> Top psychologists and senior officials in the American Psychological Association (APA) secretly collaborated with the Bush Administration's interrogation programs. The secret 'rendition'

---

143 National Whistle-blowers Day, Whistle-blowers Australia website, 30 July, 2015.

laws ensured that we too were a part of it. If we are ever to learn anything from history, then this is the time to learn that this shocking behaviour is the natural endpoint of laws introduced to normalise wrongdoing and justified as needed to combat the wrongdoing of our geopolitical enemies. It is a race to the bottom with tragic human consequences.[144]

Walking down Wilson Street at the back of Newtown, beside the abandoned railway sidings, Old Alex stooped, the beachcomber in him, to pick up a discarded book: George Orwell's *Nineteen Eighty-four*. The book was entirely prophetic. He should have called it *Two Thousand and Sixteen*.

It was literally 1984 the last time he read the book, living in Finchley in London – in love, fit, always on the move, always doing something, both wild and wildly happy, the closest perhaps he ever came to being content, life an adventure.

For the first time in more than thirty years he read the slogans of Big Brother:

WAR IS PEACE

FREEDOM IS SLAVERY

IGNORANCE IS STRENGTH

How apposite they were for the Australia of 2016: a country involved in perpetual war, where the government threw every legislative threat they could at small businesses while encouraging people to become wage slaves; where the population was being kept in deliberate ignorance and journalists doing their jobs were threatened with jail.

After all those years, he read the passage:

Behind Winston's back the voice from the telescreen was still babbling away about pig-iron and the over fulfilment of the Ninth Three-Year Plan. The telescreen received and transmitted simultaneously. Any sound of Winston made, above the level of a very low whisper, would be picked up by it; moreover, so long as he remained within the field of vision which the metal plaque commanded, he could be seen as well as heard. There was of course no way of knowing whether you were being watched at

144 Whistle-bl.owers Australia, National Whistle-blowers Day, Dr Cynthia Kardell, 30 June, 2015.

any given moment. How often, or on what system, the Thought Police plugged in on any individual was guesswork. It was even conceivable that they watched everybody all the time. But at any rate they can plug in your wire whenever they want to to. You had to live – did live, from habit that became instinct – in the assumption that every sound you made was overheard, and, except in darkness, every moment scrutinised.[145]

This was long before the invention of smartphones and smart TVs, both of which could now both broadcast and receive information, both of which were snitch devices – the phone picking up every conversation, movement, even change in body temperature, while the television picked up every movement and every conversation in your own lounge room.

After the Leong affair, and the hornet's nest it provoked – for-no one liked to be caught in a lie, and the police most certainly did not like their conduct exposed – Glen and Joy moved from their pokey little room above the Carlisle to a smart apartment down the south of King Street.

Alex could hear, or thought he heard, the buzz of anger from the ice dealers who thought he was a rat and wanted to bash him; and from the police whose comfortable little scams and obnoxious behaviour had been exposed.

The pair had never looked right in the dodgy atmosphere atop the pub, just weren't the types whose lives had gone off the rails sufficiently to end up there, and Alex occasionally wandered down to visit them in their new, far more fitting abode.

He knew the cover story was a sham, but played along; and knew he himself was a POI; person of interest. There were multiple stories depending on the listener, different tricks afoot; but didn't much care. He liked them and that was that. He should probably have been more careful.

A police siren went by Glen's apartment in South King Street one evening.

"Someone's had an original thought," he quipped, and they all laughed. It didn't seem so improbable anymore.

He was trying to make connections in a complex matrix. He was trying to find a solution to that which ailed.

"Nobody ever talks to you directly," Old Alex complained, in one of their curious multi-level conversations where it became apparent that Glen knew far more than he ever let on.

145 *Nineteen eighty-four*, George Orwell, Martin, Secker and Warburg, 1949.

"The books are evolving. It's as if they are from somewhere else."

It was a curious path.

Trying to get organised, he came across a story he had written in London in the early 1980s, an interview with the founder-manager of the Sex Pistols, Malcolm McLaren.

The interview had ended with a question from the photographer, Richard Trevaskis, long since dead, who asked: "One last question, is all this scratching making you rich?"

To which the at the time fabulously famous McLaren replied: "I hope so."

And to which Old Alex had butted in: "All this scribblin' ain't making me rich."

And their idol replied: "The life of a writer is a hard one."

Both Richard and McLaren were dead now; while Old Alex survived, a shard of glass into the future, with no-one to report back to.

The conversation on the balcony turned more serious.

"You have to trust someone," an operative known as Brian told him on that balcony in South Newtown, as weaving protective filaments spread across the sky and pieces of an invisible jigsaw began to fall into place. Unfortunately, he had heard the line before.

And then he asked Brian, who seemed both particularly independent-minded and well-informed on the subterfuges and institutional oddities, the false accusations which flew through their kind of shadow work: "Why are they so bad? Is it because they operate in secret, because they are totally unaccountable?"

And the response: "You have to realise, there are some good people."

The line would keep recurring to him in the following months as he tried to seek some reassurance he would survive.

Later, he expressed surprise when Glen explained to him that their new television was picking up everything they said, all part of the Samsung terms and conditions which almost every customer clicked on without reading.

Nothing could be kept secret.

"Well, I've only got one thing to say," Old Alex said. "What the fuck?"

It was indeed a Brave New World, just without the bravery.

There were some strands of kindness. "You're in the process of being un-fucked," he was assured, after annoying the Watchers on the Watch for days by giving every microphone in range the benefit of his views.

But he knew, could hear, there were multiple faces, and never knew who to trust.

Stray facts clung in his increasingly feverish imagination.

International security agents had for a time been extremely exercised by the fact that they had been unable to track phone calls made on international flights, opening up a narrow window for private communication.

Of course that crack in the panopticon was soon plastered over.

The stories came thick and fast, there in that dank summer; as Alex, too, just like the fearful spirits slouching towards Bethlehem, struggled to be born anew.

Appropriately, he did a story on the surveillance state and could feel the ancient instinct to hide – in caves hewn into high dusty cliffs with views down across the plains. No-one could approach unseen. But those steep inclines did not always save their huddled families when the Gods were roiled.

The story was headlined: "The Govt is Reading What You Post Online."

The net is tightening for all Australians.

Last week the government proudly announced that it was monitoring social media websites, including Facebook, to crack down on welfare fraud.

Centreline is trawling not just Facebook but Twitter accounts and eBay.

The revelations came on top of the introduction of metadata laws in October, which critics saw as the biggest invasion of privacy in Australia's history.

The mass surveillance is already altering behaviour through self-censorship and the inhibition of normal behaviour, the so-called "chilling effect", and has greatly expanded the reach of the state into the personal lives of individuals.[146]

In the fevered backyard he shouted at his tormentors.

It did no good. There was no time-out to be had. Instead there was bracing for a hot, angry wind; before the guardians declared themselves.

---

146 The Govt is Reading What You Post Online, John Stapleton, *The New Daily*, 9 February, 2016.

He could hear all the strange rustlings: the seaweed-like fronds of stray thoughts, the chatter of televisions, spattered dreams, soap operas. They dreamt of everything from Pokémon to profiteroles, even of cabinet meetings and parliamentary divisions, but most of all of true love, football, pizzas and death. "She's flatlining."

He heard the police changing shifts in the early morning, their caustic descriptions of the night's detritus. "He's harmless," he heard one of them say about a gentleman of the street, as the derelicts had once, in a politer age, been known.

And he tried to concentrate on the story in hand.

The government announced that as a result of its surveillance of social media, including Facebook and eBay, it was recovering two million dollars a year from people avoiding taxes or cheating on their dole payments by working more than the prescribed number of hours. The money was peanuts in terms of a federal budget and a massively resourced department like Human Services; but that didn't stop the boast.

The government wanted people to know one thing: they were watching.

The level of surveillance of the ordinary citizen was more or less the same as that feared by the clinically paranoid, one commentator said, and at that, Old Alex laughed. Vice Chairman of the Australian Privacy Foundation David Vale told him the monitoring of social media sites by government agencies was now ubiquitous:

> When people discover this it comes as a shock. Because a lot of it is done in secret and is not transparent, you can't audit back up the chain, were they justified, did they have a warrant? The uncertainty and invisibility of who is at the other end is a significant, corrosive influence.
>
> Facebook exposes a lot of people to privacy and security risks. Whether it is for a government to say 'suckers', whether that is morally and ethically and policy-wise appropriate is another question.[147]

In the process of the story, just acting like an old-fashioned general news reporter trying to beat a deadline while not repeating the government press

---

147 The Govt is Reading what you Post online, John Stapleton, *The New Daily*, 9 February, 2016.

release word for word, he asked the PR hacks at the department and the minister's office how many public servants were involved in trawling the nation's social media. Hundreds? Thousands? For what? A slip of thought, a letter of defiance, a moment of individual enterprise, the sale of a couch or a twenty-year-old car, a radical idea, the vaguest sign of independent thought?

Such as: "Get Off Our Backs."

Was there any cost-benefit analysis, as in, was the government spending tens of millions to claw back two million?

He asked. There was no answer.

The attitude of the government flaks was entirely different to when he had first entered the profession. Once they would have been doing their job, massaging the story to get out a positive outcome for their bosses or their institution. Equally, having come from the same democratic, journalistic tradition as himself, they would have displayed some earnestness of mission to answer the question and help him meet his deadline.

The function of the media as an essential wing of democracy was, at least at the individual level, between journalists and government media officers, respected.

Not any more.

The attitude: We're not going to tell you and that's that. We've said what we're going to say in the official release and who on Earth do you think you are to question us?

No obligation. No duty of care. No responsibility.

The journalist was the enemy. Open inquiry was the enemy. Truth was the enemy.

More than sixty government agencies were seeking to access telecommunications data gathered on every Australian citizen in the name of counter-terrorism. Typical of the nightmare of secrecy and out-of-control government abuse that now characterised Australia, the information was only released following application under Freedom of Information legislation, a deliberately tedious, complex and expensive process beyond the capacity of most Australians.

Those wanting access to metadata included the Australian Health Practitioner Regulation Agency, the Australian Postal Corporation, the Australian Taxation Office, as well as many government departments and financial control agencies. A sampling of these included Australian Transaction

Reports and Analysis Centre, the Civil Aviation Safety Authority, the Clean Energy Regulator, the Departments of Agriculture, Defence, Environment, Foreign Affairs and Trade, Health, Human Services and Social Services; Fair Work Building and Construction, the National Measurement Institute, as well as a plethora of state government departments, all wanted your metadata.

Even the Royal Society for the Prevention of Cruelty to Animals wanted access to your personal information, including emails, every website ever visited, every phone call made and the Targeted Individual's location at any given time. Were your pets sleeping at home? Were they sleeping with a government official? Were they checking dissident websites?

Were they in the middle of a forest barking: "Leave me alone. Leave me alone. Leave me alone."?

There was plenty of blame to spread around.

In another piece of Orwellian crushing of dissent, early in Malcolm Turnbull's watch metadata laws came into force. They were passed with bipartisan support. The laws, while using terror as a cloak, were aimed squarely at journalists, specifically at circumventing the ethical traditions of the profession which mandated the protection of sources.

As a last-minute piece of *Animal Farm* nonsense, the parliament created a so-called "safeguard" – the Journalist Information Warrant scheme; and as part of the scheme, yet more useless bureaucratic machinery: the Office of the Public Interest Advocate.

It might as well have been called The Office of the Window Dresser.

The laws enabled at least twenty-one government agencies to access journalists' metadata in secret, to identify and pursue a journalist's sources without the journalist's knowledge, including whistle-blowers who sought to expose instances of fraud, dishonesty, corruption and threats to public health and safety. The measures had nothing to do with counterterrorism, the lie under which the public had been sold the pup.

The government was already doing a lousy job. Now they could do so with impunity.

- The Journalist Information Warrant scheme was introduced without consultation with the profession.

- It operated entirely in secret, with the threat of a two-year jail term for anyone reporting the existence of a Journalist Information Warrant.

- Public Interest Advocates, the only course of appeal, would not represent the interests of journalists. A journalist could never challenge a Journalist Information Warrant.

- Each Journalist Information Warrant could scope the entire cache of telecommunications for the previous two years, in one giant fishing expedition, trawling through the journalist's metadata in the hunt for sources, thereby exposing every source.

- There was no public reporting or monitoring of how the warrants operated. That was, no accountability whatsoever.

- Journalists would not know if a Warrant has been taken out against them and if by some means discovered that one has been taken out against them, could be jailed for two years for publishing the fact. The first they were likely to know about this was when they or their source were prosecuted.

- Journalists and media organisations never knew how much of their data had been accessed nor how many sources and news stories had been compromised.[148]

Someone should write a book *Metadata and the Mega Rich*, Old Alex thought, for all the laws did was protect powerful vested interests in the government and corporate spheres while putting the entire Australian population, including himself, under permanent surveillance.

Could someone who first began publishing pieces of journalism in the 1970s and had just written a book called *Terror in Australia: Workers' Paradise Lost* possibly be the subject of a Journalist Information Warrant? Or was it illegal to even speculate?

It was mind-boggling stuff.

---

148 Criminalising the Truth, MEAA, 2016.

HOLD FAST THE TRUTH

AMIDST THE daily welter of commentary on overwhelmed national security services, stricken democracies, no-go areas in a failed pluralism, the fall of the Old Europe, the increasing tensions as millions of Muslim refugees poured onto the Continent, thousands of allied bomb drops on the mujahedeen, slaughtering men, women and children alike, came one short sentence: "There are things that can't be mentioned, sacred secrets."

What secrets?

That souls in agony were the easiest to harvest?

And if the Abrahamic God really did rule the heavens, he did not require peace.

Confused by the welter of encroachments into his own life, the deliberate haunting as he tried to re-establish himself after being adrift for so many years, bullied by low life thugs and invisible assailants, his head full of peculiar visions in narrow streets, Old Alex walked past the graffiti-coated walls of Sydney's inner-west.

One piece tilted to the area's bohemian past: "Newtown has never been about Yuppie Life. Respect the locals."

The best-known piece of street art in the suburb was against a large wall set back slightly from the main thoroughfare of King Street: an image of Che Guevara with the words of Martin Luther King, "I have a dream" against the Aboriginal colours: black, yellow, a deep, earthen orange red.

One, superimposed over the image of a newspaper, recorded the words: "Australia hits the wall."

Some spoke of drunken nights and happy longing: "Shout, shout, let it all out."

Another well-crafted piece of street art showed a picture of a man spray-painting a wall with the words "Free speech. Conditions Apply."

Another, emblazoned with the image of an armed extra-terrestrial and the words: "Australiens. Come in Piece."

In a nearby Stanmore Lane was a quote frequently, and incorrectly, attributed to George Orwell: "During times of universal deceit telling the truth becomes a revolutionary act."

There was talk of a new Dark Age. All was not well.

It had begun in blood, with Abraham, the monotheist who founded the Jewish, Christian and Islamic faiths, killing those who worshipped not God but His creations. He was the first of his time, in a world of animists and ancestor worshippers, of spirits of place, of magic and powerful gods, many gods, of idols and rituals, to mark the difference.

> Therefore God gave them up in the desires of their hearts to impurity for the dishonouring of their bodies with one another. They exchanged the truth of God for a lie, and worshiped and served created things rather than the Creator, who is forever worthy of praise! Amen. For this reason God gave them over to dishonourable passions. Even their women exchanged natural relations for unnatural ones....[149]

The blood, the deaths, had spilled down the centuries, from the extreme cruelties of the Early Church into the present day.

In the wider world, a US intelligence report showed that Islamic State now held provinces in Afghanistan, Pakistan, Yemen, Libya, Iraq, Syria, Egypt, Algeria, Nigeria and Saudi Arabia.

The group was heavily armed and well equipped with military hardware originating in the West, much of it looted, captured or illicitly traded from poorly secured Iraqi stocks – another consequence of the disaster of the Iraq War to which Australia had been such a willing partner. The country was flooded with arms during the war, many of which went missing or ended up in the hands of IS.

Amnesty International's report Taking Stock: The Arming of Islamic State, recorded:

---

149 Romans 1:24-26. Berean Study Bible.

IS fighters are now equipped with large stocks of mainly AK variant rifles, but also US military issue M16, Chinese CQ, German Heckler & Koch G3 and Belgian FN Herstal FAL type rifles . . . and Russian, Chinese, Iranian and American artillery systems. In addition, IS has captured more sophisticated equipment, such as guided anti-tank missiles and surface-to-air missiles. The quantity and range of IS stocks of arms and ammunition ultimately reflect decades of irresponsible arms transfers to Iraq and multiple failures by the US-led occupation administration to manage arms deliveries and stocks securely, as well as endemic corruption in Iraq itself.

These arms flows were funded variously by oil barter arrangements, Pentagon contracts and NATO donations. The bulk have been seized from or leaked out of Iraqi military stocks. [150]

In Alex's own increasingly claustrophobic world, trails of stories from previous few years continuing to loom and vanish.

"You could have held me by the hand, you could have spoken to me directly."

"We tried to reach out. We tried to tell you."

In the narrow streets around The Big White House, the drifts of damp winter leaves were beginning to rot as summer struggled to be born.

Alex was back in Australia, where he had so not wanted to be; and although he was yet to acquire a room of his own, was often sleeping over at the Big White House. He had walked slap bang into a hyper-real world. Under perpetual surveillance, he had done his best to shut down every trace of psychic disturbance that could be tracked, every trawl rope catching trails of fortune.

What had once been talk of a new style of consciousness was now a sentimental tug, a failure to thrive. The grand project of social reform, all the multiplicity of words, inclusive, harmonious, diversity, all of it was a chimera, a black pointed star scything into a world that never was and never could be.

"There's nothing wrong with what he's written," a voice said; while a soldier poured scorn anyway: "Fuck him." Of course a bullet would have been cheaper.

---

150 Taking Stock: The Arming of Islamic State, Amnesty International, December, 2015.

They were living on the edge of a savage and rapidly devolving situation. Where the threat lay? It lay everywhere, from within and without.

Even in this far-off outpost, Sydney, Australia, there was mounting disturbance: the street-mad homeless talked faster, schizophrenics shouted louder, the random spasms of dementia forming patterns as they flung out their arms ever wider. The platitudinous statements and puerile debates emanating from the nation's politicians in no way reflected the reality on the ground.

"You need help," one of the Watchers on the Watch said after a change in personnel. "We're here now. We will protect you. We've got your back."

But he did not know who to trust, what was true and what was not.

George Orwell's *Nineteen eighty-four* was being frequently referenced around the world, befitting of the times. And to reference it once again, Alex thought, there is only one solution: we will meet in the place where there is no darkness, that is, in the middle of the torture chamber. For where else, in a totalitarian world, with so many cameras, so many mobile devices, so many laws that the state itself was gridlocking, was it possible to exchange information but under fluorescent lights and white spaces, in a place where everybody could see and nobody could see, where terror reigned?

Where else could there be an act of kindness?

But most of what he heard in the garden of the Carlisle, amidst the students from the nearby colleges and universities, were the passions of youth, of a search for justice and fairness, the confidence of a new generation that they knew best. Little did they know that all the normal desires to make the world a better place, characteristic of the young, were taken up with deliberately manufactured concerns; their lives dictated by a poorly educated rabble of self-appointed elites clutching their degrees to differentiate themselves from the common muck, their limitless egotism making it impossible for them to acknowledge the pragmatic common-sense wisdom which once characterised the culture.

While the public space was taken up with such heartfelt issues stirred by the bureaucracy and government-owned media, the people were being robbed of every freedom they had once enjoyed – including the simple freedom to disagree.

The state was co-opting everyone into its blanket singularity; those who opposed it were stunned into silence, marginalised, ridiculed or denigrated.

Like the gods who lined the bar each afternoon for happy hour, they soon learnt sport was the only safe subject.

An assault on journalists was an assault on the nation.

Freedom of speech was a foundation pillar of democracy; and no one had ever conducted an assault on freedom of speech like the present incumbents, the so-called Liberal Party, a piece of oxymoronic nomenclature if there ever was.

Legislators had gifted extraordinary Star Chamber powers to a grab-bag of anti-corruption bodies, including NSW's independent Commission Against Corruption, characterised by secrecy, coercion and compulsion.

And the better they did their jobs, the more journalists were being hauled before them.

> The journalist is ordered by the Star Chamber to appear. Failure to do so incurs a fine or a jail term or both. The journalist must appear in secret – only the journalist's lawyer can know they have been ordered to appear. If the journalist tells anyone aside from a lawyer that they have been called to appear, they face a fine, a jail term or both.

> The journalist can be compelled to produce documents, notes and recordings. Failure to do so can incur a fine or a jail term or both. If the journalist respectfully refuses to divulge information from a confidential source, or refuses to identify a confidential source – as they are ethically obligated to do – the journalist faces a fine, a jail term or both.

> Caught in an ethical nightmare, the journalists who have been called to appear and produce their work before a star chamber have been unable to inform their editor or even their professional association about their predicament. They have been unable to seek advice about their professional and ethical responsibilities. To do so could immediately lead to a fine or a jail term or both. And, of course, they cannot even tell their family.[151]

This was a freedom-loving country?

This was a democracy?

---

151 Criminalising the Truth: Suppressing the Right to Know, MEAA Report into the State of Press Freedom in Australia 2016.

This was a farce.

And that was by no means the end of the suppression of free speech in Australia. The country's outlandishly dysfunctional family law and child protection systems and the many shonky operators therein were protected by rafts of legislation ostensibly aimed at protecting the privacy of the children involved, but in fact concealing scandal after shocking scandal.

Alex's old colleague at *The Australian* Caroline Overington, one of the best operators in the business, lamented that newspapers were prevented from telling the truth:

> It's gone too far in our democracy. I cannot impress upon you all enough how much you don't know. At any point in time in Australia there are more than a thousand suppression orders on stories that you have a right to know. Now I am prohibited by law from telling you what those suppression orders cover. But just use your instincts for a moment . . . there is so much you don't know.[152]

Australia's second most populous state, Victoria, whose members of the judiciary in particular liked to preen themselves as "progressive", operated in the shadows, protecting themselves and abrogating power well away from the disinfecting sunshine of news coverage.

The same people who liked to talk about freedom, diversity, open-mindedness and tolerance ad nauseam, were more than happy to keep the public ignorant. As Andrew Fowler recorded: "The courts are fond of issuing what are known as super-injunctions – gag orders so tight that even reporting their existence is a breach of the court order and thus a crime. They handed out 1502 of them in one five-year period."[153]

Tailgating physical and internet surveillance targeting journalists every move, Star Chambers where you couldn't even tell a relative you had been summoned, Journalist Information Warrants which mandated that no-one was allowed to reveal their existence and yet brought the target under the surveillance of 21 different government departments, courts so secretive even to reveal the existence of proceedings was a crime.

Could it get any worse?

---

152 Supplied.

153 *The War on Journalism*, Andrew Fowler, Random House, 2015.

Most certainly it could.

At the same time as it was introducing into the national security laws enabling the labelling of journalists as "Persons of Interest", the Australian parliament introduced yet further assaults on freedom of speech.

The controversial piece of legislation was section 35P of the ASIO Act. It allowed for ten years' jail for journalists revealing details about Special Intelligence Operations.

Even if the journalist had no idea that what they were reporting on was a Special Intelligence Operation, known in the acronym-laden jargon as an SIO, they could be imprisoned.

The definition of what constituted an SIO was determined by ASIO itself.

There was to be virtually no political dissent, as one of the most Orwellian pieces of legislation ever to grace the national parliament breezed through the chambers and into law.

The provisions were yet to be tested in the High Court of Australia. Old Alex just hoped that by some terrible accident he didn't report on a botched SIO, and become the first to face the High Court. That was the point, of course: writers, journalists, pundits and protesters, they were all being bullied, harassed and frightened into submission and self-censorship, into joining the gods lined along the bar talking of nothing but football. Those who didn't live behind polite suburban facades or charades of normality, who dared to challenge the government narrative, deserved all they got.

The Independent National Security Legislation Monitor, which the government had previously attempted to abolish, was headed by senior retired judge with the Federal Court the Honourable Roger Gyles QC. One of the most admired legal minds in the country, he had an Order of Australia for his services to the legal profession and the judiciary.

Following an outcry from media organisations over the all-encompassing nature of the new laws, in early February of 2016 the Monitor produced a report on the impact on journalists of Section 35P, the part of the legislation most directly impacting on the media. Public interest was not a defence. A demonstration of any harm to an individual or to the organisation was not required. Nor was the fact that the information disclosed may have been previously published or be in the public interest. In other words, journalists could go to jail for ten years for reporting information that was already in the public domain.

It didn't get much more totalitarian than that.

The impact of section 35P on journalists is twofold:

A. It creates uncertainty as to what may be published about the activities of ASIO without fear of prosecution. The so-called chilling effect of that uncertainty is exacerbated because it also applies in relation to disclosures made to editors for the purpose of discussion before publication.

B. Journalists are prohibited from publishing anywhere at any time any information relating to an SIO, regardless of whether it has any, or any continuing, operational significance and even if it discloses reprehensible conduct by ASIO insiders.

Section 35P is not justified. It does not contain adequate safeguards for protecting the rights of outsiders and is not proportionate to the threat of terrorism or the threat to national security.[154]

Submissions from some of the world's leading experts on terror legislation were blunt. Professor Clive Walker of Leeds University in the UK said there was no equivalent to 35P in British law – with security agencies granted relatively few powers for intrusion on property, privacy and the power to hold people in detention, these functions normally being carried out by the police.

Unlike Australia, in Britain it was also a defence that the individual charged with such a breach did not know and had no reasonable cause to suspect disclosure was likely to affect a terrorist investigation. Or that it was in the public interest. There was also a general requirement of proof damage had been caused. In Australia the mere disclosure of an operation was enough for a journalist to attract a ten-year jail term.

The country founded by convicts charged with crimes as paltry as stealing a loaf of bread for their starving children was excelling itself.

It is important to allow for the raising of reasonable excuses by way of a defence, including the public interest in the disclosure of wrongdoing. This recognition is insufficiently reflected in section 35P. As a result, it may be argued that section 35P

---

154 Report on the impact on journalists of section 35P of the ASIO Act, the Hon Roger Gyles AO, QC, Independent National Security Legislation Monitor, October, 2015.

is unprincipled, especially since Australian Commonwealth law lacks any general domestic law statement of protection equivalent to article 10 of the Human Rights Act 1998, despite endorsing the value of free speech at common law and in international law.[155]

Another submission, from the Centre of Public Law at the University of NSW, included contributions from Professor George Williams, one of the nation's preeminent experts on terror legislation and another Order of Australia recipient. He said the criminalising of the disclosure of any information relating to a Special Intelligence Operation was likely to have a clear chilling effect on freedom of the press. A journalist would face imprisonment of up to ten years for revealing, for example, that an officer with the Australian Security Intelligence Organisation had physically harmed a suspect during a Special Intelligence Operation or posed a risk to the safety of the general public.

> The offence prohibits journalists from reporting on SIOs, even where this would reveal that ASIO officers were involved in substantial wrongdoing or unlawful conduct during the course of an operation.

> No comparable nation has seen it necessary to grant the same level of immunity to officers of their domestic security service for committing unlawful acts during undercover operations.

> For a person to commit an offence under s 35P, they do not need to know that the information relates to an SIO. The information need only relate to an SIO in some minor or indirect way, and the person need not intend to harm national security or the public interest.[156]

---

155 Submission to the independent Security Law Monitor, Inquiry into section 35P of the Australian Security Intelligence Organisation Act 1979, Professor Clive Walker, University of Leeds, 3 April, 2015.

156 Submission to the Inquiry into section 35P of the ASIO Act, Dr Keiran Hardy, Professor George Williams, Professor Anthony Mason, Centre for Public Law, Faculty of Law, University of NSW, 2 April, 2015.

Exactly why would Australian legislators and bureaucrats feel the need to develop such ludicrous legislation, unless it was to protect their own malfeasance?

The politicians kowtowed to those in a secretive, essentially parallel government; while the public, with no great regard for journalists, couldn't have cared less.

But whether or not there was a sting of public rebuke, there was a price to pay.

Perhaps it might be all well and good if the laws protected the national interest; but they instead protected ASIO and the bank of security agencies behind them.

ASIO, as the best known of the agencies and thereby one of the few to garner any sort of public recognition had, it could best be said, a mixed reputation.

In early February the government tabled its response to parliament:

> The Government has accepted and will implement all of the recommendations made by the Monitor providing added safe-guards to journalists reporting on national security.
>
> New amendments to the ASIO Act will establish two separate offence regimes for 'insiders' and 'outsiders' in recognition that ASIO employees and its affiliates should be held to a higher standard in relation to the disclosure of sensitive information. The Government will ensure that an inadvertent disclosure by an outsider will not result in a criminal offence.
>
> A defence of prior publication will also be available to journal-ists and other members of the community.[157]

Media outlets and the journalists' union welcomed the reform at the time as if it had already been introduced into law.

In the end the promise to reform the laws targeting journalists became just another broken promise. The government misled the public and the profession while defying one of the most respected legal minds in the country.

Old Alex contacted the author of the report, Roger Gyles QC, himself

---

157 Government response to INSLM report, Attorney General for Australia Media Release, 2 February, 2016.

sounding frustrated by the lack of progress. He continued to work within the Department of Prime Minister and Cabinet.

His response was marked as "Unclassified":

> There has been no amendment to the legislation as yet, although the government did announce that the recommendations were accepted.

> I hope that my review of security legislation over my term will give perspective on the broader issue. I am unlikely to tackle that issue until I am further into the task. I welcome interest in this important area.[158]

Old Alex had always been fascinated by secret societies, secret, hidden parts of the city, clandestine, rapidly shifting scenes – the opium dens, in a sense, of modern Australia, worlds hidden away from view. Nobody knew, no one should know what really happened in these places, who embraced who, what information or emotion was or was not passed.

Most government departments were now hidden behind walls of bright, self-righteous, self-serving bureaucratic effrontery – but it was natural to become fascinated by the world behind the world, what lay behind the mask.

The truth was far worse than he knew from personal experience, or so the more decent of the Watchers on the Watch whispered to him. Let go your own experience, look beyond yourself, there are greater issues at play, greater injustices than a single malicious vendetta aimed at a single man.

Everywhere he walked there was a trail of the dead, people he had known and loved and were gone. The Joni Mitchell song drifted through:

> The last time I saw Richard was Detroit in '68
> And he told me all romantics meet the same fate someday
> Cynical and drunk and boring someone in some dark café
> You laugh he said you think you're immune
> Go look at your eyes they're full of moon...

> All those pretty lies, pretty lies.[159]

The dogs of war had been unleashed, and they turned on their masters.

---

158 Unclassified email response from Roger Gyle in the Prime Minister and Cabinet Office of Australia, dated

159 Last Time I Saw Richard, Joni Mitchell, 1970.

Decades before, as his own career was beginning to take off at *The Sydney Morning Herald*, Old Alex had lived next to the Sydney residence of the author of *The First Casualty*, a classic history of war reporting by renowned journalist Phillip Knightley.

As they got to know each other, they exchanged media gossip on their doorsteps. Knightley had been an inspiration to generations of journalists.

The first casualty, of course, is truth.

The world-famous John Pilger, admired by the public but never much liked by fellow journalists because of his ceaseless grandstanding, had once refused to be interviewed by Old Alex at a function down by Woolloomooloo's Finger Wharves because he was from the so-called right wing press, that is the country's national newspaper *The Australian*.

Not deigning to speak to him, and thereby his audience, simply because of the perceived political bias of his employer Rupert Murdoch, was, as far as Old Alex was concerned, simply ignorant.

But he did get one thing right. He began his introduction to Knightley's book with a quote from Britain's First World War Prime Minister Lloyd George: "If people really knew (the truth) the war would be stopped tomorrow." To which *The Times* correspondent Sir Philip Gibbs, who was knighted for his services, insisted the truth was told, "apart from the naked realism of horrors and losses, and criticism of the facts".

Robert Miller, a United Press correspondent during the Korean War was less subtle: "There are certain facts and stories . . . that editors and publishers have printed which were pure fabrication. Many of us who sent the stories knew they were false, but we had to write them because they were the official releases from responsible military headquarters and were released for publication even though the people responsible knew they were untrue."

> Almost every word of these testimonies could apply to the wars of our time... Knightley's work (is) the most comprehensive j'accuse of journalism as propaganda in the English language. It is the author's lament that for all the dazzling advances in media technology, the media has little or no memory, as the same bogus "truth" is served up again and again. I wondered when journalism's modern breeding grounds, the media studies courses, would begin to address the most important issue raised in the book, the virulence of an unrecognised censorship, often

concealed behind false principles of objectivity, whose effect is
to minimise and deny the culpability of Western power in acts
of great violence and terrorism.[160]

In waking dreams, there in that confined network of laneways and graffiti-coated walls, Alex knew the mother of souls was dismayed that millions
of the progeny she had sown across galaxies were being drawn into the dark
heavens, their devotion empowering Dark Lords. The gift of souls, to which
humans had, oddly for such a violent species, been such ready receptacles
had created an unintended outcome. Despite all their prophetic gifts the
celestials had not foreseen how rogue gods could come to harvest and to
gain power from the mother's beloved souls, how a cyclonic darkness would
spread like a stain across the heavens and across worlds.

> Those who dream by day are cognisant of many things which
> escape those who dream only by night. In their grey visions they
> obtain glimpses of eternity, and thrill, in waking, to find that
> they have been upon the verge of the great secret. In snatches,
> they learn something of the wisdom which is of good, and more
> of the mere knowledge which is of evil.[161]

In the material world the news itself was no less fantastical than in all
those waking dreams.

"Could the Islamic State Get a Nuclear Weapon?" was just one headline.

Spreading its profound sense of disturbance, IS claimed it could purchase
its first nuclear weapon from Pakistan through weapons dealers with links
to corrupt officials.

Captured British photojournalist John Cantlie produced a string of
propaganda videos for Islamic State, dressed in the orange jumpsuit which
mirrored the prison garb of Guantanamo Bay.

In 2015 he claimed there was no doubt Islamic State had nuclear weapons
in mind.

> Let me throw a hypothetical operation onto the table. The
> Islamic State has billions of dollars in the bank, so they call on
> their wilāyah in Pakistan to purchase a nuclear device through
> weapons dealers with links to corrupt officials in the region.

---

160 *The First Casualty*, Philip Knightley, The John Hopkins University Press, 2002.
161 Complete Tales and Poems, Edgar Allan Poe, Barnes and Noble, 2008.

It's the sum of all fears for Western intelligence agencies.

They'll be looking to do something big, something that would make any past operation look like a squirrel shoot, and the more groups that pledge allegiance the more possible it becomes to pull off something truly epic.[162]

A year later and the warnings were more explicit still.

Extremist madmen from IS would not hesitate to launch a catastrophic nuclear attack, US President Barack Obama warned an international gathering of leaders at a Nuclear Security Summit in Washington.

Obama, who was leaving the world a far more dangerous place after eight years as President, painted an apocalyptic picture:

ISIL has already used chemical weapons, including mustard gas, in Syria and Iraq. There is no doubt that if these madmen ever got their hands on a nuclear bomb or nuclear material, they most certainly would use it to continue to kill as many innocent people as possible.

Just the smallest amount of plutonium – about the size of an apple – would kill and injure hundreds of thousands of innocent people. It would be a humanitarian, political, economic and environmental catastrophe with global ramifications for decades.

It would change our world.[163]

Entire cities burned.

It hadn't been long after arriving at the Big White House that Old Alex realised that he was once again under surveillance.

With greater games afoot, Alex sat in the back garden, with its malfunctioning water feature and tangle of pot plants, just as cluttered as the house itself. He churned inside, fearful of invisible enemies, their draped artifice creeping across every tile, every plank. No-one he met, none of his perceptions, nothing could be trusted.

---

162 Isis claims it could buy its first nuclear weapon, Heather Saul, *The Independent*, 23 May, 2015.

163 Obama warns Islamic State madmen would gladly use nuclear weapons, ABC, 2 April, 2016.

"I serve Allah," said one of the Watchers on the Watch.

"I know," he replied. "That's what makes this situation so dangerous."

There they were, in a seemingly cosy corner of the world. A place which should have been safe simply was not, a refuge destroyed.

Old Pete the Aging Opera Diva, sipping expensive wine or swilling champagne, expounded on how friendly his community was, how supportive everyone had been after Declan's death. Alex had heard the story numerous times, of how casserole dishes would be left at the front door, because everyone knew he couldn't cook.

However real or illusory these neighbourhood friendships were, in a fractured time everyone wanted a sense of belonging, to be held with affection, esteemed for their place in the world. In the out-of-phase, increasingly disturbed external world, people found meaning in private routines, a narrow domain upon which order could be imposed. Disengaged, they turned inward because the wider world did not make sense.

My focus has always been on my home.

Politicians and the like are stuck in some sort of fantastical game or theatre. Seemingly unconscious of the consequences. Playing out their crazy role without any vision of a socially just society.

To that end, I expect nothing and try not to be disappointed. I no longer hang out for a politician or political party to set out a clear vision or roadmap to create a better society.

At this point I think about growing vegetables, or rearranging a chair, or at best doing something that creates a social connection in my village.[164]

A wet spring was turning into an even wetter summer. Old Alex had felt cold ever since he returned from Vietnam, uncomfortable despite the surface familiarity of streets he had known so well twenty years before.

And then, as if opening up, in one great clasping moment the heavens provided a way forward; and he knew, as far left of field as it might appear on the surface, what had to be done.

Who was being killed and why, the Australian public did not know and therefore did not care.

---

164 Correspondence with Cara Macdougall, 28 June, 2015.

Loss of life, treasure and credibility meant nothing.

It was all being done in secret, and was therefore subterfuge.

There was no national pride in the war effort because, through deliberate manipulation, the country knew almost nothing about it. The many billions being spent on a discredited war created no national pride, no sense of sacrifice for a noble cause, no resultant feeling of safety. It did not make sense.

Public support there was none. Consent, if it could even be called that, was only achieved through the cloak of extreme secrecy which had characterised Australia's military involvement in Afghanistan, Iraq, Syria and elsewhere.

Climate change was a much more comfortable subject than war. On that they could all agree. Everyone knew what the science said.

There might be no immediate or apparent consequence in the anaemic, washed-out environment that constituted public discourse, but there was a very high price to pay nonetheless for the Australian government's willingness to involve itself in futile, unjust wars and the resultant extensive waste of public resources.

Secrecy, malfeasance and political dishonesty all came at a higher price than the obvious.

The illusion of consent was only manufactured by the elimination of any coordinated opposition, greatly assisted by Australia's embrace of the surveillance state; for organisation of any protest without ceding prior knowledge to the authorities had become impossible.

The targeting and intimidation of journalists was an essential part of the strategy.

In his own case, and as a journalist of several decades standing, the surveillance had been so extensive and long-lasting it could only have been conducted with approval of or on the say so of the highest levels of governance. At the peak of that disturbance were the then Prime Minister Tony Abbott and the head of ASIO, former Army General Duncan Lewis.

Either that or there were rogue elements in the agencies prepared to target a journalist of more than thirty years standing, in which case they needed to be brought under control.

Control of the media was essential to the maintenance of perpetual war.

As Major General John Cantwell wrote in his book Exit Wounds: *One Australian's War on Terror:*

I approve scores of media updates, make or release dozens of newsy videos, provide commentary on our challenges and progress, and look for every opportunity to tell the Australian people what our troops are doing, and how well they're doing it. Most of these sink without a trace in the Defence and parliamentary precincts of Canberra. I get more mileage from the story of sending home a long-lost and rediscovered explosive-detection dog, Sarbi, than from all my other media engagements combined. In general, the work of our service men and women seems to be invisible in the Australian media. It's partly the fault of the press, but largely due to the draconian control of information by the Department of Defence Public Affairs Office and the Defence Minister's office.[165]

The pace of events was accelerating.

The centre could not hold.

Despite the depleted, increasingly proscribed nature of public discourse, on occasion details which might once not have been revealed for decades rose quickly to the surface.

In the gathering storm his own discomfort was nothing, dead leaves ripped away in early winds, a cyclone coming.

For all its numerous faults, the national broadcaster the ABC could sometimes be devastatingly effective, playing the role that journalism was meant to play: confronting power, forcing the nation to face the consequences of its worst decisions.

As a wintry summer began to turn to autumn, the ABC broadcast a much-lauded documentary series, "Afghanistan: Our Longest War". It was a war which had cost the lives of 41 soldiers and left a further 261 injured. Afghanistan saw more Australian casualties than any conflict since the Vietnam War, in which 521 were killed and 3,000 wounded.

In the end the truth would always out, this time driven by the stories of lost mates and riven conscience, the voices of the soldiers themselves.

Every two to three weeks they would come up with new ways to kill us...

You are in a position where you are more than likely going to die.

165 *Exit Wounds: One Australians War on Terror*, Melbourne University Publishing, 2013.

How do you encourage people to risk their lives when you your-self are having doubts?[166]

The ones that came off looking the worst were the politicians who had sent their own people into those beautiful valleys and harsh mountain land-scapes.

Just as they did the Americans, the Afghanis hated the invading Austra-lians.

Beyond Post Traumatic Stress Disorder lay Moral Injury, the result of military being asked to do something which defies their own conscience.

> We received a report there had been a strike. Instinctively I knew it was the Sarab Pass. I also knew that I could have prevented it … We waited for the casualties to arrive … When the dual cab utility vehicle stopped next to the RAP, the police and some of our troops started unloading the wounded children from the back seat. I didn't want to look at the children and focused my attention on the tray. I could see two large mounts in the back of the vehicle, covered by blankets.

> My first nightmare about this incident happened a few days later. I often dreamt that the 'mounds of flesh' in the back of the ute came to life like zombies and started chasing me, deter-mined to get their revenge for what I had done to them. The dreams evolved to include my family members in place of the Afghan civilians. On one occasion the woman in the back of the ute became my sister and I killed her with a broken broomstick. It entered her head through the mouth and came out the back of her skull.

> In those dreams the 'living dead' are always trying to bite me. The only way I can stop them is to drive something through their mouths.[167]

The infrastructure that was built – mosques, schools, hospitals which were meant to rebuild the country and usher in democracy – was frequently destroyed the minute the troops departed.

At last it was over. Previously, the only time the war made it onto the

---

166 Inside Australia's Longest War, Episode 2, Australian Broadcasting Commission, 2015.
167 Moral Injury, Ed Tom Frame, University of New South Wales Press, 2015.

nation's screens was when a succession of Prime Ministers fulfilled a tradition to attend the funerals of soldiers: Howard, Rudd, Gillard, Abbott, a conga line of justification. There was learned discussion as to whether the prime ministers really needed to bring unwanted attention to the war by doing so.

On a flying visit, then Prime Minister Tony Abbott spoke to the final deployment:

> Australia's longest war is ended, not with victory not with defeat, but with, we hope, an Afghanistan which is better for our presence here.
>
> Our armed forces and our officials have done their duty. That duty never ends, although our duty here has.[168]

As former head of Australian Army Peter Leahy said dismissively, hope is not a strategy: "Afghanistan might have slipped from our attention, but the mission goes on. Over time our politicians did not tell us much of our strategy. There is a good excuse – we didn't have one."[169]

The minute that shameful war was over, it was barely ever mentioned again, certainly not by the politicians. Another shameful episode in the nation's history, conducted at the behest of the Americans, was swept under the carpet.

Those who lost their lives included:

> Jacob Moerland, 21, a sapper in the 2nd Combat Engineer Regiment, serving with MTF 1. He was killed on 7 June 2010 by an improvised explosive device while participating in an Australian patrol conducting operations in the Miribad Valley region of Oruzgan province.
>
> Mathew Hopkins, 21, a corporal in the 7th Battalion, Royal Australian Regiment. He was attacked and fatally injured on 16 March 2009 while on patrol as part of a mentoring and reconstruction taskforce patrol operating with members of the Afghan National Army, near a village 12 kilometres north of Tarin Kowt.

---

168 Long war ends with hope, says Tony Abbott, Phillip Coorey, *The Sydney Morning Herald*, 29 October, 2013.

169 Afghanistan: We had no strategy in this war and the details were kept from us, Peter Leahy, *Sydney Morning Herald*, 22 February, 2016.

Andrew Russell, 33, a sergeant in the Special Air Service Regiment (SASR). On 16 February 2002, Russell was travelling through southern Afghanistan with four other Australian soldiers when their Long Range Patrol Vehicle struck a land mine.

Matthew Locke MG, 33, a sergeant in the Special Air Service Regiment. On 25 October 2007, Locke, who was serving a second tour of duty in Afghanistan, was engaged in a fire fight with members of the Taliban militia, when he was shot in the chest.

The terrible list went on.

In 2016 the Taliban surrounded Tarin Kot, the capital of Uruzgan Province which had served as the Australian base for a decade. Little if anything of the infrastructure Australian taxes built remained.

Straight-faced, former lawyer, Australian Foreign Minister Julie Bishop, denied on the national broadcaster that 41 Australian soldiers had died in vain.

With all due respect to my learned colleague, as lawyers were wont to say, Old Alex did not agree.

He had interviewed a lot of former soldiers over the years.

They were almost invariably traumatised by their experiences, regarded war as a mistake and held little but contempt for the politicians who had sent them into harm's way.

Prime Minister Julia Gillard attended 24 funerals for Australian soldiers while she was in office.

In a rare display of self-doubt, she said: "Somewhere inside you it does wear away. You really have to sit and reflect to yourself, you know, am I still sure this is worth it? And I would always get to the conclusion that it is, but there was a tussle."[170]

No, it was not "worth it".

The dead weren't her sons, her brothers, her husband, her father, her friends. She could dismiss them, rationalise their deaths, because their funerals were simply part of her political duties. But their families could not.

Those men, yes, they were all men, died not because their homeland was

---

170 Ibid.

under threat, not to help the people of another country, but for the sake of a military alliance built around multibillion dollar procurement contracts and intelligence sharing; because, just as it had done in Vietnam, Australia always unquestioningly followed America into conflict no matter how patently unjust, counterproductive or clearly mismanaged.

Because the nation's politicians did not have the mettle or the moral fibre to stand up and say: This is wrong, to sacrifice the lives of our compatriots for the sake of a US alliance which is costing the nation a fortune in cash, credibility and life, and which has turned a country that should have been a hideout from an impending apocalypse into a farmyard directly in the path of the coming storm.

One long afternoon at News Limited headquarters, one amongst many long afternoons, as disillusion with journalism crept through every bone in his body, Old Alex had spent frantic hours doing a story on another Afghan tragedy of dead and injured soldiers. The government had point blank refused to release even a simple statistic about the number wounded in the conflict.

Why?

Because if the public knew the truth they would never have supported their government's war.

Why should Australian soldiers be injured in secrecy, details of their deaths almost impossible to obtain?

One of the most telling indictments in the series came from General John Grantwell, who suffered from post-traumatic stress and wrote a book about his experiences in both Iraq and Afghanistan, *Exit Wounds: One Man's War on Terror*.

In contrast to the platitudes of politicians, General Cantwell said the Afghan cause was not worth dying for; that the trade-off, whatever it amounted to, was not worth the price.

> I reached to a nearby shelf and extract a blue surgical glove and pull it onto my right hand and take a slow breath and step close to each man placing my hand on his shoulder and turn.

> The chill of their bodies reaches my heart, looking down at each dead soldier. I say how sorry I am that they have been claimed by war.

I thank them for their sacrifice and tell them they are on their way home.

It feels perfectly natural to be speaking to the dead.

After a moment of contemplation I say 'goodbye Jacob' and then I pause and say 'goodbye Darren'.[171]

While government-funded refugee, climate change and feminist lobby groups dominated public discourse, one of the few groups speaking out against Australia's involvement in American wars was Australians for War Power Reform, which had begun in 2003 as an attempt to expose the reasons why the country joined the Iraq War. The group argued that the power to go to war should not rest in the hands of a single person, the Prime Minister.

> Australia's decision to join the United States bombing campaign in Syria was mired in deceit, disinformation and obfuscation from the outset. When the Australian government announced in August 2015 that they were going to consider the legal ramifications involved before committing to a decision, they omitted two crucial facts.

> The first fact was that the then Prime Minister Tony Abbott had already solicited an invitation from the Americans to join the bombing campaign. The second omitted fact was that the legal opinion had been sought and obtained a year earlier.

> In mid-September 2015, without any parliamentary debate (then or since) Australia committed itself to yet another war on behalf of the Americans. Bombing raids ("sorties") commenced almost immediately.[172]

The braggadocio of politicians, the ceaseless beating of the national security drum, the demonisation of the Muslim minority, the appalling losses of life, treasure and credibility, the injustices committed in the name of the war on terror, all of it was coming into play in a world beyond the world, behind the shallow narrative prosecuted by politicians and the nation's media.

---

171 *Exit Wounds: One Australians War on Terror*, Melbourne University Publishing, 2013.

172 Open letter to PM Turnbull: RAAF Operations in Syria and Related Matters, Australians for War Power Reform, Posted in blog 28 September, 2016.

The consequences were clear for all to see, including an abandonment of sovereignty.

In an open letter to Prime Minister Malcolm Turnbull, former Secretary of Defence and President of Australians for War Powers Reform Paul Barratt wrote:

> We believe that Australia has since the start of this century been too ready to resort to military operations as the solution to complex political religious and cultural problems that are unlikely to benefit from Western military intervention; conversely, lacking in willingness to pursue diplomacy to achieve the desired outcomes or to explore other non-military options; too reluctant to counsel our major ally to exercise restraint, or to ask the necessary hard questions about the wisdom of our ally's proposed interventions; insufficiently heedful of the likely humanitarian consequences of military action on the civilian populations of the affected countries; and notoriously reluctant to provide international humanitarian assistance commensurate with the scale of our military activities and the destruction to which we have been party. We believe that the involvement of the Parliament in decisions about these matters, and the Government taking the Australian public into its confidence, would produce a better outcome in all of these respects.[173]

Decide in haste, repent at leisure. The consequences of these decisions had moulded the nature of the country, had been moulding it for more than a century.

Prime Minister Andrew Fisher took the nation into the First World War after having famously declared: "Australians will stand beside the mother country to help and defend her to our last man and our last shilling."[174]

More than 60,000 were killed and 156,000 wounded, gassed or taken prisoner. The ANZAC tradition of loyalty, self-reliance and mateship was born.

Australia's longest serving Prime Minister, Sir Robert Menzies, took the nation into the Second World War. In a sombre address to the nation he

173 Deployment of Special Forces, Letter to Prime Minister Malcolm Turnbull, Paul Barratt, Australians for War Powers Reform, 29 April, 2016.

174 'To the last man' – Australia's entry to war in 1914, Jonathan Curtis, Research Branch, Parliament of Australia, 31 July, 2014.

said: "There can be no doubt that where Great Britain stands there stand the people of the entire British world. May God in His mercy and compassion grant that the world may soon be delivered from this agony."[175]

More than 27,000 were killed and 23,000 wounded.

Menzies served for so long he was around to follow the Americans into the Vietnam War in which 521 Australians were killed and more than 3,000 injured.

It was then John Howard's turn to follow America into Afghanistan and then Iraq. Tony Abbott took the nation back into Iraq and then Syria. All this rush to war occurred without popular support, or with extensively manufactured nationalism.

And the price had become extremely high.

By one of those peculiar twists of fate and journalism, Alex interviewed David Kilcullen, one of the world's leading counterterrorism experts, on the occasion of the publication of his book *Blood Year: The Failures of the War on Terror*.

> This conflict threatens not only to destroy the lives of millions of people, but also to destabilise the world economy by massively disrupting global energy flows, shipping routes, air transportation and telecommunications systems, to create unprecedented refugee flows, to redraw the borders of half a dozen nation-states (with huge loss of life in the process), to drag regional and world powers (Iran, Israel, Russia, Egypt, China, Pakistan, Turkey) into an escalating – potentially nuclear – conflict, to encourage radical violence in scores of countries worldwide, and to enable the aggressive expansion of the Islamic state by means of military conquest. Some of this is already happening.[176]

Kilcullen had been a fierce critic of the 2003 invasion of Iraq, "the mother mistake" to which Australia had been such a willing party.

He told a story, and then immediately expressed his regret at conveying the information to a journalist, about how he had been present at a background briefing between military officials and one of the nation's leading politicians.

---

175 Prime Minister Robert G. Menzies: wartime broadcast, Australian War Memorial, 3 September, 1939.

176 *Blood Year: Islamic State and The Failures of the War on Terror*, David Kilcullen, C Hurst & Co Ltd., 2016.

He thought to himself, I'm never going to have this chance again, and asked the question, "Why are we doing this?"

The politician replied with words to the effect, "You're asking the wrong question. The Americans are invading, should we be with them or not?"

In other words, all the palaver about making Australia safer from terrorism and liberating the people of Iraq was baloney. The public had been peddled a lie. Australia was there because America was there.

The senior politician in Australia at the time had been Prime Minister John Howard.

He could tell that Kilcullen, whose fortunes relied heavily on government and News Limited contracts, instantly regretted his indiscretion, and in subsequent questioning Kilcullen refused to confirm that the identity of the senior politician was indeed the PM.

Howard had been the driving figure in taking Australia into the Iraq War in 2003, against a significant body of Australian opinion.

But as always in the end the truth would out.

> Some parts of Blood Year are deeply shocking, including the extreme barbarity perpetrated by all sides in a collapsing Iraq. It records, for instance, how, under the noses of Coalition forces, commercial kidnapping gangs auctioned off terrified children for slaughter in a makeshift night market. "A whole underground industry grew up around the making of sectarian snuff videos. Like any drug, blood-lust demands progressively bigger hits to satisfy its addicts."[177]

All the way Australia had been a compliant, uncomplaining ally. But by failing to urge caution, Australia had proved a very poor ally indeed.

Australian soldiers were being put at risk for the sake of an American alliance and multibillion dollar defence contracts. Always follow the money.

Writing for the Australian Strategic Policy Institute, former Ambassador to the US Kim Beazley confirmed, Australia was there because America was there.

Not to defend the homeland, not for justice, not to protect the defenceless, not for any honourable reason whatsoever; we were there because America was there.

---

177 David Kilcullen: *Blood Year*, John Stapleton, 17 February, 2016.

Both globally and regionally, our strategic situation has deteriorated. We confront a fraught situation in the Middle East, where we support fragile local allies struggling with the fundamentalist extremist side of a confessional dispute in the Muslim community. We do so because our American ally is there, we have been engaged in Iraq and Afghanistan and we know that, although this aspect of the struggle is local to the Middle East, it's global in impact.[178]

One of the prices the Americans demanded from their allies was the expectation that they would spend 2% of their Gross Domestic Product on defence – much of which flowed directly to American military contractors. Australia rushed to comply.

From our point of view, access to the best American technology is now critical for any chance of an Australian capability edge in this strategic zone. This is the post 'revolution in military affairs' or 'second offset' event acting out in our procurement program. It took effect in the early 1990s. We spend $13 million a working day in the US defence industry. The Australian Embassy in Washington DC manages over 400 foreign military sales programs. To cite one example of the fruit of this, one could point to the most effective air defence of our approaches we have ever had. For surveillance—satellites, over-the-horizon radar, AEW&C aircraft, P-8 anti-submarine aircraft. For sustaining the effort—inflight infuellers. For strike and interdiction—classic Hornets, Super Hornets, Growlers and F-35s. It's all American or American origin.[179]

Australia's politicians had betrayed the nation's sovereignty, handing responsibility for its foreign policy to the Americans.

It was a shameful set of extremely dangerous circumstances which desperately needed review.

That Australia's involvement in foreign wars had been chaotically mismanaged by the country's political class was no secret.

For one story Old Alex was commissioned to do he quoted head of

---

178 Agenda for Change 2016: Strategic Choices for the Next Government, Australian Strategic Policy Institute, June, 2016.

179 Ibid.

the Australian Strategic Policy Institute Peter Jennings as saying one only needed to read recent works such as Niki Savva's *The Road to Ruin* on the Abbott era or a slew of memoirs from Labor's shell-shocked casualties of the Rudd–Gillard–Rudd era, to see how disastrously cabinet government had run off the rails.

> Rapid changes in prime ministers and ministers has the effect of wildly shifting basic policy objectives, for example from Tony Abbott's enthusiastic support for extending the air campaign to Syria in August 2015 to the much more cautious position of Malcolm Turnbull which started to shape policy from September 2015.

> Blame the 24/7 media cycle. Blame battalions of staffers relentlessly texting each other. Blame tweeting internet trolls, twerking populists and ranting radio shock jocks. Blame a 'responsive' rather than a thoughtful Australian public service. Just don't expect a return to the calm nostrum that good process makes good policy.[180]

Australia had entered that state of perpetual war which the ever-prophetic George Orwell cautioned about so strongly. To survive it needed an enemy. To justify the unjustifiable – vast military expenditure without scrutiny – it needed not just a broken, servile media to pump out its propaganda and a compliant, unquestioning population, but a distant, inhumane enemy. The minute the enemy acquired a face the battle was lost.

> Terrorists, terrorists. terrorists. In the Middle East, in the entire Muslim world, this word would become a plague, a meaningless punctuation mark in all our lives, a full stop erected to finish all discussion of injustice, constructed as a wall by Russians, Americans, Israelis, British, Pakistanis, Saudis, Turks, to shut us up. Who would ever say a word in favour of terrorists? What cause could possibly justify terror? So our enemies are always terrorists.[181]

The acceptance of perpetual war required a good deal of dehumanisation.

---

180 Former PM Tony Abbott made Islamic State sound cool, John Stapleton, *The New Daily*, 7 June, 2016.

181 *The Great War for Civilisation*, Robert Fisk, The Fourth Estate, 2005.

Australian intellectuals were on the whole against the country's involvement in the Iraq and Syria wars, but their voices failed to resonate. Their views were confined to a few rarely read and poorly distributed literary magazines – most of which, in any case, had been defunded by mid-2016.

Renowned British philosopher Bertrand Russell, with whom Old Alex had been fascinated in his youth, when he still retained some mental agility, was also staunchly anti-war.

Ever prolific and one of the pre-eminent intellects of the 20th Century, Russell received a six-month sentence in Brixton prison for his anti-war campaigning. Of upper class background and even then a world famous Cambridge don, he was given preferential treatment, allowed to read and write.

Of his time in prison he famously wrote: "I was rather interested in my fellow prisoners, who seemed to me in no way morally inferior to the rest of the population, though they were on the whole slightly below the usual level of intelligence, as was shown by their having been caught."[182]

For one of such aristocratic origin, with the best education that Britain's renowned institutions could provide, with world fame and remarkable intellectual gifts, it was Russell's ability to appreciate the various virtues of his fellow man that led him to his pacifist stance. It was a pity the gods had not granted Australia's politicians the same gift.

Despite his towering intelligence, Bertrand was an essentially humble, largely cheerful, good-natured man. He wrote his book *Introduction to Mathematical Philosophy* while in prison and began work on *Analysis of Mind*. His writings would go on to influence the development of diverse fields including theoretical logic, mathematics, set theory, linguistics, as well as those disciplines so crucial to the present day: artificial intelligence and cognitive and computer science. Also the author of *A History of Western Philosophy*, in that realm he was particularly influential in the fields of epistemology, language and metaphysics.

He was awarded the Nobel Prize for Literature in 1950.

Dying at the age of 97, Russell had lived long enough to become not just a campaigner against British conduct in World War One; in the modern era he also campaigned against the Vietnam War and in favour of nuclear disarmament.

---

182 *The Autobiography of Bertrand Russell*, Routledge, 2000. Originally published in 1967.

In a letter to *The Guardian* during the First World War opposing conscription he wrote:

> There are no doubts many kinds of reasons which lead men to become conscientious objectors, but I am convinced that the chief reason, and the most valid, is precisely that sense of "the solidarity of mankind," of "our membership one of another" ... The conscientious objector does not believe that violence can cure violence, or that militarism can exorcise the spirit of militarism. He persists in feeling "solidarity" with those who are called "enemies," and he believes if this feeling was more widespread among us it would do more than armies and navies can ever do to prevent the growth of aggressive Imperialism, not only among ourselves, but also among potential enemies.[183]

Hence "the death cult".

Hence the drones.

Hence the smart bombs.

Hence the blowback.

The price was too high.

Most, although by no means all, humans were born with a conscience, or at least a semblance of one.

Despite being more than 7,000 miles from their targets in the Middle East, American drone operators, and the Australian drone operators who were embedded on training programs with them, would come to feel their own haunting:

> Ever step on ants and never give it another thought? That's what you are made to think of the targets – as just black blobs on a screen. You start to do these psychological gymnastics to make it easier to do what you have to do – they deserved it, they chose their side. You had to kill part of your conscience to keep doing your job every day – and ignore those voices telling you this wasn't right.[184]

The hauntings were worse at night, in dreams:

---

183 Letter to *The Guardian*, Originally published 19 March, 1917. Republished by *the Guardian* Research Dept, 21 May, 2011.

184 Micahel Haas, quoted in Life as a drone operator: 'Ever step on ants and never give it another thought?', Ed Pilkington, *The Guardian*, 20 November, 2015.

I'm in the radio unit flipping switches, with my boss yelling at
me to get it up and running. Then all of a sudden it does start
working and I realize with a jolt what I've done. I run out of
the control station and now I'm in a village in Afghanistan and
the whole place is burnt out and there's a woman on the ground
covered in soot and a child crying over her. I go up to help the
child, but half of her face is blown off and there's nothing I can
do.[185]

Australian personnel had dropped more than 1400 bombs on Iraq and
Syria in the previous two years. The government released no figures on estimated civilian and military casualties. The voices of military personnel were
not heard.

But Old Alex had interviewed enough old soldiers to know that they, too,
would come to feel their own hauntings; become, if they were not already,
permanently traumatised. In the cloaks of secrecy that enveloped Australia's
wars, and the sledgehammer legislation which protected the government's
secrets, the public were unlikely to ever hear their tortured thoughts.

The operations they undertook were at the behest of political masters not
driven by a desire for gainful employment, interesting careers or the need to
support their families, but by personal greed, religious zealotry and geopolitical convenience.

An anger and suffering Australia had made a great contribution to, as it
swung wholeheartedly behind America's invasion of Iraq. Former conservative Prime Minister John Howard strutted the world stage as one of the
Coalition of the Willing, honoured with a visit to George Bush's ranch.

The country was taken back into this dangerous quagmire in 2014 by his
ideological heir Tony Abbott.

The decision to invade Iraq in 2003, the "mother mistake" as former
Australian Army officer and now world-renowned analyst David Kilcullen
described it, had by 2016 been almost universally discredited.

There had been a deliberate dumbing down of the Australian population – and when it came to matters of defence, warfare and international
conflict, never more so. While millions around the world took to the streets
in 2003 to protest the Iraq War, their voices were ignored. Both the ABC
in Australia and the BBC in Britain were heavily criticised by their govern-

185 Cian Westmoreland, Ibid.

ments. In Britain, defence reporter Andrew Gilligan reported that Blair had "sexed up" the dossier justifying the invasion of Iraq. In Australia, then Communications Minister Richard Alston sent a much publicised and blistering complaint alleging 68 separate incidents of bias in the national broadcaster's coverage of the war. Gilligan was ultimately forced to resign, Alston disappeared into history. By 2016, the critics of the war were vindicated.

Old Alex was asked to do a news story on the 12 volume Chilcot Report, the result of three years of forensic work by Sir John Chilcot and his team into the British decision, taken by former Prime Minister Tony Blair, to join the American invasion of Iraq.

The Iraq Inquiry had extensive powers, and unlike any previous inquiry was able to access papers, minutes of meetings, cabinet memos, communications between politicians and government personnel and all government documents relevant to the invasion. The Inquiry received 150,000 such documents. As the report stated:

> The material agreed by the Government for disclosure by the Inquiry is highly unusual in its scale and sensitivity.
>
> This Report therefore contains, exceptionally, material of a kind which would normally be regarded as highly sensitive and confidential, including:
>
> • extracts from Cabinet minutes;
>
> • extracts from, or summaries of, exchanges between former Prime Ministers and the former US President; and
>
> • material drawn from or otherwise relating to very sensitive security and intelligence sources, including a large number of Assessments by the Joint Intelligence Committee (JIC).

Two seminars were also held with a bevy of experts, examining the evolution of international policy towards Iraq between 1990 and 2003 and the causes and consequences of Iraq's descent into violence after the invasion.

Chilcot dismissed Tony Blair's defence that the chaos which was still enveloping Iraq, with some 300 people being killed in bomb blasts in Baghdad in the week of its release, could not have been foreseen.

Given the chance to apologise to the Australian people for taking the nation into a discredited and counterproductive war on the basis of a lie, former Prime Minister John Howard refused. "Do I apologise for the core decision? I defend the decision that I took. I don't resile from it. I don't believe it was the wrong decision. There were errors in intelligence, but there was no lie."[186]

It was one of the most inglorious points in his long career.

Howard knew perfectly well at the time that the "intelligence" he was flogging to the Australian people as justification for war was deeply flawed; and yet still chose to play a pivotal role in the propaganda war.

> The news flashed around the world that the White House had 'confirmed a report in *The New York Times*' that Saddam Hussein has been attempting to get equipment to enrich uranium to produce nuclear weapons. Australian Prime Minister John Howard added to the misleading game, saying the intelligence that had come out of the United States 'if accurate confirms the intelligence that we have been given'. The fact is it was the same intelligence that the United States had already given to Australia.[187]

The New York Times story was fabrication, a direct planting of misinformation by the US government accepted, uncritically, by discredited journalist Judith Miller. Despite all her self-justification, her reputation promptly became that of the journalist most responsible for taking the US into a war in Iraq based on a lie.

And Howard knowingly played right along. If there was any possibility he did not know, he was incompetent.

The forensic nature of the Chilcot Report vindicated critics of Howard's decision to go to war.

Former Defence secretary Paul Barratt said Howard should stop blaming the intelligence community for his own poor decision-making.

> He took Australia to war on false pretences, that he either knew or should have known.

The remarkable thing about it was just how little a role intel-

186 Howard defends Iraq War after damning report, John Stapleton, *The New Daily*, 7 July, 2016.

187 *The War On Journalism*, Andrew Fowler, Random House, 2015.

ligence played in the decision to go to war. It was completely politically driven.

It was clearly the wrong decision because it was a disaster for all concerned. The intelligence community was warning that if they were going to do it they should be prepared for a messy aftermath. The current mess is a direct result.[188]

Andrew Wilkie, former intelligence analyst with the Office of National Assessments, who subsequently became a politician standing as an independent, was the only intelligence officer in the country who was prepared to sacrifice his job in order to tell the public the truth – and the only one to come out of the debacle with any credibility.

In a public statement he said the three men most responsible for taking the world to war, George Bush, Tony Blair and John Howard, should face charges as war criminals:

That he has never been held to account, and that his foreign minister Alexander Downer is now Australian High Commissioner to London, is quite simply outrageous.

Moreover, the Iraq debacle turbocharged al Qaida and created the circumstances for the eventual emergence of Islamic State. In other words the terrorist danger confronting Australians to this very day is a result of Australia's involvement in Iraq.[189]

Old Alex couldn't have said it better.

Britain lost 179 military personnel in the conflict.

Australia's intelligence community lost all plausibility and honour, thanks to the misconduct of a politician.

Estimates of the number killed in Iraq during and since the invasion ranged up to and over one million.

Just like Howard, Tony Blair defended his decision:

There were no lies. There was no deceit. There was no deception. But there was a decision and it was a controversial decision: a decision to remove Saddam and a decision to be with America. Now, many people would disagree with both of those decisions.

---

188 Ibid.

189 Ibid.

That's fine. But if you're going to do that, you have to say what the consequences of the opposite decision would have been. 'Cause the point about being prime minister is: you're the decision maker. You sit in the seat and take the decision.[190]

I believe we made the right decision and the world is better and safer.[191]

But what was most remarkable of all, was that in 2016 Australia was back in Iraq, dropping bombs at the behest of the Americans. Who they were killing, how many civilians were dying as a result, that they did not have the guts to tell the Australian people.

The legality of Australia's involvement in Iraq remained an open, unresolved question. The war which Howard had drawn the country into, a dirty, immoral and dishonest war, continued to curdle Australia's standing in the world – and ultimately, for the dead would have their way, on the nation's conscience and moral standing.

The Australia of 2016, a place where whistle-blowers were hunted and surveillance universal, where the authorities could run amok without consequence, where all faith in politicians had been shut down and almost all genuine public debate quashed, was born from the Howard era, and in that decision to go to war.

The rising of religious and ethnic tensions within Australia was due in no small part to the nation's involvement in the Middle East. Everything got worse. There was undoubtedly blowback and increasing danger to the civilian population, another price too high to pay.

Thirteen years after that fateful decision in 2003, and having re-entered Iraq, Howard's war became Turnbull's war and bombs paid for by Australian taxpayers continued to rain down on a country half a world away.

In Britain, Sarah O'Connor, whose brother Bob died when his plane was shot down over Iraq in 2005, said: "There is one terrorist in this world that the world needs to be aware of, and his name is Tony Blair, the world's worst terrorist".

---

190 Tony Blair defends Iraq war in the wake of Chilcot Report, Steve Cannane, ABC, 7 July, 2016.

191 Tony Blair unrepentant as Chilcot gives crushing Iraq war verdict, Luke Harding, *The Guardian*, 7 July, 2016.

From Baghdad to Washington, Sydney to London and many places in between, the words stung.

There was increasing acceptance that the planet was entering World War Three, and that nuclear weapons were on the table.

Yet in Australia the power to go to war remained in the hands of a very few political operatives – in particular the Prime Minister, who could take the country to war without the approval of either the people or the Parliament.

In the wake of the Chilcot Report a group of Federal MPs, former military chiefs and lobbyists ramped up calls to change the war powers invested in the Prime Minister and Cabinet.

The decision to go to war in 2003 had been John Howard's decision. Despite some show of consultation there had been no vote in the parliament. Former Australian Army Officer James Brown said the learning process was only halfway done.

> I think we're unlikely to see an inquiry as forensic and extensive as Chilcot in Australia but it would be good to see more on the public record about how some of these decisions were made. That's why we're seeing calls for war powers reform in Canada, New Zealand and particularly in the United Kingdom.[192]

Labor Senator Lisa Singh broke ranks, claiming the decision to go to war is too important to be left solely to the Prime Minister. "We're talking about one of the most important policy areas that our country has to face. And yet the decision is made by one person."

Kellie Merritt, whose husband Paul Pardoel was killed in the Iraq war, also pushed for the power to go to war to be taken out of the hands of the Prime Minister: "We invaded another country and the fallout from that has been catastrophic. The gravest decision a government can make must also be the most robust, considered, rationally grounded one and the process we have now hasn't leant itself to giving us that sort of outcome."[193]

Australia, either directly or by failing to protest the behaviour, had been an all too willing partner to the tortures of Abu Ghraib, to the killing and maiming of children, to the destruction of a country and to the escalating spates of terrorist attacks occurring after the 2003 invasion.

---

192 MPs and former military chiefs push to broaden war powers beyond PM, Cabinet, David Lipson, ABC, 26 August, 2016.

193 Ibid.

As Gwynne Dyer put it in *The Mess They Made*:

> The occupation of Iraq was the most spectacularly incompetent and corrupt operation carried out by the government of any developed country in many decades, and it turned the high probability of a major insurgency in Iraq after the invasion into the certainty of countrywide violence, despair and anarchy.[194]

Yet John Howard, the Prime Minister who took the country to war and was the man most singularly responsible for the mess the country now faced, refused to apologise.

The days when he did his Bantam strut with Prime Minister Tony Blair and President George Bush had disappeared into ignoble history.

"There was no lie," claimed Howard. And nobody believed him.

---

194 *The Mess They Made*, Gwynne Dyer, McClelland and Stewart, 2007.

AN IDIOT WIND

OPERATIVES, dressed in black, all equipped with night vision goggles, crept through the undergrowth. There were many dangers afoot. Military trained empaths circled the encampment. Old Alex sat in that cluttered Newtown garden and knew no peace, the rustling movements of the Neighbourhood Watch types everywhere, in the neighbouring yards, a room that overlooked the house, the drifting clamour from the Courthouse Hotel, down into a once wooded depression which had never been safe.

It was a peculiarity of Australian consciousness that the stories of a previous landscape and the first peoples kept breaking through into the present day: "To take a strange land as one's home/Is folly beyond compare." No one had felt safe from the ravaging of the white ghosts; and the latter-day attempts of the invaders at absolving their own guilt were feeble indeed.

> For outsiders in the bush do not, on the whole, think magically, or see the ceremonial logic of that world and the compelling force it exerts upon those plunged within it. The ideas western observers apply to the Aboriginal realm come, rather, from social science and cultural frameworks. They are the ideas of the Bohemian, the intellectual, the aid worker or the enlightened functionary, and they bring confusion in their wake . . . an administrative order, elaborate, with constantly shifting priorities.[195]

---

195 *Quicksilver*, Nicolas Rothwell. Prepublication copy supplied by author.

Into their conquering, colonial deceits the white ghosts brought with them their own collapsing and decaying reversals of spiritual belief.

> The primal order of the world has been shattered, it lies in fragments; the sparks of the divine are spread over the expanses of the earth, and it is essential to gather them up, each last scintilla; to go down into the darkness where they are disseminated, down into the furthest reaches of the world, and there embrace sin and falsity. Such paradoxes had a natural appeal, in a time when the adherents of the faith were constantly persecuted; when established rituals brought nothing; when God's protection had so manifestly failed. It was this climate of ideas that paved the way for the religious cataclysms ahead.[196]

That sacred land, which the white men transgressed every day with arrogance and filthy belief, was still being ransacked and sold off for profit to foreigners centuries later without so much as a nod to the descendents – beyond comprehension.

They had been a tribal people. Wise souls travelled down their lineages for thousands of years. Did the ghosts think there would be no revenge for their desecration?

If the indigenous regarded a piece of ground as unlucky, or dangerous, infested with mischievous or hostile spirits of place, those elements remained despite the terrace houses and the 21st Century automobiles.

That, Old Alex most certainly felt, was the case in the hollow, once hallowed ground, trailing away behind The Big White House.

In mid-November came the first in a rolling wave of mass casualty attacks on the West, killing 130 people, including 89 at the Bataclan Theatre in Paris. Another 368 people were injured.

In a statement to parliament, the Prime Minister Malcolm Turnbull used the Paris attacks to highlight the importance of the military activity of the international community in defeating Islamic State in the field in Syria and Iraq:

> Late on the afternoon of Friday, 13 November, Paris, the city of light, was assaulted by godless ISIL murderers who blasphemously claimed to be killing in the name God, who claimed to be killing in the name of Islam, but defame and blasphemed Islam itself.

196 Ibid.

It reminds us that a few fanatics with automatic weapons and explosives can do great damage and strike at the heart of free, open and democratic societies. This was not just an assault on French lives and French freedoms. It was an attack on all humanity, on all our freedoms, freedom to gather and to celebrate, the freedom to share time with our family and friends, the freedom to walk our streets without fear.[197]

Rumours would emerge that some of the victims had their eyes gauged out, genitals mutilated or were beheaded. Where the truth lay was difficult to determine. But it was enough that the stories spread. The jihadists had succeeded.

Ramping up the fear levels in the Australian community, a fear likely to favour the incumbent government in the coming election, Prime Minister Malcolm Turnbull warned that another terrorist attack in Australia was likely "in the current environment".

Turnbull claimed Australian authorities were doing everything possible to keep the nation safe and that Muslim nations were "utterly united in their commitment to defeat terrorism".

There were many times in Turnbull's tenure when his glib verbal facility so typical of a trained lawyer stretched credulity wafer-thin.

He said:

Claims by the terrorist group, by Daesh or ISIL speaking in the name of God or in the name of Islam, are absolutely blasphemous. Their leaders, they do not speak in the name of Islam, they defame Islam, they are an abomination.

I've spoken this morning as I have every day with our key security agencies, the head of ASIO Duncan Lewis, the Commissioner of the Federal Police, Andrew Colvin, and my ministerial colleagues.

Our security agencies are the best in the world. We recognise that risks exist, attacks are possible, attacks in this environment are likely to happen in the future, but Australians can be assured that we have the best security agencies, they are monitoring the

197 Statement on Indulgence – Terror attacks around the world, Australian Parliament, Prime Minister, 23 November, 2015.

situation and seeking to protect Australians at home in so far as we can and abroad.

So I have every confidence that our security environment, while challenged of course, in this context of terrorism, is nonetheless being well managed by the best security agencies in the world.[198]

Australians were always being told they were the best country on Earth, possessed "the world's best security forces", "the world's most successful multicultural society", "the world's best border protection".

It did not jell with the reality on the ground and did nothing to provoke a realistic assessment of the nation's plummeting standing in the world.

One of the critiques Alex got of his recent writing was: "How could you possibly criticise Australia? We're lucky to live here."

What, you're lucky to be betrayed? You're lucky to see your own society transformed into a prison cell?

But he never bothered to respond.

As for the best security agencies in the world, that was not the story he heard either in academic journals or whispered in the wind; instead he heard mindboggling tales of vast and vastly incompetent bureaucracies, the word "malfeasance" frequently spoken.

Australia also had the most expensive, and some of the world's slowest internet, some of the world's highest costs of living and most expensive housing, the world's most expensive electricity, the world's most rapacious and most profitable banks and one of the most miserably over-regulated societies on Earth.

Indigenous males also had the world's highest suicide rates, and Aboriginals health standards were falling across almost all categories in all states.

Despite all the high-flying rhetoric and the pledging of billions of dollars, educational standards were also falling across the nation.

In the wake of the Paris attacks Major-General Duncan Lewis, head of the Australian Security Intelligence Organisation, the most visible of the agencies, denied there was any nexus between Australia's involvement in Iraq and Syria and the domestic terror threat:

These people are anti-Western. Australia has been a terrorist

---

198 Paris terror attacks: Malcolm Turnbull warns of 'likely' strike on Australia, Mark Kenney, *Sydney Morning Herald*, 16 November, 2015.

target long before we became engaged in the Middle East, but we are as a culture, we are as a society objectionable to them.

They want to attack us. They want to destroy us. We must be enormously resolute in the way we approach this.

This [the Paris attacks] is an act of criminality; this is a grotesque distortion of one of the world's great religions to provide an excuse or cover for their actions.[199]

The claim that there was no link between Australia's foreign policy and the escalating domestic terror threat was contradicted by some of the nation's and the world's leading terror experts.

Martin Chulov was a former colleague from *The Australian*, too smart to stay there. He always had excellent contacts in the federal police and national security circuits. In 2015 year he won of the one of world's most prestigious prizes for journalism, the very appropriately named Orwell Prize.

In his book *Australian Jihad: The battle against terrorism from within and without*, he wrote:

We have been far more central to radical Islamists' priorities than we ever recognised – and the radicalism they are peddling took root in Australian society more than a decade ago. The lightning rod of Afghanistan has to a large extent been replaced by Iraq, which continues to have a profound impact on radicalised Muslims in Australia and Southeast Asia. Home-grown radicals are drawing strength from what they see as the anger and suffering of their brethren abroad.[200]

The book had been withdrawn from sale after suppression orders restricting coverage of one of Australia's most famous terror cases, Operation Pendennis, were made. While the court orders were lifted several years later, the book had never been reissued and copies were difficult to find. It should have been compulsory reading. The actions against the book smacked of deliberate suppression.

In the wake of the Paris attacks Alex was commissioned to do a piece on the growing power of Islamic State.

---

199 Islamic State wants to attack and destroy us, ASIO chief Duncan Lewis warns, James Massola, *Sydney Morning Herald*, 16 November, 2015.

200 Australian Jihad: The battle against terrorism from within and without, Martin Chulov, Pan MacMillan, 2006.

For all the talk of degrading Islamic State (IS), the group has grown even more deadly this year.

Despite a whole host of books in 2015 warning of its increasing power and numerous cautionary tales from some of the world's most gifted analysts, Australians still seem ill-informed on the subject.

It is as if town criers have swarmed through the streets shouting "Hear ye, hear ye" but no one listened.

Until Paris ripped away the fog.[201]

It was a different style of journalism to the past, driven by click rates and anchored in a sea of competing, attention-grabbing stories. Flashier, more immediate, less learned in tone. He liked it.

The Australian population was disengaged from the political process, distrustful and disbelieving of their politicians. The attempts to heighten alarm over terrorists fitted ill with the decades of multicultural propaganda, and the simplistic rhetoric of Tony Abbott's government had fed misunderstandings and lulled Australians into believing Islamic State was an easily defeated "death cult".

It was hard to believe that this revolution in geo-political reality had occurred in the space of two short years.

Again Alex quoted Martin Chulov, who was now based in Beirut and had become one of the world's foremost experts on Islamic State. He said the group spent its first eighteen months establishing a caliphate, which successfully "stripped the authority of regional countries, fed off grievances of disenfranchised Sunnis and imposed itself as a 'true' authority, acting out a divine will".

At the same time, it has been preparing for its next incarnation, which is exporting chaos far and wide. We had already seen that in part, with satellites in Egypt, Libya and Yemen swearing allegiance, but the attacks in Paris reveal just how far that capacity has evolved in such a short time.

In a sense, it now matters less whether IS can hold on to the

201 There's a new and deadlier Islamic State coming, John Stapleton, *The New Daily*, 22 November, 2015.

contiguous strip of land it controls from Aleppo to Mosul. Its base has been convinced of what it can do. The rest of the world has taken notice.[202]

In the distress of the days following the Bataclan attack, French President Francois Hollande called the Islamic State "an army which threatens the world".

Australian politicians had never officially declared the nation to be at war, while in an address to a joint session of Parliament the French President made it clear, war had been declared. He said the country was facing an enemy which had a territorial base, financial resources, and military capabilities. Since the beginning of the year Islamic State's terrorist army had struck in Paris, Denmark, Tunisia, Egypt, Lebanon, Kuwait, Saudi Arabia, Turkey, and Libya. Every day, it massacred and oppressed populations.

> France is at war. The acts committed in Paris and near the Stade de France on Friday evening are acts of war. They left at least 129 dead and many injured. They are an act of aggression against our country, against its values, against its young people, and against its way of life.
>
> They were carried out by a jihadist army, by Daesh, which is fighting us because France is a country of freedom, because we are the birthplace of human rights.
>
> Their objective was quite clear: to sow fear in order to divide us and to keep us from fighting terrorism in the Middle East.[203]

The President proclaimed a state of emergency, ordered the reestablishment of border controls and initiated a string of airstrikes on the Islamic State capital of Raqqa.

War had been declared. And Australia was right in its path.

Australian politicians had long had a habit of telling their constituents what reasonable Muslims thought, rather than letting them speak for themselves. There was a reason for that. They rarely said what the politicians and the champions of the state creed of multiculturalism would like them to say.

---

202 Ibid.

203 Speech by the President of the Republic before a joint session of Parliament, Versailles, 16 November, 2015.

Turnbull was no exception to the rule:

> The leadership of Muslims around the world in condemning
> ISIL is another key factor, and I want to commend the Muslim
> leaders – Presidents of great nations and Presidents of commu-
> nity associations alike – who have spoken out for an authentic,
> moderate and tolerant Islam. Extremism is a challenge all Austra-
> lians must address. Extremists aim to sow discord by driving a
> wedge between Muslims a non-Muslim, dividing us as a society.
>
> We are the most successful and harmonious multicultural
> society in the world. The richness of our diversity is one of our
> nation's greatest strengths and we must protect and defend it
> dearly.[204]

Lie layered upon lie, that was the Australia of the day. The oft-repeated
claim by the Prime Minister that Australia was the world's most successful
multicultural country would be sorely tested in the months to come. A
theory like any other theory, designed to break up the hegemony of the
ruling culture, it had been embraced by generations of bureaucrats and
social engineers as an unassailable, unalloyed good; while governments
spent literally billions of dollars to convey the message.

But however desperately the governing class attempted to paint over
obvious fissures, as in every other Western country, questions of immigration and national identity were now at the forefront of community debate.

Grand Mufti Dr Ibrahim Abu Mohammed had long made it clear that
the country's Muslims did not need advice from the Australian government
and would not participate in their propaganda. That is, they would not
present a united stand with the authorities, cooperate in their own oppres-
sion and paper over the numerous points of division.

> These recent incidents highlight the fact that current strategies
> to deal with the threat of terrorism are not working.
>
> It is therefore imperative that all causative factors such as racism,
> Islamophobia, curtailing freedoms through securitisation,
> duplicitous foreign policies and military intervention must be
> comprehensively addressed.

---

204 Statement on Indulgence – Terror attacks around the world, Malcolm Turnbull MP,
23 November, 2015..

In addition, any discourse which attempts to apportion blame by association or sensationalises violence to stigmatise a certain segment of society only serves to undermine community harmony and safety.

Credit goes to those who have called for calm and responsibility. We call upon all people of goodwill to stand against fearmongering and injustice.[205]

A subsequent "clarification" notwithstanding, the comments set off a mini-firestorm, with Immigration Minister Peter Dutton saying the Grand Mufti needed to "make it very clear that he condemns these acts of terrorism, these murderous acts, without reservation". Treasurer Scott Morrison, an evangelical Christian, said: "I was very disappointed for Australian Muslims ... I thought Australian Muslims were let down by the Mufti yesterday."[206]

The Telco Optus was forced to remove a new advertisement, written in Arabic, from a Sydney shopping centre after staff were allegedly threatened.

Alex was commissioned to do a story on Captagon, a variant of amphetamine popular in the Middle East, and its use by Islamic State: headlined The Drug Creating Islamic State Super Soldiers.

It seemed appropriate, with that apocalyptic drug ice so readily available upstairs at the Carlisle opposite, within metres from where he slept. The drug was being linked to terror attacks across Europe and the Middle East. Captagon gave the users a sense of omnipotence and allowed soldiers to stay awake for days on end. Feuding jihad groups across the Middle East may have had little else in common, but they were all rumoured to be using methamphetamines, the drug credited with helping to create the "super soldiers" of the Islamic State.

While the drug is virtually unknown in Australia, it mirrors some of the effects of ice, a methamphetamine with which Australians are becoming all too familiar.

The calmness that jihadists have shown while committing terrorist acts, such as that displayed by the perpetrators of the recent Paris attacks, is being directly attributed to the drug.

205 Media Statement, ANBIC Mourns Loss of Innocent Lives to Terrorist Attacks, Australian National Imans Council, 15 November, 2015.

206 Muslim community distances itself from Grand Mufti Dr Ibrahim Abu Mohammed's comments on Paris Terror attacks, Miles Godfrey, *The Daily Telegraph*, 17 November, 2015.

Numerous reports suggested the perpetrators were strangely composed.

One witness said: "I saw a man who was peaceful, composed, with a face that was almost serene, contemplative … He sprayed the terrace (with bullets) as anyone else would spray their lawn with a garden hose."[207]

In the collapsing state of Syria, the black money generated by the drug trade was being used to fund jihad groups.

In the collapsing Australian state, drug money was also ending up in the hands of jihadists, with the Australian Crime Commission acknowledging that hundreds of millions of dollars from the Australian drug trade was being channelled to terror groups.

High unemployment rates, both official and concealed, high levels of disengagement, low levels of national pride, zero levels of social cohesion, increasingly large percentages of the population cut out from the national discourse, numerous bureaucratic blockages to personal endeavour and self-sufficiency, an economy where it was impossible for many small business people to realise their dreams, strangulated as they were by onerous taxes and ludicrous regulation… it was a perfect petri dish for an ice epidemic.

Disaster was fomenting. Pity the poor prisoner.

Old Alex had been a close observer of the Australian underclass throughout his professional life. He had never seen things worse, not just in sheer numbers but in the level of abasement and personal disintegration so easily observed on the streets.

The honour amongst thieves strung through the traditional camaraderie of Australia's working and criminal classes had disappeared. Now the under-class ripped each other off as quickly as they stole from the bourgeoisie.

Rifling around for someone who may have used Captagon, he quoted an old friend:

Michael Prato, an Australian who has used Captagon, albeit some decades ago, said it was widely available in Bangkok in the 1970s.

"The packet said it 'heightens efficiency and readies one for effi-

207 The Drug Creating Islamic State Supersoldiers, John Stapleton, *The New Daily*, 13 January, 2016.

ciency'. At the time I thought, 'that will do me. I used to walk around with a packet of the things in my pocket. It was easy to get at any Chinese chemist in Bangkok.

"Captagon gives you a lightening of mood, a lightening of steps, unlimited energy. Nothing is too much trouble. It doesn't surprise me at all jihadists are using it. It is a well thought out tactic."[208]

The words across time reflected a friendlier, more gifted era; sunshine in a forest grove, long ago.

There was no camaraderie, no creativity, no fun, no "up yours" hilarity in the present day scenarios.

Opposite, upstairs at the Carlisle, he could hear through those long hours of the early morning the Mordor-like insanities of the ice addicts, shuddering, jumping, desperately degraded spurts of consciousness, and the cynical, broken treacheries of a police informant.

There was already a camera in his own attic.

There was no privacy.

He slept when exhausted, climbing up the narrow stairs and passing out fully clothed, fitfully escaping for a few hours into the night, another night.

Hunted in perpetuity, he truly hated his pursuers, appalled at the maladministration which had gifted them the power to behave the way they did. As far as he was concerned, it was criminal misconduct. The more he heard, the more he hated them; the homophobes and boofheads from the federal and local police, militant gender warriors from the agencies. Nobody had the decency to tell him the truth.

The Adoration of Bertrand Russell had reached ludicrous levels in his youth, and in a sense remained with him still.

So it was his old mentor Bertrand who intoned:

No matter how powerfully or beautifully expressed, anger and frustration do not a clear analysis make. You are not the only person this is happening to. You need to examine the social, legal, cultural and bureaucratic processes which have made these operations an acceptable part of modern day law enforcement.

In his base heart of hearts all he wanted to do was fulminate about low-life thugs and the primitive behaviour of the mob.

---

208 Ibid.

None of which was very helpful, in that cloistered garden, as others died on the world's battlefields, courtesy of the Australian taxpayer.

All he could do was get up and do the best by the day, hope that things would blow over, that a transitory refuge might turn into a permanent one.

There were nights when he could not believe what he heard, our taxes at work.

"Danger, Bashers About," sprang up one headline, one of the hundreds of old stories he had begun collecting onto an internet site. There was no such thing as coincidence.

The summer slid, briefly, into a silken time. Try as he might to watch a bit of news on the television, Pete the Opera Diva would rapidly switch channels to old musicals or repeats of *Downton Abbey*.

He should have been born in the Edwardian Era, he insisted. It never occurred to him that he might have been reincarnated downstairs, as a footman or a butler, not upstairs as Lord of the Manor.

Peter was a walking composite of everything about the wealthy gay community in Sydney Old Alex disliked: its narrow self-importance, elitism, their ever prattling presences, the constant reliving of youth, outdoing each other in their obscene expenditures as they picked over expensive meals in restaurants. Nonetheless the two of them spent a lot of time together that summer, as if in the early stages of romance, although there was no romance. But there was a curative element in their peculiar friendship, perhaps because the times had been so harrowing for them both.

It was Christmas and there were many parties to attend. The world might be sliding straight towards cataclysm, but in The Big White House it was a time for festivity, Peter's second Christmas without his beloved Declan.

Decorations went up: trails of green and red crepe, a ridiculous looking reindeer draped in glitter.

Peter simply had to throw a party.

After considerable fuss, invitations went out.

Alex's idea of a party was just to invite everybody, buy lots of grog and a few nibblies, and let things take their course.

That was not the way things were done at Ardmore House, aka The Big White House.

The preparations went on for weeks, with extensive discussions amongst the inmates, those likely lads, about what to wear, the best alcohol, the right brand of champagne, the appropriate food, the guest list, the music.

Nathan, who swanned around Ardmore House in his dressing gown pecking at his smartphone, checking out Facebook and Grindr every few minutes, was in a complete lather, simply could not decide on anything, what to wear, who to invite, the best dishes to serve.

Lee was in a flummox over his first outing in drag, worried most of all about what his boyfriend would think. He had a bright red dress made especially for the occasion.

Old Alex had been cold ever since returning from Vietnam, and took friendship where he could find it.

The air changed texture, warmer, less hostile.

He stopped shouting at his invisible tormentors: "I'd sue you for harassment if I could."

They would try once again to come for him, in their own time, wreathed in their own darkness, their secrets eating at their souls like an invisible leprosy.

But for a time there was peace.

He heard one of the annoyed intelligence officers say: "We should have listened to the journalists in the first place."

As in, he wasn't the person mafia-linked police officers and security agents on a vendetta had made him out to be. They had fallen into a trap of their own making.

The Christmas party came with a great fussing: trips to pick up the especially printed invitations, flowers and champagne to be bought.

Alex's contribution was a couple of bottles of schnapps, and during the party he wandered through the crowded rooms dishing out shots: peach, apple. That got them going.

It was an old-fashioned party: plenty of booze, plenty to eat, friendly mix of all-sorts, good crowd.

An old lover from the 1970s came; and Alex thought, as the conversation flowed freely and the guests became increasingly inebriated, "I hope I never grow that old."

But of course he was that old.

There was a kind of poignancy wherever he looked.

A gangster friend who ran sex shops had dressed up for the occasion and held court, middle aged women yearned for the castoffs, old girls of both genders gathered around the piano and sang as if they were back on stage, as if they were all still fabulous.

In the morning there were those enduring signs of a successful party: guests still drinking, the music still playing as night turned to dawn, the usual jostle of who was going to sleep with whom, as if anyone really cared. He stayed above the fray, or wasn't in the fray.

"I went up to bed, and there were two men waiting for me," Peter boasted, determined to believe the good times weren't yet over.

The same bed in which Declan had died.

Alex did not come from a family which celebrated Christmas, and so on the day itself, having made it clear he was not going to function simply as a taxi driver, he drove some of the household out to the home of yet another set of Peter's wealthy friends.

There, on the outskirts of Sydney where mansions sat on five or ten acre lots, the electronic gates swung open and The Beast, his old blue Ford, drove down across a bridge and swept up past the banks of azaleas, rhododendrons and camellias to a Gone with the Wind house.

They were given Christmas punch on arrival; and Alex was given a tour of the garden – regularly featured, of course, in the annual Open Garden scheme. The lifestyle cost not just a fortune to maintain, but a lifetime to create. A wall-to-ceiling panel of lights and switches maintained the property, the gate at the entrance, the lights beside the pool, the elaborate sprinkler system through various corners of the property.

A full traditional lunch in the antique stuffed formal dining room was followed by naked, drunken antics in the pool. He remained shy and aloof. In the evening there was Cherries Jubilee, a dish devised for Queen Victoria's Diamond Jubilee.

They clutched at their status symbols while he acted as the chauffeur, driving his passengers back through twenty-five kilometres of almost deserted highway, the town ghostly quiet; as if the revenants were already massing before a terrible dawn.

That December the Royal Australian Air Force dropped 81 bombs on Iraq from a total of 539 flying hours and 73 sorties flying the aging F/A18 Hornets, ordered through the US government's Foreign Military Sales program.

The aircraft also dropped 21 bombs on Syria from 10 sorties.

Hundreds of men, women and children were likely to have been killed as a result. The government issued no information on casualties.

Thanks for the Christmas present, Daddy.

Malcolm Turnbull, the man most directly responsible for the killings, wished the Australian people a Merry Christmas and a safe and happy New Year: "This is a very special time as the year comes to an end and we draw closer to family and dear friends. Christmas is a time of love, hope and joy. Bright eyed children waiting for Santa, grandparents welcoming home their far flung brood – the mystery of a thousand Christmas services in churches large and small."[209]

Authorities around the world were on high alert as New Year dawned. But there were no massacres, a burning building in Dubai, cancelled celebrations in Brussels, evacuated train stations in Munich – but none of the mass casualty events so feared on a day of pagan celebration.

A day which until recently had been a cause for celebration, not fear.

2016: a year Alex had never expected to see, was dawning on edge, the pictures of fireworks and exultant crowds one final delusion of a departing world.

David Bowie, that God of his youth, died ten days later.

In the inner-city milieu of the 1970s in which he had once thrived, all his hard-partying friends had been awed by the rush of takeoff:

Ground Control to Major Tom
Commencing countdown,
engines on
Check ignition
and may God's love be with you

And even more by denouement:

Ground Control to Major Tom
Your circuit's dead,
there's something wrong
Can you hear me, Major Tom?
Can you hear me, Major Tom?

And yet even more when the truth would out:

Ashes to ashes, fun to funky
We know Major Tom's a junkie

209 Seasons Greetings 2015, Malcolm Turnbull's website.

> Strung out in heaven's high
> Hitting an all-time low[210]

Back in the 1970s Keith Stead had been a frequent visitor to his home in Hargrave Street, Paddington, next door to the Bellevue Hotel.

Every David Bowie album was treated as the second coming – his music ringing from the whitewashed streets of Greek villages to the back lanes of Paddington, everywhere he went.

The religious iconography was already there: the red light of Mars, the black lapping seas, the high priestesses bowing to touch the ground, images of isolation and pain, an infinite sense of longing and loss, of a spiritual essence beyond the physical realm; all of it bathed their consciousness.

Keith had been a handsome, charismatic, maliciously clever, unconscionably funny man who was also splendidly out of it. Drug dependence, they would have sniffed decades on. Then it was The Doors of Perception: "The road of excess leads to the palace of wisdom."

Keith would die that terrible year: a miserable death in diminished circumstance, reclusive, sick, obsessed with God.

They had fallen out decades before, when Alex held an End of Sydney party before moving to London.

Sydney's not ending just because you're leaving, Keith tried rather pointlessly to point out – as he pursued Alex around an otherwise extremely successful party, with the crowds spilling out onto the pavement.

Keith became a torment; and the days when every new Velvet Underground, Lou Reed, Iggy Pop and David Bowie album was a cause for a week-long celebration vanished into their respective histories.

Alex went on into mainstream journalism, a different life; and tried never to look back.

Most of those he had partied with from that bygone era were dead – victims of the twin evils of the age, AIDS and overdoses.

He was the guilty party who introduced Keith to his good friend Jenny, in one of whose many houses he happened to be happily living. The only good result from that terrible, violent and mercifully short relationship was a daughter to whom, all these decades on, Jenny remained devoted.

He saw the daughter's sad tribute on Facebook to a father who was gone,

---

210 Lines from Space Oddity and Ashes to Ashes by David Bowie.

and her natural desire to believe that things were better than they actually were. He messaged her words of comfort: "You are the light that came from some very dark days."

And she shared the pain of those times when all she wanted was a phone call from her Dad on her birthday.

There was no comfort in such a dismal waste of life, except in new life and private, family routines.

The old rebel Jenny was now a very proud grandmother; the clandestine past banished by the years.

Even in summer that cloistered Newtown backyard felt dank, over-watered.

With Glen and Joy he sat and listened to Bowie's last great work, Dark Star. Ashes to Ashes, Tom's a Junkie, Strung Out in Heaven's High, it had all spilled down the decades to become something else.

They were too young to understand, their lives before them. They were clever, yet they still believed they could help make the world a better place. He understood that, too.

In Bowie's final performances it was also clear: be careful what you pray for, who you pray to.

The same themes continued: solitude, the conviction he was from somewhere else, a grieving, unquenchable sense of loss.

Major Tom was going home… to be reborn on another pain rack.

The icon his entire generation had adored from afar, the news of bisexuality electric through the orgies of the era, justifying almost anything, was now an old man.

Demonic bodies quivered; the hand-held mirrors to other worlds, the serious intent, the belief that words and music were a kind of magic which transmitted spiritual messages, it was all there.

Dark Star was released on the 8th of January, 2016.

Bowie died two days later:

> Something happened on the day he died
>
> Spirit rose a metre and stepped aside
> Somebody else took his place, and bravely cried
>
> I'm a blackstar, I'm a blackstar
> How many times does an angel fall?
> How many people lie instead of talking tall?

He trod on sacred ground, he cried loud into the crowd
I'm a blackstar, I'm a blackstar, I'm not a gangstar
I can't answer why I'm a blackstar[211]

There was a reason why figures such as David Bowie stood so far outside their times, geniuses of their age.

The aching loneliness which Bowie projected was exactly that of a cluster soul without the cluster, a hive mind without the hive.

The era was sometimes called The Age of Loneliness, and for whatever reason, millions of people instantly related, as they had related to other towering figures down the ages.

In the beginning was the Word. Alex had never understood it before. He did now.

Bowie understood more than anyone that words, written words, were the symbology, the instruments of saints and shamans, priests and magicians, a kind of magisterium from one plain of existence to another.

In the days when he half-believed Glen's aspiring writer story, he flicked him a quote he found from *Brain Pickings* by Maria Popova, one of those brave souls struggling to trigger an Enlightenment in a darkening world, before the harvesting of souls could begin in earnest:

> With all peoples the word and writing are holy and magical; naming and writing were originally magical operations, magical conquests of nature through the spirit, and everywhere the gift of writing was thought to be of divine origin. With most peoples, writing and reading were secret and holy arts reserved for the priesthood alone.

> Without the word, without the writing of books, there is no history, there is no concept of humanity.[212]

He did not relay the rest of what Herman Hesse had to say:

> The laws of the spirit change just as little as those of nature and it is equally impossible to "discard" them. Priesthoods and astrologers' guilds can be dissolved or deprived of their privi-

211 Black Star, David Bowie, Published 8 January, 2016.

212 *My Belief: Essays on Life and Art*, Farrar, Straus and Giroux, Herman Hesse, 1974 & The Magic of the Book: Herman Hesse on Why We Read and Always Will, Maria Popova, Brain Pickings.

leges. Discoveries or poetic inventions that formerly were secret possessions of the few can be made accessible to the many, who can even be forced to learn about these treasures. But all this goes on at the most superficial level and in reality nothing in the world of the spirit has changed since Luther translated the Bible and Gutenberg invented the printing press. The whole magic is still there, and the spirit is still the secret of a small hierarchically organised band of privileged persons, only now the band has become anonymous.

If today the ability to read is everyone's portion, still only a few notice what a powerful talisman has thus been put into their hands.[213]

As King David's seer Nathan said to his young charge Solomon, recorded in that magnificent piece of literary channelling *The Secret Chord*, by Sydney-born Pulitzer Prize winning author Geraldine Brooks: "Did you know the Mitzrayimites call their writing 'god signs'? They understand that words have power." We turned our attention to deciphering the glyphs, and he, delighted and puzzled, threw himself fully into this new challenge.[214]

In the following days he could hear Blackstar and the old Bowie hits playing everywhere, the lines jumbling together, at the Carlisle, from car radios, in the distance – as he sat in the backyard struggling to concentrate on work.

We were born upside down
The wrong way round
I can't tell you why…
On the day of execution
Ashes to ashes
Fun to funky
The stars are out tonight
I hope they live forever

There were uncanny links down through the ages; but was now the time to tell of those peculiar cluster intelligences sliding through a cascading succession of lives and coagulations?

---

213 Ibid.

214 *The Secret Chord*, Geraldine Brooks, Viking Press, 2015.

There is no doubt that there is strung across the eons – a strong and fiery-wrought chain of lights, and that each glint and ray represents a great work, a great wisdom preserved. The lights on this infinite ligature have been added to, and continue to be added to, link by link. A few of the names of those who have added such lights are remembered, but the names of those who ignited most of the lights have been lost in time. However, it can be said that we are descended from them all. This phenomenon of the necklace of lights should not be understood as some mere trinket. Its reality is that it has acted, since forever, as a swaying, glowing life-line for human souls trying to find their way through the dark.[215]

They were one of the Great Mysteries of history – these people who stood so far out of, or above, their time. But they were in danger now, these powerful yet fragile, mystical yet corporeal figures, easily targeted through the same technologies they had originally used to identify each other; to recognise that they were not, as they had been throughout much of history, alone. The same technologies which had briefly promised the greatest democratisation of knowledge in human history had been swiftly turned into threat by authoritarian governments and the stalking Soldiers of God. They could be targetted. They could be disappeared from history.

They had been appearing in public, these peculiarly gifted people, here at the end of days, as if on request. Then they disappeared as quickly as they emerged, cloaking themselves once again in the traditional modes of concealment, the ordinary. As if they weren't so extraordinary after all but were just like everybody else, subservient, submissive, conformist.

He was given Colin Wilson's *The Outsider* by an early lover, in the fevered, ground-breaking atmosphere of the late sixties, when Alex had been another wild-eyed kid on the streets of that bohemian and underworld paradise Kings Cross.

The book was a revelation. It seemed to explain everything. It was, in a sense, a guide setting out a pathway to an artistic life, to finding your own wellspring of creativity. The ultimate point being that the outsiders were valuable to any society; they saw the world in a different way, they thought in a different way, and therefore had much to contribute.

---

215 Introduction to the 2004 Commemorative Edition, Clarissa Pinkola Estes, *The Hero with a Thousand Faces*, Joseph Conrad, Princeton University Press.

He had a habit, in his early days, of hunting down the famous. One of the great privileges of journalism was that it provides an excuse to meet and write about the people who most fascinate you.

Colin Wilson was boundlessly prolific, and for a time Alex consumed most of his books.

But nothing beat meeting the legend himself.

Alex had been living in London and doing freelance stories for the papers back home. The interview was arranged through Wilson's publishers, as these things usually were; and, surprisingly for someone who had once been so instantly recognisable, the God of his youth, he agreed readily.

English publishers could be very snooty about a book market as small as Australia, but there was never a shred of that from Wilson.

By the time Alex met him he was well past the height of his fame, and he seemed rather honoured, if that was the right word, to be asked; pleased that people still remembered him.

The Outsider made Colin Wilson instantly famous around the world, but as each subsequent title received damning reviews and sold fewer and fewer copies, his reputation shrivelled.

Alex and Wilson met in a London pub for lunch, but with the ridiculous licensing laws of the English he was shortly thereafter invited to continue their session at his Club.

It wasn't the grandest club in London, Wilson explained, but they had been welcoming to him before he was well off, and he liked it still.

> What can be said to characterise the Outsider is a sense of strangeness, unreality. Even Keats could write . . . in a letter just before he died: 'I feel as if I had died already and am now living a posthumous existence.' This is the sense of unreality, that can strike out of a perfectly clear sky . . . the Outsider is a man who cannot live in the comfortable, insulated world of the bourgeois, accepting what he sees and touches as reality. 'He sees too deep and too much,' and what he sees is essentially *chaos*. For the bourgeois, the world is fundamentally an orderly place... For the Outsider the world is not rational, orderly. When he asserts his sense of anarchy in the face of the bourgeois' complacent acceptance, it is not simply the need to cock a snoot at respectability that provokes him; it is a distressing sense that *truth must be told at all costs*, otherwise there can be no hope of

an ultimate restoration of order . . . truth must be told, chaos must be faced.[216]

The thronging, bohemian streets of the Cross Alex had known as a young man were no longer, most of the bars shut, the streets empty and dangerous.

But in those best of times, everyone he knew had wanted to be a painter, a writer, an actor, or at the very least to make their own lives a work of art, to be a star in their own movie.

Now the best anyone hoped for was a job, to become a serf. The higher paid a slave they were, the happier it made them.

This was the Age of Extinguishment.

Creativity had been destroyed.

"An innovative learning community" flashed the sign outside a local school on the South Coast.

This was followed by promotion for a Mufti dinner and a Multicultural Story Competition.

As the Hizb had always said, believe in everything and you believe in nothing.

The local library did not even have basic texts of the English canon like *Animal Farm*, *Brave New World* or *The Varieties of Religious Experience*.

The culture was being redacted.

Ideas were contagious, and this was a government and a society frightened of ideas.

Colin Wilson died in 2013.

In Australia fear was widespread: of another Great Depression, of an impending apocalypse, of a new Dark Age, the faith in orthodox stories crippled by a lack of distrust in all the stories being told.

In that backyard, he could see the fissures in the sky, darting into the ordinary.

He went quiet, very quiet, in this country ridden with hypocrisy, false trails and make believe tales.

The place he had once loved, a city where he had danced till dawn, had become a place where creativity was no longer celebrated, where submission was the only trait required for survival.

A country once girt by flashing surf and winsome flesh, characterised by

---

216 *The Outsider*, Colin Wilson, TarcherPerigee Reissue Edition, 1987.

a wild delight in the pleasures of life and disrespect for authority was now orthodox, conformist.

It was only one short step from here to the next terrible step in the country's iron-grip devolution, to a destitution of soul and spirit which, wreathed in threat, would gift ever greater powers to the dark: "They discover a frightful queerness has come into life. Even quite unobservant people now are betraying, by fits and starts, a certain wonder, a shrinking and fugitive sense that something is happening so that life will never be quite the same again."[217]

The brutality of the pursuit and the Psychological Operation targeting him would never cease to amaze, there in that encroaching space, that tiny Newtown back garden. Alex told no-one because it was so unexpected, so difficult to believe, as if it were happening beyond the border of the real.

He passed funereal daisies massed along a bank, and the harassment never stopped.

"Why give up hope now?" a voice asked.

There was a chorus of dismay, but this time the anger was directed at themselves, squabbling agencies, terrible mistakes.

"There's nothing wrong with what he's written," an intelligence officer said; while a soldier poured scorn anyway: "Fuck him."

Another muttered "Enemy of the State"; as if journalists were the enemy, truth was the enemy.

He read, it seemed to fit the mood, Graham Greene's *The Power and the Glory* – perhaps 40 years to the day after he first read it. The whisky priest climbing to the plateau, the dead child. Nobody could make our lives worse than we could make them ourselves.

A place which should have been a home was not a home, the Watchers on the Watch made sure of that. He ate dinner with the Old Opera Diva as they watched Downton Abbey, and pretended that everything was normal.

Instead the night was an overheated grey and there was treachery blanking in and out of nightmare.

Above the sky burned, below the furnaces roared.

As he bashed out news stories, he heard the schemes of the Watchers going on around him, the changes in shift at the nearby police station, the briefings and debriefings on all the usual walk-in casualties of the night.

---

217 *The Mind at the End of Its Tether*, H.G. Wells, Heinemann, 1945.

There was an occasional Muslim intelligence officer, or an Islamic specialist. No-one was planning to blow up the local shopping centre.

Locals, university students, young families, gathered at the nearby Camperdown Park, drinking and arguing their issues of the day, agreeing to agree on refugees and climate change and marriage equality.

Scenarios, haunting scenarios, moved in and out of the fabric.

"Enough, enough," a raised arm. "We surrender." "We apologise." But he just pretended to not hear whatever was the murmur in the wind of the day. "Better to be undetectable," he said to no-one in particular. "The gifts come and go. Safer to be invisible."

For, the waking dreams told him, truthsayers had always been hunted, across galaxies, across time.

Nothing was a greater threat to the existing power structures than the truth.

"This case has been mismanaged from the beginning," an annoyed voice said in the dark reaches. Perhaps it was Glen. "There's so many things wrong with it."

"I'd be careful of Glen," an old friend amongst the Watchers told him. "He works for..."

"Yes, I know," he replied.

Someone had to be smart enough and arrogant enough to sort out the mess. The wastes of money, resources, reputation, the downward spiral of bitterness and confusion, it had to end, for all their sakes.

Three a.m. on an Australia Day morning, more precisely Invasion Day.

Endlessly politicised, poorly managed, the country could not even celebrate its own story.

He could hear the disturbed voices of the ice addicts; the frustrated voices of the Watchers on the Watch, the muffled quiet of party goers trying not to attract too much attention to their drug use.

There would be no forgiveness on this day, as the slate grey skies tumbled overhead. Like many Sydneysiders, he would go down to the Aboriginal-themed Invasion Day events; and watch, if he watched at all, the triumphalism of the flyovers and celebrations on Sydney Harbour on television.

"War Footing" David Kilcullen wrote in a piece summarising the likely progress of the year ahead: Iraq: Situation dire, politics problematic. Syria: Increasingly bloody conflict. Afghanistan: An impending crisis. Libya: Islamic State to cement its control throughout the year, exporting terrorist violence and ideology throughout North Africa and the Sahara. Africa: Increased terror risk. Europe: Deepening migration crisis. The backlash to escalate as European border security broke down.

Closer to home, Southeast Asia is also likely to see an uptick in terrorist activity.

This is partly driven by the spreading influence of Islamic State, which established a wilayat in the southern Philippines at the end of last year, sent militants into Thailand last October to attack foreign tourists, and claimed last week's attack in downtown Jakarta. But older separatist and jihadist groups are also still active in the region and, as in other parts of the world, the emergence of Islamic State has created a competitive dynamic, with each group seeking to outdo the others, raising the general terror threat from a range of Islamist Thai, Malaysian, Bangladeshi and Indonesian officials have also expressed concerns about the potential for foreign fighters in Iraq and Syria returning home. All this is likely to generate a higher background threat level for many countries in Southeast Asia, including Australia.[218]

Every time he tried to watch the news the Opera Diva declared: "Boring, boring. The news is boring. Let them kill themselves. I don't care. Why would you want to watch that rubbish?"

As the world drifted towards calamity, his head became more active. In his waking dreams, the military-trained empaths roaming the perimeter increased in number. Two black cats, psychic animals, sat on the rooftop next door in the early hours of the morning… until he shooed them away.

Driven to distraction by the surveillance, Old Alex tried to order the empaths to stay beyond the outskirts, threatened to turn their brains to jelly, suck them out through a straw and hose what was left of their dismal consciousness down the gutter.

They paid no heed.

The imagery didn't work.

As for the rest of them, he threatened to rearrange the brains of the mundanes so they would never harass, bully or intimidate anyone ever again; in the same instant their faith in the old gods to be destroyed.

---

218 War footing: 2016 hot spots from the Middle East to Asia, David Kilcullen, *The Australian*, 23 January, 2016.

They couldn't even hear him.

> Now is the winter of our discontent…
> Cheated of feature by dissembling nature,
> Deformed, unfinished, sent before my time
> Into this breathing world, scarce half made up…[219]

The previous tenant, Nathan, having to everyone's surprise fallen for a woman on the South Coast, and the attic vacated, Alex officially moved into what he had hoped could be the bolt-hole in Sydney that he sought, a place to come and go.

He had the nomad's blood; and just like the nomads on the Steppes of Russia his children had been born barely a year apart – a survival mechanism in harsh conditions.

And just as with the nomads, he never stayed in one place long, but he needed a base.

The air was a clinging, unpleasant damp, summer itself born scarce half made up; the wettest, coldest summer he could ever remember.

He was advised: "You will have to accept that you will live the rest of your life in a glass cage."

Once he had lived crushed on the bottom of an aquarium filled with liquid lead. Now he was trapped inside a prism.

Glass was made to be broken. He accepted nothing.

What sort of country put its own citizens in cages?

> As I write, Western countries (several, particularly the US, now with severely reduced international credibility) face a larger, more unified, capable, experienced and savage enemy, in a less stable, more fragmented region, with a far higher level of geopolitical competition, and a much more severe risk of great-power conflict, than at any time since 9/11.[220]

A Sydney man, Mehmet Biber, 23, returned from the battlefields of Syria with a warning posted to Facebook and subsequently removed by the Australian authorities:

> Let the general public know that home ground attacks such as the likes of the one we seen at Parramatta will start to become more

219 *Richard III*, Shakespeare, Act 1, Scene 1.
220 *Blood Year: Islamic State and the Failures of the War on Terror*, David Kilcullen,

frequent as the Australian government sticks its hands deeper into the blood of the Muslims via joint attacks on Muslims overseas. If you attack Islam and Muslims for years on end indiscriminately then it's stupid and naive to think there wont be retaliation and consequences... just sayin' [221]

It was safe to assume Biber would spend the rest of his life under the lash of surveillance, would hear the voices of derision only he was meant to hear, and become angrier with every passing year.

In his waking dreams Alex saw a cabin cruiser docked outside a wealthy man's heavily curtained residence, there in the luminosity of the over-rich colours of Sydney Harbour; a once pink granite wall, a stretch of green grass, the shriek of sea-birds.

There was no shortage of money with these people – Saudi money, often as not. The transfer of arms took place under the cloak of night. Subterfuge, malice, threat.

The clairvoyant camera eye of remote dreaming, a prophecy from the increasingly roiled gods, a fantasy in the short-circuiting synapses of an over-worked brain, he had no way of knowing.

The moment was past, the weapons stashed; the hour yet to arrive.

Scene overlaid scene.

"There are multiple plots afoot across the country."

Old Alex was reminded of the day the Emir of Kuwait came to town and he was sent down to cover the event; struck by the gloomy, generational wealth.

Did Australians really have any idea who they were going to war for, or why?

The story, in *The Sydney Morning Herald*, was headlined: "The emir says thank you, but not much else" and began:

> So here was the man the Western allies went to war for, the Emir of Kuwait, Sheikh Jaber al-Ahmed al-Sabah.
>
> Appearing serious, almost withdrawn, he did not so much as look sideways at the gaggle of television and still photographers who were allowed on to a nearby barge to photograph him as he boarded the cruise ship John Cadman III yesterday.

---

221 Mehmet Biber Syrian returnee warns of homegrown attacks, *The Sydney Morning Herald*, 31 January, 2016.

The emir arrived in Sydney on Friday evening and has been staying at the Regent Hotel, where the party is reported to have booked 112 rooms, most of them at the Kuwaiti government's expense.

He is travelling with a retinue which includes personal bodyguards, servants, and senior members of the Kuwaiti government.

The current issue of *Fortune* lists him as the seventh richest man, with a personal fortune worth $US7.5 billion.[222]

The year was 1992.

The man could have paid for the entire cost of Australia's contribution to the First Gulf War and had billions left over in spare change.

A quarter of a century later, Australian taxpayers were still paying for Middle Eastern wars.

The thing that struck him the most was how, after being driven in a cavalcade the short distance from the hotel, the Emir and his party had moved so rapidly down a gangplank and onto the cruise ship.

These people were afraid to be outside.

The news that the visit was ostensibly to thank Australia for their war effort was left to Australian officials to convey.

Then Prime Minister Paul Keating said: "I welcome the Emir's visit as an opportunity to reaffirm our commitment to peace and security in the Gulf."

All the themes were coming into play. It was six months since he had finished *Terror in Australia: Workers' Paradise Lost*, and the story had continued to expand in the interim. The world was already transforming beyond recognition. 119, or was it 120, the day's reports varied, people were killed in Islamic State bomb attacks in Syria. At the same time, the "Coalition" announced there had been 38 bomb strikes in a single day. How many dead? How many injured? How many civilians? How many mujahedeen? Nobody would ever know.

Certainly not the Australian public paying to participate in this debacle. Events which would have once been front page news for days barely rated a mention in the back of the papers. Australia's population officially topped 24 million – that vision of Malcolm Fraser, the aristocrat from

---

222 The emir says thanks, but not much else, John Stapleton, *The Sydney Morning Herald*, 7 September, 1992.

country Victoria who had dreamed of a big Australia. Well, they had their big Australia, these so-called visionaries – and it was the aristocrats who benefited.

He had admired the bold analysis of Australian-born author David Kilcullen for some time, and when the opportunity came to interview him, jumped at the chance.

Kilcullen, highly intelligent, utterly scathing of the original decision to go to war, the idiot decision of John Howard to go all the way with the U S of A, could say things nobody else could.

The result of Western intervention in the Middle East had been the creation of battle-hardened terror groups wealthier and more dangerous than ever before.

His new book *Blood Year: The Failures of the War on Terror* slammed President George Bush's invasion of Iraq as a diabolical mistake. He was no more complimentary towards President Barack Obama – who, Kilcullen said, had mistaken brave talk for effective action and increased the terror threat worldwide. Tens of billions of dollars and hundreds of thousands of lives wasted.

So how did Australia get into this mess? Kilcullen replied: "It was a mad f...ing idea to go into Iraq in the first place. It is an American screw-up, but we are all participants. There's plenty of blame to go around."[223]

Prime Minister Tony Abbott had been accused of misusing national security for his own political ends, but Kilcullen said politicians of all stripes had an interest in exploiting terror to attack opponents in the trench warfare that passes for political process. "You may as well criticise a dog for barking. Politicians manipulate public opinion. It is what it is. All sides are trying to spin up the terror threat."[224]

Kilcullen said one of the reasons he wrote *Blood Year* was to force a rethink. Ways to defeat Islamic State being rolled out in the West, including Australia, involve pre-emptively detaining people on the suspicion they may be planning to commit a crime, mass surveillance and treating all Muslims as a threat. "What are we trying to protect? We are destroying society to save it. There is a real risk of that happening."[225]

---

223 *Blood Year*: David Kilcullen, John Stapleton, 17 February, 2016.

224 Ibid.

225 Ibid.

Of the war fatigue that had settled over Australia, even as increasing numbers of bombs paid for by Australian taxpayers rained down on the Middle East, Kilcullen put it down to the length of the conflict. He said he expected "this enormous slow-motion train wreck" to last at least another five years.

Exactly whose side Australia was on amid the competing terror groups and proxy wars of the Middle East was becoming increasingly hard to follow; the point of the nation's involvement lost on the public, to just about everybody.

Occam's Razor, the simplest truth is the best truth. "What's it got to do with us?" asked one of his children.

The fact that Australia had handed over its sovereignty to America was clearly evidenced when he asked the Australian Defence Department which countries they were in military alliance with.

The answer came back with a link to the US State Department.

A budget running into the tens of billions of dollars, and all the Australian Defence Department could do was link to another country's website. They should have been embarrassed.

The page began with the already failed mission statement of President Obama made two years before: "Our objective is clear: We will degrade, and ultimately destroy, ISIL through a comprehensive and sustained counterterrorism strategy."[226]

Now it was mission creep, and a manifest disaster. And the politicians from Australia's major parties raised not a word of protest.

The alliance of 66 nations included Saudi Arabia, one of the world's most socially oppressive states, involved in everything from executing homosexuals to funding terrorism to the military atrocities in Yemen, the Arab League, Kuwait, the United Arab League, Egypt. Of all the countries in the so-called alliance, Australia claimed itself as the second largest contributor to the war effort.

It was stark, it was useless, and it reeked of dangerous motive.

In that final month of the summer that never arrived, Old Alex went to the book launch of Kilcullen's *Blood Year*.

It was no ordinary book launch.

Most Australian authors struggle to make ends meet or to generate much of an audience beyond inner-city enthusiasts.

226 The Global Coalition to Counter ISIL, US State Department.

Here, barely rippling below the surface, millions of dollars were at play.

The launch was held in the auditorium of Macquarie Private Bank, the so-called millionaire's factory, and hosted by the US Study Centre. Security was tight.

In the auditorium itself, located high within the building, large screens relayed the delivery to a packed audience. Kilcullen spoke airily of his analysts in the world's hotspot.

Later Old Alex wandered the expansive veranda, high above the city streets, and spoke to one of the bodyguards provided by the Army. Waiters plied food and drink.

After Kilcullen's accomplished speech and question and answer session, the book signing created a queue across the auditorium. Few authors are so lucky.

A former Army Officer, Kilcullen had, Alex surmised, grown wealthy and influential on the back of government contracts.

As insightful as it was, there was a sense in which, Alex felt, *Blood Year* was a glossy brochure for his company Caerus Associates to garner yet more military contracts, in that secret world of which the public would never know.

There was plenty of money in failed wars.

Outside the building, Old Alex watched as Kilcullen left, surrounded by security, publicity officers and government officials.

Afterwards, not having been invited to join them for dinner, although he had proposed just such an option to one of the publicity women, he wandered through the empty streets of the business district.

"We are all being played," was his one summation of the evening, and the phrase kept playing in his head for days: "We are all being played."

KILL THE ARTISTS KILL THE WRITERS

SUMMER struggled to be born, slouching towards Bethlehem. Jerusalem. Rome. The ruins of Aleppo.

Gifted with a vital mission, it all had to do with the minutest variations in the timeline.

In the practice room it had been almost impossible to predict; for it came not from some grand gesture but, in the nature of a story, a throwaway line.

The humans called it the Butterfly Effect.

Old Alex was blanking into fright at the same time as the drone of tennis matches filtered out of houses; the Australian Open and the run-up tournaments a general feature of languid, cicada-screech Australian summers; a hymn to ordinariness and bygone days, to a kind of dishonesty, for all was not at peace.

On TV, decades-old replays of MASH, Everybody Loves Raymond, Seinfeld, Antiques Roadshow; endless cheap-as-chips programming. Out there, somewhere, bureaucrats talked of that greatest of all lies: community.

The commissions just kept on coming – and he was not in a position to refuse them.

One of them involved his old *bete noire* and antagonist, that most dangerous of Australia's Prime Ministers, Tony Abbott:

> Former Prime Minister Tony Abbott and his controversial Chief of Staff Peta Credlin manipulated public opinion in relation to national security and the terror threat "on a mass scale" in a desperate effort to stay in power, according to a new book published this week.

In a government run by a remote Prime Minister and an intimi-
dating Chief of Staff who had helped create a climate of fear
across the government, the few Liberal MPs brave enough to
express the view that hyping the terrorism threat could backfire
were drowned out.[227]

Old Alex took himself off to the new Fairfax building to interview
the author of *Credlin & Co: How the Abbott Government Destroyed Itself*,
respected journalist Aaron Patrick, a deputy editor at *The Australian Financial Review*.

The Fin, as it was universally known amongst journalists, had been on the
floor above *The Sydney Morning Herald* in the 1980s when it had been situ-
ated on Broadway, one of the ugliest buildings in one of the ugliest parts of
town; a building that wreaked of atmosphere and the smell of printer's ink.

When the print run started on the lower floors, literally the whole building
would shake.

Trucks lined up outside at midnight to deliver the first edition. Scraps of
newsprint drifted in the street in the early mornings.

All of it gone now; in 2016 Fairfax was located in just another smart
office building with a high level of security; smart receptionists and glowing
screens.

Now on the outside rather than on the inside, they sat in a smart cafe
downstairs for the interview on the topic of the moment: terror, national
security, the manipulation of public opinion and the abuses of politicians.

> Abbott and Credlin believed the threat of terrorism from Islamic
> fundamentalists was one of the government's most potent polit-
> ical assets. It also illustrated the weakness at the heart of the
> government. After the failure of its first budget, Abbott mostly
> dodged issues of substance and concentrated on crowd-pleasing
> gestures aimed at middle Australia. Supported by backroom
> operatives ... Abbott and Credlin stoked the public's fear of
> terrorism on a weekly and sometimes daily basis. They exploited
> the media's natural respect for the prime minister and national
> security policy.[228]

227 Tony Abbott 'used terror threat as political weapon", John Stapleton, *The New Daily*,
1 February, 2016.
228 Ibid.

In the welter of "death cult" rhetoric and the triumphalism in delighting in the misfortune and deaths of Australian jihadists who had the courage of their convictions to die on the battlefields of Iraq and Syria, Abbott held a press conference nine months after 18-year-old Numan Haider was shot dead outside the Endeavour Hills police station in Melbourne during an incident with a police officer.

Abbott organised the event to publicly thank the officers involved.

They might have more appropriately been disciplined for unprofessional conduct in failing to recognise a "death by cop" suicide scenario; leading to the unfortunate death of a teenager.

Abbott described Haider as "Australia's first actual terrorist".

It was not just an historically inaccurate claim; the first religiously motivated deaths occurring at a picnic in Silverton, a dusty little highway town outside Broken Hill. In 1915 two camel drivers from present day Pakistan flew the Ottoman flag, killed four people and wounded seven others.

One of the camel drivers, Gool Mahomed, left a note which was almost identical to notes left by jihadists a century later: "I must kill you and give my life for my faith. Allahu Akbar."

There is no God but God. Muhammad is his Prophet. God is Great.

Police had to block a mob from attacking a local Afghan camp the following night.

A century later, Australian bombs were killing far more Muslims than Muslims were killing Australians. As author Aaron Patrick observed, to turn the suicidal actions of a teenager and the tragedy of his death into a photo opportunity showed zero understanding of the forces driving Australian Muslim youth into the arms of Islamic State.

Zero empathy.

Abbott, as Patrick pointed out, was ably assisted by the utterly irresponsible coverage of the tabloids, some, including Sydney's best selling tabloid *The Daily Telegraph*, even badging their terror pages with the slogan "Death Cult", despite all the expert warnings the slogan was acting as a recruiting tool. Terror was good for ratings.

> Mainstream media outlets, desperate to staunch the loss of their audiences to the internet, were willingly used. *The Daily Telegraph* and the *Herald Sun*, Australia's two biggest daily newspapers, ran front-page stories about terrorism dozens of times.

The commercial television news bulletins mentioned terrorism almost every night.

"It was quite effective," Patrick said. "The Prime Minister had the News Corp tabloids and the TV networks with him.[229]

The right wing power brokers got away with their manipulation of public opinion. There were a few people, Patrick recorded, who said it was all going too far, "but overall most people were too nervous to take on Abbott over terrorism because it was a life and death issue."[230]

Alex bashed out the stories, and roamed the hunched webbed streets; tried to relax in the Carlisle amid the loose cannons and miscreants who frequented the bar.

To supplement the written word, or as an alternative to it, many people who are "un-villaged" recreate villages wherever they go. Thus they gather with each other at crossroads, or at a certain cafe, the gyros shop, the bakery, the breakfast-place, at the curb or on street corners, all to "jape and jaw," that is to talk long-windedly and jokingly with one's peers about each one's latest exploits. And in between the exploits, they tell all the old personal and mythic stories each can remember. These are all reassertions of tribal story gatherings.[231]

But threat and betrayal were already gathering in a place which should have been safe.

He dreamt, constantly, a kind of longing, of being rescued; of returning home.

But it was not to be.

Friends were not friends. His instincts did not run true.

He did Buddhist exercises in a Christian cemetery; and there were no natural feelings, here at the end of days.

In those waking dreams his visitors – guardians, one might have called them if they were not so dismissive of a single life – could barely contain their delight. Far more malevolent than he could ever have imagined; their

---

229 Ibid.

230 Ibid.

231 *The Hero with a Thousand Faces*, Joseph Campbell, New World Library, Originally published 1949.

grey wings half-furled, perched in window cells, along cracked wooden fences… watching, waiting. Hoping he would fall.

They could hardly wait to feed on a coming sacrifice, not of him but of millions; and gave him lectures in the long night on good and evil, dualities, the necessity of one to create the other.

Radiation did not frighten them.

They did not need to breathe.

Thousands drowned at sea.

The body of a dead child on a beach moved the world for a brief media moment, and was gone.

The world was more interested in Brangelina.

His heroes continued to die.

Harper Lee died.

Umberto Eco died.

Peter Matthiessen died.

He thought of Desmarquet often now, the clack clack clack through the night of the old man playing chess in his dreams; "I've been here for a hundred million years and you've been abducted by aliens," he remembered the moment once again, their farewell; their joint laughter, for Alex needed protection now.

He had not felt safe since he left that Vietnamese island.

Russia warned of "a new world war" starting in Syria, after a dramatic day in which Gulf States threatened to send in ground forces. Both countries escalated their aerial bombardment.

Foreign and defence ministers of the leading international states backing different factions in the war-torn country met in separate meetings in Munich and Brussels following the collapse of the latest round of peace talks.

Russia and the United States demanded ceasefires in the long-running civil war so that the fight could be concentrated against Islamic State – but each on their own, conflicting terms.

Australian taxpayers continued to pay for their fair share of the drama.

While at home the surveillance state grew apace. And everywhere he looked, everything he heard, confirmed what he already knew.

He dreamt constantly of the City at the End of Time.

He had woken up in the future of his own life and something was calling, old souls trapped in fragile frames, every day crueller than the last.

Come to me darling, the devil's heads had said, while all around everything drained away. I'm not sure whether I'm here on an anthropological study, or really am here, a man said to him, and to that he could relate. He dreamt of exploits forty years before: the Miami Hotel in Bangkok, the Bunny Club in Chiang Mai, sleeping under cars in Paris, hitchhiking across America. When all was future – and he was embarked on the greatest adventure in human history; a rickshaw in an isolated part of town.

And of the future, he became obsessed with writing a book

The Fall of Rome, although someone had already beaten him to the title.

It's not linear, a voice said. Why did you think it would be? There beyond the border of the real.

We dream of a city at the end of time. Of course we do.

The surveillance was meant to create a compliant, docile and frightened population, leaving those who stood outside the government narrative hunted down or harassed.

He was angry that the chilling effect was already working on him.

He avoided people who would not benefit from additional surveillance, entirely unhelpful for a journalist; he put in links to government information in stories to make it clear he was not the enemy; when he wasn't giving them the full benefit of his views he tried to make appeasing comments where he knew there were microphones; and he was overly cautious about checking out jihad sites, also extremely unhelpful for a journalist.

He even at one point, desperate to escape, suggested they put him on retainer as a media adviser. God knows, they needed one.

He tried boring them witless, outraging them, insulting them, all to no avail.

Appeasement never worked. He should have known better than to think there was some rationality in the system.

Infinite government funding; billions of dollars in a small pond, intelligence funding having tripled in the decade post 9/11. They would not let go. Why should they?

> Australia's current total intelligence budget is artfully hidden deep within annual reports and spread across multiple agencies. Commentators and analysts cannot be absolutely sure of the accuracy of publicly available figures and have to contend with layers of opaqueness and even undeclared or "black" programs

designed to confuse and deceive the enemy. This makes it difficult to judge the value for money provided by the nation's intelligence agencies.[232]

The government's narrative was a febrile terrace strung across failed state creeds, infested with career bureaucrats and riven by personal, financial, political and organisational self-interest.

It stank.

Writers and artists who might once have celebrated ideas, dissention, even confusion of aims and the messiness, the squalling, mewling nature of human existence, all of it was banished.

Kill the Artists. Kill the Writers.

One of the only art forms that continued to exist in any sense was painting. Flags flew from the light poles of Sydney advertising the Archibald portrait prize.

The same poles the state government had sold to the Chinese on a 99-year lease.

Portraits were safe.

Ideas were not.

What was worth saving?

Freedom of speech? There was none.

Privacy? There was none.

Was it a brave, courageous and independent media?

It didn't exist. The privately or corporate-owned media championed the causes of the ultra-rich and the ultra-right, which ran closely parallel to the interests of government; while the publicly owned media parroted the narrow fields of debate which also suited the government.

What remnants of artistic life remained had been entirely subsumed by government sponsorship or restricted by a plethora of laws; or made obsequious, deadened by the constant need of small art companies to ensure their funding.

Islamic State chanted: We will kill the artists; we will kill the writers.

For all their support of creative endeavour, the Australian government might as well have been chanting the same thing.

Stone those who worship the creations not the creator.

The Louvre would burn. The van Gogh Museum would burn. The British

---

232 Bigger budgets = better intelligence? Peter Leahy, in *Spooked: The truth about intelligence in Australia*, edited by Daniel Baldino, University of NSW, 2013.

Museum would burn. The Tate would burn. The cathedrals of Europe would burn. The libraries, the intellectual achievements of thousands of years, would burn. Cities which had championed freedom of personal expression, freedom, tolerance and diversity lifestyles, freedom of religion, they would all burn. Amsterdam would burn. Paris would burn. The Cities of Light would be turned to ash. The sails of Sydney's world famous Opera House would sink back into the harbour.

Every triumph of man would be destroyed, to leave the masses bowing down in worship to their Dark Lord.

There was, after the expenditure of tens of billions of dollars to enslave the world, to deliver it up to the Lord of All the Worlds, only one solution: The Enlightenment.

Ideas were contagious, and ideas in and of themselves could appear magical. Technologies used to enslave could also be used to liberate; and technologies which once seemed magical became mundane.

For Old Alex, the journalistic assignments came thick and fast. It was simple, really: he needed the money.

The one he had most wanted to do concerned the escalating number of bomb drops in Iraq under the new Prime Minister.

Malcolm Turnbull had sold himself to his left-leaning electorate as a progressive, a supporter of gay marriage aka marriage equality, a climate change true believer, a feminist, multicultural advocate, a supporter of indigenous causes and refugee rights: all the touchstone identity politics of the era.

But the dove was no dove at all.

When it came to the crunch, in the hands of Turnbull all the fashionable causes which his diminishing number of supporters and his electorate once assumed he believed in became tools for social manipulation, to fill a space with pointless debate, snuffling up the social justice instincts of the well intentioned, filling with detritus what would otherwise be dead air.

The government could take the country to war in an afternoon; but climate change had curdled political debate for twenty years while achieving precisely nothing; and equally in 2016 a tortured and religiously charged dispute over gay marriage was doing exactly the same.

When it came to the war, a war about which the Australian public was neither consulted nor informed, Turnbull proved even worse than his forebears.

That was the point of the story; that Turnbull was responsible for killing even more Muslims than his predecessor.

And that sure as night followed day, there would be a very high price to pay – beyond the already astronomical costs in terms of military expenditure and national crackdowns on dissent and freedom of speech.

There would come a haunting for the man who had stained the soul of the country and betrayed the people he was elected to represent; a haunting in what Alex always felt would be a foreshortened life:

> Former secretary to the Department of Defence Paul Barratt described Australia's involvement in Iraq as insanity: repeating the same mistake and expecting a different result.
>
> "The Americans have always been more relaxed about collateral damage than we are," he said.
>
> "We went through the whole of the Iraq War with the Americans saying we don't count the bodies."[233]

Australia was not counting bodies either. And while its rules of engagement were stricter than America's, that would soon change. The body count was rising. And there was no accounting.

In January there were 111 bomb drops on Iraq from 74 sorties. In Syria there were 11 bomb drops from six sorties, out of a total flying time between the two countries of 518 hours.

In February there were a total of 69 bomb drops on Iraq out of 62 sorties; and four bomb drops out of four sorties on Syria.

Alex's dealings with the government were as fruitless and as futile as ever.

The Prime Minister's office referred questions on the bomb drops to Defence.

In other words, the man most singly responsible for the bomb drops and the resultant deaths – numbering one could only assume in the hundreds if not the thousands – was taking no responsibility whatsoever and was offering no explanation for the increasing number of bomb drops, and therefore the increasing numbers of deaths at the hands, ultimately, of Australian taxpayers.

Turnbull's office referred his inquiries to the Defence Minister Marise

---

233 Figures show increase in RAAF bombings of Islamic State, John Stapleton, The New Daily, 16 December, 2016.

Payne – who also did not bother to justify, defend or explain Australia's increased military actions.

These people were paid many times the average citizen's salary, and could not be bothered to answer simple questions – or to even make an attempt to defend the increasingly indefensible.

This was a democracy?

> No official estimates of casualties are ever made public and the Australian government does not make available details on its specific targets. The only target information is released by US Central Command, with Australia's involvement included in the larger Coalition tally.

> Clive Williams, Adjunct Professor at the Australian Defence Force Academy, said it had been foolish for Australia to get involved.

> "Most people in strategic studies are saying the airstrikes won't achieve anything in terms of a political outcome," he said. "There are a lot of negative aspects."[234]

On gaining office, Canada's new Prime Minister Justin Trudeau announced that his country would be ceasing aerial bombardment. No such commitment came from Australia's new Prime Minister Malcolm Turnbull.

> "I fear for our long term outlooks as a result of the civilian casualties caught up in this conflict," former military analyst Dr Clarke Jones said. "There are always civilian casualties, you would be naive to think otherwise. There are mistakes. Islamic State use civilian shields. Naturally there will be civilian casualties.

> "There is no doubt that the sentiment in relation to allied bombing does contribute to radicalisation within communities within Australia. Without a doubt it is radicalising Muslim minorities."[235]

Dr Jones said Muslims within Australia were overwhelmingly against the war, and Australia's military intervention was bringing them into conflict with their own country.

---

234 Ibid.

235 Interview with author, December, 2015.

We have to be careful about the enemies we generate in the region, in our neighbouring countries and the overall Muslim sentiment around the world, including in Australia, you bet you. I don't have to go very far, even inside Canberra, to get that sentiment. We are playing into Islamic State hands. I can't understand why we are continuing down this path.[236]

Muslim spokesman Keysar Trad told him the Coalition went out of its way to cover up the number of its victims; and they failed to understand they were creating a hardened generation of orphans.

The net result is a lot of death and killings and children raised in desperate conditions. The Holy Qur'an describes a group of people who will be raised towards the end who will...not display the compassionate hesitation. They are more likely to see the world in black and white terms, just like a certain flag.[237]

Professor Tanter said the bombs being dropped were 500-2000 pound bombs whose impact could be felt 700 metres away. There was no way of knowing how many combatants, along with civilians, men, women and children, were being killed by Australian Defence Force bombs. "In the defence of Iraq? That's ridiculous. We are adding to the misery."[238]

Former head of the Australian Strategic and Defence Studies Centre Professor Des Ball argued civilian casualties were high: "I would not be surprised if the total number of children exceeds the total number of terrorists."[239]

Australia was also directly involved in one of the most inhumane forms of warfare ever devised: unmanned drones.

The drones are capable of hovering for days over targets before unleashing their payloads, and are blamed for driving radicalisation in Muslim territories.

In the dying days of the Abbott government the Australian Defence Force announced five RAAF personnel were embedded

---

236 Ibid.

237 Interview with author, December, 2016.

238 Drone Wars: Australia's Dirty Secret, John Stapleton, *The New Daily*, 4 December, 2015.

239 Ibid.

with the US Air Force, performing operational duties including piloting and operating MQ-9 Reaper Drones.[240]

French Philosopher Gregoire Chamayou argued in his book *A Theory of the Drone* that as more and more drones are launched into battle, war is becoming a realm of secretive, targeted assassinations beyond the view and control of citizens of the perpetrating democracies.

In Australia, the lack of parliamentary debate breached recommendations from a Senate Report into drones released in July, which suggests the Australian government make a policy statement affirming that armed unmanned platforms will be used in accordance with international law and include appropriate transparency.

Apart from the obvious damage on the ground, there were already plenty of stories on the psychological damage being done to the drone operators themselves. They might be sheltered, or cowering as some would have it, in military installations thousands of miles away from their targets, but guilt knows no boundaries.

Professor Tanter said Australia's accelerated involvement with drone warfare was a "very serious" development: "This is more than just training. This is participating in warfare."[241]

Australians were not being informed of the number of drone strikes with which their military was involved. Nor was there any public information on the likely number of civilian or combat casualties.

Professor of International Relations at UNSW Clinton Fernandes said:

The big problem is the affect on everybody else in the territory.

The society can be patrolled basically indefinitely. The sense that you might die at any moment is dreadful.

An air campaign makes a society more religious because it is more helpless. The sharpening radicalisation in Yemen is due in part to the drone campaign.[242]

---

240 Ibid.

241 Drone Wars: Australia's Dirty Secret, John Stapleton, *The New Daily*, 4 December, 2015.

242 Ibid.

Emily Howie, a senior researcher at the Human Rights Law Centre, called on the Australian government to open up about its role in drone attacks.

> The very central concern is that Australia could be participating in extra-judicial killings or other violations of human rights law or the laws of war and the rest of us would know nothing about it.

> This is being done beneath a shroud of secrecy. There is really no way of knowing, no proper independent evaluation that occurs, that enables a proper assessment of whether laws have been violated.

> What is frightening about drone strikes is they essentially enable government's role to go completely unsupervised.[243]

Just as with the bombings, there was no way of knowing how many were being killed in the drone attacks, ably assisted by the Australian taxpayer. The price to pay did not come just in terms of the damaged and lost lives of military personnel, in inappropriate expenditure of the nation's finances, in international credibility and lost opportunities.

While useful fools parroted "diversity" at every turn, the culture had been leached of colour – destroying what, despite its remoteness, had been a bubbly, challenging, talented artistic community.

In this Brave New World of ever lengthening bureaucratic overreach, the impacts of rafts of legislation meant even the smallest art and theatre groups were obliged by law to possess public liability insurance and faced a raft of other measures just in order to perform or exhibit.

The cost of compliance ensured that almost any creative activity required government funding in order to survive. Those performances that did make it through the morass of legal and financial constraints were inevitably sponsored by large corporations, or by government in one form or another, local, state or federal. The restriction of the artistic and creative life of the country solely to that funded by the government also gifted it the ability to crush dissent.

The bureaucratic mindset, "just say no", had permeated through every form of endeavour. The weekend boot markets where people could gather at an oval and sell second-hand goods out of the backs of their cars had

---

243 Ibid.

died off because they were forced to acquire licences and public liability insurance. Even street buskers required a licence. Most parks no longer had children's playgrounds because they were a health and safety issue, and exposed councils to the threat of a lawsuit. Drivers were booked for eating an apple behind the wheel. Grocery stores could no longer sell Christmas trees outside the front of their shops during the festive season because they required an Environmental Impact Statement to do so. Flowers could no longer be left in cemeteries except in approved plastic containers. There was even talk of sending government inspectors around to check the kitchens of the normally genteel, cheerful older women who occasionally held charity stalls selling homemade cakes, scones and jams.

In the arts, the result had been the contraction of almost every community-based project, to be replaced by a corporatised world performing risk-averse recycled crowd pleasers.

It had all been done blatantly and quickly.

The world may always have been born anew, rewritten every day, but this was an era without historical memory, with zero respect for those who had gone before. The artists weren't standing on the shoulders of giants; they were paddling in a flash crowd pond that worshipped success and success only.

The vivid, urgent, imperative creative voices which had once made Australia such an interesting place to live despite its isolation and small population had been all but eliminated.

> Australian artists have faced many desperate moments over the past three years, particularly in the last 12 months following the 2015/16 Federal Budget announcement . . . which revealed devastating cuts to the funds distributed by the Australia Council. However, Friday the 13th of May 2016 is now a date that will be remembered in infamy by many as one of the blackest in Australia's artistic history. Published this morning, the Australia Council have announced . . . many unsuccessful applicants, including 62 organisations, previously funded by the Australia Council, are now facing uncertain futures as their operational costs are no longer underwritten.
>
> The full extent of the damage that has been inflicted upon Australia's arts ecology . . . is still coming to light...[244]

---

244 Black Friday: Australia Council cuts defund dozens of art companies, Maxim Boon, *Limelight*, 13 May, 2016.

Defunded organisations included Sydney-based dance company Force Majeure, youth music organisation Gondwana Choirs, percussion ensemble Synergy, Sydney's street theatre company Legs on the Wall, Adelaide's Vital-statistix, Melbourne's independent acting companies Red Stitch and Actors' Theatre. Dozens of them. Even the 75-year-old literary magazine Meanjin, to which as a teenager Old Alex used to submit stories.

Chair of the Next Wave Festival Board Janeene Willis said: "A healthy and flourishing community needs a healthy and flourishing arts community. We need voices that challenge, question and provide ways to think anew. Artists provide that critical voice."[245]

In a statement the Confederation of Australian State Theatre Companies (CAST) said the cuts would lead to hundreds of job losses and increased instability throughout the arts industry:

> CAST considers these cuts and subsequent defunding of arts organisations to be a deeply concerning outcome that will cause a devastating cultural and employment deficit with widespread and long-lasting impact.
>
> These cuts have an impact just as dramatic and negative as the arts industry has feared and will cause irreparable damage across the sector – one that contributes over $4.2 billion to GDP in Australia.
>
> Small to medium companies are the lifeblood of the theatre sector across Australia and where some of the most innovative new Australian work is generated and presented.[246]

It was not just the painters and performers. The same tool for redacting the culture had been applied to the literature board.

Even historically important magazines of ideas, with essentially miniscule readerships, became a target.

Quadrant Magazine had a reputation for being right wing simply because some its articles often ran against the prevailing group-think. As Old Alex was fond of saying: "The right is not always wrong, and the left is not always right."

---

245 Ibid.

246 Cast calls on Federal Government to Reinstate Australia Council Funds, Malthouse Theatre Bog, 13 May, 2016.

Quadrant had also been entirely defunded. For the first time in its sixty-year history, in 2016 it would receive no government support.

The magazine published more poetry than any other outlet in Australia and was an important literary incubator. Its Literary Editor was one of the country's greatest living poets, Les Murray.

Quadrant had the largest readership amongst the literary magazines, around 6,000 subscribers – of no significance really, but not even that tiny level of dissent could be allowed.

Ideas, those contagious things, were in themselves now viewed as a threat.

Curiously perhaps, this dissent was coming from the right and not the left.

But a perusal of *Quadrant* was enough to see why it had been defunded. Its article and letter writers all railed against bureaucratically imposed state creeds and the rise of group-think, the mid-winter edition particularly concerned with multiculturalism and warning of the advent of no-go suburbs and Sharia law.

Ultimately it didn't much matter where you stood. Control, the power to influence outcomes, the voices of the voiceless, the power to provoke debate, to float the disease of ideas into the zeitgeist, had been wrested into the hands of the machinery of Big Brother.

There was more than one way to eliminate dissent. Just defund the bastards.

The Australian government fear of ideas and intellectual debate reached into every aspect of the culture, including an attempt to destroy the $2.2 billion book industry.

It was this very act of suppressing debate which was curdling the country; and even that act had to be concealed.

Kill the Writers.

In 2016 the industry combined to distribute free a compilation of work, titled #SaveOzStories, from some of the country's most esteemed writers, including David Malouf and Geraldine Brooks. The book was a response to an Australian Productivity Commission Report which recommended changes to copyright and importation rules.

It added to a long list of attacks by the Abbott/Turnbull conservative governments on journalism, whistle-blowers, actors, artists and writers, essentially on all independent thought.

Esteemed Australian writer Richard Flanagan, who won the Mann Booker Prize Winner for his powerful book *Narrow Road to the Deep North*, wrote:

The Abbott and now Turnbull Government's record drips with a contempt for writers and writing that leaves me in despair. They want to thieve our past work, and, by ending parallel importation restrictions and territorial copyright, destroy any future for Australian writers.

Be under no illusion: they want to destroy this industry. And with it, Australian literature.

Vassals of an outdated ideology unrelated to the real world, they can, when questioned on this issue, only mumble neoliberal mantras that have delivered the world economic stagnation, rising inequality and global environmental crisis. Hollow men, stuffed men, their words rats' feet over broken glass. The only thing these people read are the Panama Papers to see if their own name has cropped up.[247]

Flanagan said the decision to destroy the book industry by removing parallel import restrictions was consistent with the government's relentless attacks on thought and debate.

He asked: "Who benefits from ignorance and silence other than the most powerful and the richest?"

The democracy of thought and discussion that books make possible, the possibility of empathy that books are known to engender, the sense of a shared humanity and the transcendent possibilities that books give rise to, all will be diminished by this profound attack on Australian writing. And we will have returned to being what we were fifty years ago: a colony of the mind.

Flanagan described the disenfranchisement of the imagination as the disempowerment of the individual, and therefore profoundly political.

This government, which again, and again, has brought Australia only global shame with its follies of cowardice and cruelty has no right now to destroy such a good in our nation as this: the voice of our experience, the words of our people, the tongue of our hope—our culture of writing.

This is a government that despises books and views with hostility the civilisation they represent.

---

247 #SaveOzStories, Melbourne University Press, 2016.

In this time of fracture we need more than ever the things that can bring us together as a people, not fear, not the resentments of the many, carefully cultivated to cloak the privilege of the few, but the hope of a society that might discover in books the liberating possibility of a shared humanity.[248]

Artists. Writers. And Journalists.

On the chopping block.

Alex went to a reunion for those who worked on *The Sydney Morning Herald* in the 1980s and 1990s; held, appropriately enough, at Machiavelli's, once the eatery of choice for every backstabbing corporate and editor-in-chief in town.

It was a rare event, and attracted many of the main players of the era, some of the country's best news photographers, a plethora of talent. Young journalists he had sat next to thirty years before; as he peered at people and adjusted his mind's eye and tried to remember the names of people he hadn't seen in decades.

Some were still grateful, all those years later, that in those first terrifying days on the job he had been kind: telling them to relax, they would soon learn the ropes and in any case, the editors were out to lunch. Literally, and often enough at Machiavelli's.

There was hilarity too, at the numerous absurdities of the profession. For example, although he had forgotten the event, of the day he was hunting around the office of the most prestigious newspaper in the country for a jacket and tie to go and interview the King of Tonga.

In the day, a suit and tie was a symbol of the oppressor. There was not one to be found except on the back of one of the legendary snakes of Australian journalism, the Editor-in-Chief John Alexander, who was in any case off at lunch, at Machiavelli's.

"This is the last supper," someone said. "They don't seem to realise it."

There was talk that the final print edition of *The Sydney Morning Herald* would go to press before the New Year, that once esteemed publication he had been so proud to work for.

The speeches were short, but across the crowded room Old Alex could hear former editor Eric Beecher talking of the contracting and disintegrating media, how many more outlets would be closing. "It is never talked about

248 Ibid.

in public. If we talked about it, then people would start to realise there is such incredible ramifications for democracy happening before our eyes."

At least they were the words Alex jotted down on a scrap of paper with a pen borrowed from behind the Machiavelli Bar.

More accurately, in a piece titled The Death of Fairfax and the End of Newspapers, Beecher wrote:

> The story of how Australian quality journalism fell victim to a commercial market failure has been known to insiders for years, but it has largely been withheld from consumers of Australian journalism because the mainstream media has conspired to censor and spin the truth. Australia's newspapers of record have deliberately ignored the story of their own decline, and its impact on their own readers and the health of society, instead of covering it as they would the decline of any other important industry or profession. They have shown a deep reluctance to disclose or explain that large-scale commercial journalism has become unviable, and no one has yet found a formula to subsidise "public trust" journalism in the way newspaper advertising did.

> For Australia, the story is more significant than just the demise of an industry business model. In a small robust democracy with relatively little commercial quality journalism, it has the makings of a civic catastrophe.[249]

With each step towards totalitarianism going unchecked and unquestioned, civic catastrophe was already upon the country.

The technology used to track terrorists was equally being used to track freethinkers: hunting through the shell of a democracy for any unrestrained voices.

It was no accident that the world's most famous journalist, publisher and whistle-blower, Australian-born Julian Assange, sought refuge in the Ecuadorian Embassy and not that of his own country.

The Australian Embassy would have been one of the least safe places on Earth for this genius child of a broken family who as a boy had spent his childhood moving from house to house up and down the East Coast.

As for any nomad, confinement to a single place was torture, no matter how luxurious the prison cell.

---

249 The Death of Fairfax and the End of Newspapers, Eric Beecher, July, 2013.

It was another peculiarity of history that an isolated country such as Australia, close to the Antarctic, seemingly on the border of the real, should give birth to the founder of WikiLeaks, a global game-changer in the field of journalism, delivering up its true obligation to confront state power.

Assange became frightened for his life after exposing American military misconduct in both Iraq and Afghanistan, although the public had every right to know the abuses their taxes were paying for. He was hailed as a hero by civil libertarians, and hunted by governments. Far from acting to protect one of their citizens, the Australian government, and the country's first woman Prime Minister Julia Gillard, chose instead to protect the American alliance. "The foundation stone of it is an illegal act. It would not happen, information would not be on WikiLeaks, if there had not been an illegal act undertaken."[250]

There was threatening debate over whether Julian could be charged with treason, an offence punishable by life imprisonment.

But the motivations and origins of a truthsayer were far more honourable than anything an Australian politician could muster.

What fascinated Alex most about Julian, apart from his high intellect, was his very ordinariness or humanness; including his stuffed-up childhood as the son of a single mother. As a boy, his family moved constantly from one place to another; and in adulthood his lifestyle transitory, migratory, nomadic. He shifted through hotel after hotel with little more than a laptop and a change of clothes – while those who feared, despised and condemned him the most set down roots inside giant houses and comfortable social circumstance.

And who would history see as the greater man? Those who pocketed their corporate dividends from the manufacture of armaments, or one who exposed the worst conduct of the elites and the military in their bombing of Iraq and Afghanistan? The genius child from a broken home, the era's most significant journalist, publisher and whistleblower, or the state sanctioned killers?

Julian's mother Christine Ann Assange told an interviewer that as a child he had wanted to be a physicist:

---

250 PM can't say what law WikiLeaks has broken, *The Sydney Morning Herald*, 7 December, 2010.

He wanted to discover the source of the universe. He has always been about the truth. He is not at all materialistic. He still has quite a limited wardrobe.

As a mother I wish he had never done it.

As a citizen, having investigated what WikiLeaks has done, to bring transparency to the world about the abuses of power, of corruption, kidnapping, extortion, rorting and fraud involved with big institutions, I absolutely support my son.[251]

The world's most famous whistle-blower Edward Snowden was forced to flee to Moscow. Chelsea Manning still languished in prison after revealing malfeasance on a massive scale within the US military. Truthsayers, once revered, suffered dire consequences in the 21st Century.

As journalist Andrew Fowler recorded in his book *The Most Dangerous Man in the World*, Assange had always put individual activity at the centre of his philosophy. If WikiLeaks had existed earlier, war could have been avoided and ultimately hundreds of thousands of lives saved. Instead boots landed on the ground, drones flew overhead and bombs rained down, the decision to go to war hostage to the self-interest of politicians despite widespread doubt about military operations in Iraq within military, intelligence and security services.

The application of state power to silence and control the individual would be repeatedly resisted by Assange, as it had been from the beginning of his travels . . . It was a journey that had driven him into the arms of anarchic liberalism . . . People tried to fool themselves into believing that one could 'think globally and act locally'; however, to anyone with a sense of proportion, acting locally was a marginal activity.[252]

In Sydney the bland out was all around: turn off a light and you were saving the planet from global warming. You were a good person. You could die in spiritual comfort. Never mind that the government was using your taxes for the most nefarious of purposes.

251 PM Gillard, traitor and US puppet, Julian Assange's mother, RT, Youtube. Posted 4 August, 2012.

252 The Most Dangerous Man in the World, Andrew Fowler, Melbourne University Publishing, 2011.

Standing atop the rubble, with nowhere to hide, nowhere to go, no safe place, as if drones were overhead and cameras installed throughout the house, Old Alex thought: "Trust Your Own Instincts".

But how was that possible in a world of flailing demons and under the all-encompassing malevolence of the Surveillance State? Where anyone who dared to look outside was boxing at shadows?

Always harsh, always self-interested, blessed with a myth-manufacturing media and always prepared to delude its own people, Assange's home country had labelled him a criminal.

On the contrary, Alex admired him. Almost everything he had helped expose to the world, from mass surveillance to the killing of civilians in war zones, should have been publicly known.

The malfeasance of the secretive, amoral and poorly administered government, military and security worlds he exposed, deserved to be exposed.

Assange had a far higher IQ than any single member of the Australian parliament; and far loftier motives than most of the grubs in office.

But Australia could not provide safe haven to one of its own most brilliant sons. What kind of country abandons one of its most significant figures?

Instead the nation's obsequious political class opted for the security of the American Alliance rather than the safety of one of their own citizens.

Assange was repeatedly threatened, but not one single Australian authority spoke up in his support.

What exactly was it that he published or exposed that should not have been public knowledge in the first place?

The indiscriminate or targeted extra-judicial killings in the name of terror, the deliberate geo-political destabilisation, the widespread malfeasance of the US Empire, the universal surveillance and abrogation of personal freedoms in the name of the war on terror? War crimes and human rights abuses? For exposing that Abu Ghraib was the was the tip of the iceberg, that America supported torture, that it deliberately fomented sectarian violence in Iraq, that it backed former Iraqi Prime Minister Nouri al-Maliki because he agreed to keep Iraqi oil fields open to the West, for releasing a now famous classified video showing in detail the murder of over a dozen people in Baghdad, including two journalists, with one of the helicopter pilots exclaiming: "Oh yeah, look at those dead bastards!"

The transcript of that famous video, Collateral Murder, read in part:

"Got a bunch of bodies lying here..."
"We're shooting some more..."
"Hahaha I hit 'em."
"Nice."
"Nice."
"Good shoot'n."
"Thank you."[253]

WikiLeaks release of diplomatic cables from Iraq exposed the brutality of US policies in that country that were ongoing throughout the occupation, including the killing of women and children. The home raids, creation and use of death squads, divide and conquer strategies, the use of torture and clear evidence of a military strategy aimed at generating civilian casualties and thereby sectarian violence.[254]

The importance of what Julian Assange and WikiLeaks achieved could not be overstated, exposing as they did information about the US policies which left a legacy of violence and political instability, the basis of the failed state that is Iraq; and as a result, a far less safer world.

The cables released by WikiLeaks also exposed the attempts to stamp out dissent from European governments critical of American actions. And they also exposed one of the primary aims of American foreign policy: lobbying for US arms and energy companies.

> Today, the WikiLeaked cables have become indispensable primary sources for journalists, academics, and students of history and international relations. What were initially surprising revelations concerning the nature and practice of American foreign policy have since become firmly embedded in mainstream understandings of world affairs . . . Freed from their classified seals, the WikiLeaks materials bridge the gulf between the "morons" with security clearances and nothing to learn, and us, their readers.[255]

Where was Australia in all of this?

A loyal American ally and a dangerous enemy to those who helped expose the truth.

---

253 Collateral Murder, Wikileaks, 2010.

254 The Wikileaks Files: The World According to US Empire, Verso, 2015.

255 Ibid.

But nothing, not even betrayal by his own country, stopped Assange. Destiny gave him the talent, intelligence and means to create opportunity, and he took it.

"The War on Whistle-blowers and Why America's Next President Will Kill Julian Assange" read one headline.

Tyler Durden, played by Brad Pitt in Fight Club and a rather likely pseudonym, said his concern about the welfare of Julian Assange was a pragmatic one. The increasingly hostile statements made by top state officials and their surrogates show a widespread condemnation of whistle-blowers in the halls of government. President Obama set the tone early in his administration with a number of prosecutions.

> In the case of WikiLeaks founder Julian Assange, the rhetoric goes well beyond condemnation of methodology and straight to advocating for his brutal murder.

> We already know that Obama, Clinton, Sanders, and Trump have all said they would prosecute Assange. Clinton, to get more specific, wants him extradited from Ecuador, prosecuted for espionage, and his WikiLeaks removed from the Internet.

> It is my assertion that both Trump and Clinton are likely to engage in specific military operations to dismantle organizations responsible for high-level leaks. It could very well be the next ubiquitous war.[256]

Clinton strategist Bob Beckel called for Assange to be assassinated on Fox television. TIME senior national correspondent Michael Grunwald posted on Twitter that he could not wait to write a defence of the drone strike that takes out Julian Assange. These two men, Democrat luminaries regularly featured on POLITICO and CNN, advocated the extrajudicial killing of a whistle-blower to millions of people. The stigmatisation and demonisation of whistle-blowers and hacktivists come after a decade in which the U.S. government's civil liberty abuses have been laid bare for all to see.

> What can be proven, and what should be taken far more seriously, is the metamorphosis of the state's rhetoric against Wikileaks from hostile to downright war-like. Not vitriolic, but

---

256 The War on Whistle-blowers & Why America's Next President Will Kill Julian Assange, Tyler Durden, Zerohedge, 27 August, 2016.

war-like – as in quite literally the kind of rhetoric that leads to actual war with tanks, guns, and bomber planes – or, in this case, maybe just a bomb robot or a stealthy climber.

It's a worrisome time for Assange supporters. The last two weeks, in particular, have been downright surreal. First, Obama hagiographer Michael Grunwald tweeted with maniacal delight his support of Assange being killed in a drone strike. Then, Clinton strategist Bob Beckel went on *Fox News* and jumped up and down in his seat begging for someone to "illegally shoot the son of a bitch...[because] a dead man can't leak stuff."[257]

With the Australian government in lockstep with the worst civil, military and security developments in the United States, acting already as the 53rd State, no politician rose to defend the nation's most brilliant son.

Just as jihadists worldwide had seized on the new technology and made maximum use of it, so had the most totalitarian of state elements; and Australian authorities were in there for the ride.

The anti-WikiLeaks propaganda wouldn't feel so existential if I didn't believe anti-whistle-blower messaging is soon going to escalate into an actual long-term military campaign against leakers and hacktivists around the world. In the near future, don't be surprised if there is some 'event' that catalyzes a mobilization of military campaigns against targets that are deemed 'a danger to our democracy because of their unlawful disclosures of matters of national security.' This would almost assuredly include symbolic targets like Julian Assange and Edward Snowden to achieve a "chilling effect." . . . power structures are increasingly criminalizing the dissemination of information.[258]

As dreary, as annoyingly human as it was, as a cold summer turned to autumn Old Alex came down with toothache, and became increasingly sick.

Pain was not his forte; and thus it was that he went back to Vietnam, where the cost of dentistry was no more than 20% of what it was in Australia.

And thereby hung another tale, where the Watchers on the Watch amassed, and exposed themselves. And he went slightly mad. So much for a holiday.

---

257 Ibid.

258 Ibid.

Driven to distraction by the surveillance, in his delinquent conclusions he felt morally bound to lure his pursuers out onto thin ice. As spiritual as he was, he would have happily watched them drown.

No individual should have to accept the harassment he had endured, and no government should perpetrate it.

Never think the same again, he warned the Watchers on the Watch.

Never bully, harass, threaten or intimidate anyone ever again.

But before all that, there were other twinkling falls in a dying year.

He was commissioned to do one final story before he departed that internecine web of streets; as the terror yarn continued to roll, here in this place that should have been safe, a hideout from the coming Apocalypse.

In those unprecedented times, the Prime Minister celebrated the death of an Australian citizen, Neil Prakash, aged 24, who he was claiming responsibility for helping to kill.

Australian authorities were providing targeting and identification information to the US on Australian citizens in the Middle East.

That Australia was directly assisting in the killing of its own citizens was new territory in the fight against Islamic State.

Prakash was a subject of considerable interest because he had become a leading recruiter for Islamic State, appearing prominently in IS propaganda, including in videos and on the cover of their magazine Dabiq.

Prakash was reportedly killed by a US drone strike in the northern Iraqi city of Mosul, bringing the number of Australian jihadists killed in Iraq and Syria to more than fifty.

Like many of those drawn to become a jihadist, Prakash came from a troubled background; a high school dropout who had been a Buddhist, an apprentice mechanic and a rapper before converting to Islam.

From a broken family, with a schizophrenic mother and absent father, he spent many of his formative years living in the garage of a friend.

The person he was bore little resemblance to the person he was to become.

In a twelve-minute video, professionally produced and heavily promoted by IS, Prakash, known by the *nom de guerre* Abu Khaled al-Cambodi, issued a call to arms:

> My brothers, my beloved brothers in Islam in Australia. Now is the time to rise. Now is the time to wake up. You must start attacking before they attack you.

I invite the Muslims to come here.

I tell you that this is the land of life.

The media has portrayed that we come here [because we were] social outcasts, because we had nobody we had to turn to Islam, because we were just trouble-makers in the past. This is far from the reality. We see people from all walks of life here.[259]

Malcolm Turnbull described his death as a very, very positive development in the war against Islamic State terror.

Professor Greg Barton of Deakin University said there were many paradoxes with the Australian authorities' celebration of Prakash's death and their assistance in tracking down Australian citizens:

This is a whole new area. It raises a lot of questions. There is a war going on.

It is a conventional war on the ground in Iraq and Syria, but it is also about the hearts and minds of young people in Australian suburbs.

It is dealing with very sad and tragic issues. It is good news that Prakash is no longer online trying to influence young people but his own story is a very tragic one. His story is full of pathos.

He was a lost kid who ended up in a bad place..."[260]

Old Alex was reminded of two old school friends with whom he shared passionate, youthful friendships.

One overdosed, one suicided, both at young ages, both troubled individuals. They had all been troubled, out there in an over-lit J.G. Ballard world of clashing sand and frothing surf, Sydney beachside suburbs.

As it turned out, reports of Prakash's death were premature, and he was subsequently arrested in Turkey, when again Turnbull made full use of the occasion, threatening him with the full power of the Australian courts once he was as declaring he was extradited.

---

259 Islamic State recruiter Neil Prakash calls for attack in Australia in propaganda video, Marissa Callegeros, 22 April, 2015.

260 Neil Prakash's Life before he became an IS Fighter, John Stapleton, *The New Daily*, 6 May, 2016.

As the world drifted towards calamity, his head became more active.

The constant murmur of surveillance and the electronic babble of the 21st Century had worn through the throne room, disintegrated the flesh off skulls and worn away in righteous probity the sins to which all flesh were prone. He was going to be strung out on racks between heaven and from earth, and punished for those very sins.

He dreamt frequently of living in one of his favourite cities in the world, Madrid, and writing a book about the Spanish Inquisition – as if he, too, had been held in those dungeons of the righteous; those soldiers of God who marched the cold stone corridors above. Punished cruelly for sins which were no more sins than the rising of the sun, unless decreed by one of the overlords with a devil in his heart, or in the case of the Inquisition, a devil in her heart.

Torturer-in-chief, Queen Isabella of Spain, was given the honourific Servant of God by the Vatican in 1974.

Her God was equally as cruel as the God of Islamic State.

And he heard it everywhere: "We worship the same God."

Along with many other prominent figures in Australia, the present Prime Minister Malcolm Turnbull and the former Prime Minister Tony Abbott were Roman Catholics. The Deputy Prime Minister and the leader of the Opposition also received a Catholic education.

There were certainly days when Australia's politicians seemed determine to disillusion the populace with the nature of Earthly government.

He was drawn to a quote, allegedly from the Jesuit Extreme Oath of Induction, which he had no way of verifying:

> You have been taught to insidiously plant the seeds of jealousy and hatred between communities, provinces, states that were at peace, and incite them to deeds of blood, involving them in war with each other, and to create revolutions and civil wars in countries that were independent and prosperous, cultivating the arts and the sciences and enjoying the blessings of peace.[261]

Queen Isabella owed her elevation to her driving the Muslims out of Spain.

Both Abbott and Turnbull were heavily involved in a new crusader war; and it felt for Old Alex as if, fixed between image and circumstance, blood-soaked spiritual anagrams had become suspended in the surrounding air.

---

261 Jesuit Oath of Extreme Induction, found on the website Reformation dot org.

The Spanish Tribunal of the Holy Office of the Inquisition survived for more than 350 years.

And then, far from trace memories of dark torments and the Madrid bars and clubs to which as a young man Alex had been such a devotee, twining in the Newtown streets, there were thick drifts of autumn leaves.

The last two journalists were leaving London's once famous Fleet Street, the Street of Shame – that legendary bar-filled area which, as far as Old Alex had been concerned, was a place of awe and which echoed his own early experiences of smoke-filled newsrooms and loud disputes between journalists and editors, an era of enormous creativity in the far off antipodes:

"The alcohol flowed like water in Fleet Street.

"I was working on an undercover job once for a paper, and rang an editor from a payphone, to check in with him.

"He asked 'Are you in danger, pet?' I replied 'Yes, I am'. To which he replied 'Oh, good.'"[262]

An old colleague, journalistic legend and in-house lawyer Brian Gallagher, universally known as Twitch, died that year, aged 81.

"Has the story been Twitched?" meant, has it been legalled?

Old Twitch loved a drink.

As another fine journeyman Graeme Leech wrote for the obituary: "Twitch was a most convivial man and enjoyed the late-night company of reporters, editors and subeditors after the paper had been put to bed. The stories, the anecdotes and the jokes would fill a ledger. This is one of them."[263]

Old Alex's story related to the longest running case in Family Court history and in part to a psychiatrist, a darling of the legal establishment and a favoured report writer for the state's court system. The report writers, as far as Alex was concerned, were at the core of the country's judicial corruption and dysfunctional court system.

After the publication of a double page spread titled Battered by the System, the paper was promptly hit with a legal threat from the psychiatrist's lawyers and an offer to draft the apology.

262 Fleet Street: Last journalists leave former home of national newspaper, Mario Cacciottolo, BBC, 5 August, 2016.

263 After crossing pens, Twitch had last jape, Graeme leech, *The Australian*, 18 July, 2016.

He was summoned to Twitch's office.

"We can't say this," he huffed as he perused the copy. "It'll cost us a fortune."

"Well you passed it," Old Alex replied.

"Must have been after lunch," Twitch sniffed.

As in, after several hours drinking with the like-minded down the local watering hole.

Twitch never backed down. After considerable argy-bargy and production of various pieces of evidence, there was no more talk from the psychiatrist in question of drafting apologies. Twitch won the day, and Old Alex's affection forever.

But the journalism Twitch knew, the world of heavy drinkers and contempt for the bastards, as any figure of authority was inevitably labelled, had by the time of his death, become an entirely sanitised profession.

Kill the artists, kill the writers.

Kill the journalists.

Hunt down the free thinkers. Assassinate. Assassinate.

We worship the same God.

One plane flight can change everything, and so it did.

Perhaps there would always have come a day in Alex's life when he would be sitting next to a wizened Lilly in Lilly's Bar in central Saigon, watching the workers and the tourists and the local denizens in scrappy, bar-lined streets.

He complained to her about being overcharged, and she lifted her wrist a few lazy centimetres, displaying ten heavy rings of gold affixed to her arm.

"Next time," she said dismissively.

Pleasing a Cheap Charlie such as himself was the least of her concerns.

At a booth opposite, which this famous figure of old Saigon also owned, a ceaseless queue of Westerners, NGO types and middle class Vietnamese pulled up on motorbikes, bought their marijuana and were quickly off into the busy streets.

Millions of dong changed hands every night, week in, month out.

All of this occurring directly under police cameras.

In contrast to the rampant hypocrisies of the West, sometimes in Asia things just worked. Everybody knew where they stood. Everybody was paid. There was no trouble because to cause problems meant you were dispatched from the mortal coil, promptly escorted blood spattered into the next life.

As Lilly lowered her arm to the table he had the flash thought: "People have died in this story."

Like many a Westerner, images of the fall of Saigon and the disgraces of the Vietnam War, or the American War as it was locally known, would filter through his consciousness, overlaying themselves on the present-day flicker of crowded streets and bustling enterprise.

Australia, even then, had been a willing and uncritical ally to America's barbarities, and the nation's politicians had been willing to sacrifice the welfare, resources and integrity of the country and the welfare of thousands of soldiers in a military fiasco.

No matter how noble their friendships, how courageous their conduct, how youthful their naivety or well-intentioned the motives of the soldiers themselves, nothing would ever justify the West's, or Australia's, involvement in what the Vietnamese would forever regard as an unforgivably inhumane, cruel and unjust war perpetrated by foreigners who had no right to be there.

But in 2016 Vietnam was a young and optimistic country. For most of the population born after the war it was an historic injustice rather than a present day injustice and visitors were almost invariably treated with courtesy, kindness or indifference.

The Vietnamese were a far prouder, more nationalistic people than Australians, their society more prosperous, liberal, better functioning and cohesive. The karma of history had already taken its revenge.

Long ago the French, Chinese and American invaders had all been seen off, and if they had any sense, would never come back. And if Australian politicians had any common sense or integrity, they would never have involved their citizens in another American military disaster ever again.

But in those hot, sticky, crowded streets these stray thoughts were all by-the-by.

Old Alex settled back to watch the transsexual hookers plying their trade on the pavement, doing provocative little jigs to the music belting from Lilly's Bar.

There was plenty of competition in the clutter of the surrounding streets.

Traced, tracked. An agent in a cafe opposite raised his iPhone and took a picture of him; as if another picture in what they assumed was a compromising situation would serve any purpose whatsoever.

He was exhausted by the wear and tear of the year, dreary dental problems and the inconvenience of flu. Never a malingerer, he hated to be sick.

But there he sat, hour after hour, watching the Saigon prostitutes ply their trade and the tourists come and go, in those famous streets which still felt as if an impeccably dressed Graham Greene might be just about to walk around the corner, picking his way fastidiously not through the crowds of coolies and rickshaws of old, but the motorbikes and hustlers of the 21st Century. Old Alex already felt like a character in H.G. Wells' final book *The Mind at the End of Its Tether*, a book which had no characters:

> The writer finds very considerable reason for believing that, within a period to be estimated by weeks and months rather than by æons, there has been a fundamental change in the conditions under which life, not simply human life but all self-conscious existence, has been going on, since its beginning.
>
> His renascent intelligence finds itself confronted with strange, convincing realities so overwhelming that, were he indeed one of those logical, consistent people we incline to claim we are, he would think night and day in a passion of concentration, dismay and mental struggle upon the ultimate disaster that confronts our species.[264]

Wells foresaw, or feared, a fundamental shift in the nature of consciousness; while Old Alex was disturbed by the all too familiar.

He had known from the minute he booked into the City Hotel, a cheap hotel in District One popular with Vietnamese tourists from the North, that he was under surveillance, still.

It drove him nuts, not to put too fine a point on it.

Nothing he did would allow him to escape this dreadful treacle, and either his pursuers were so incompetent they constantly gave themselves away, or it was deliberate harassment.

He chose the latter; as he listened to the monster woman stationed at the Embassy check-in daily with the Watchers on the Watch.

For years he had been listening to her and her ilk, bureaucrats with the imaginations of gnats making their dismissive comments and disappearing back to their air-conditioned offices. While he thrashed in ever more fitful circumstance, trapped.

---

264 *The Mind at the End of Its Tether*, H.G. Wells, Heinemann, 1945.

All they got, just as all they got from their surveillance of so many other targets, and their mass surveillance of the population at large, was information on the way people behaved when they knew they were under surveillance.

Which was of no use whatsoever unless you were deliberately trying to socially engineer the so-called "chilling effect".

It had begun well enough. He checked into the City Star, where he had once read Herman Melville's *Moby Dick*, and been entranced, like so many millions of other readers, by the great beast harpooned with multiple lines thrashing as it dived and died.

From his seventh floor room he looked down the cluttered Saigon street lined with tall century old trees towering past, their trunks more impressive than the thin canopy above. He walked frequently through the neighbouring park, filled with Vietnamese doing their exercises, and swam each day in the wonderfully atmospheric pool at the old French Club. The colonial trappings of the elites were now being ably utilised by the Vietnamese public.

His medical issues were more easily resolved than he expected and Alex spent many an evening with a group of local men who would gather in the evenings on cheap plastic stools outside a cafe in a neighbouring street, there to drink and feast and gossip; a group who had been kind to him on previous visits.

One of them had died in the year since he was last there but the gatherings went on.

"What is your new book about?" asked a Vietnamese woman whom he gave some English lessons to.

He tried to explain.

There was no use talking about Stephen Spender's beautiful memoir of writing and life, *World Within World*, or the concept of national snapshots or capturing moments in time or anything else much.

"You are trying to save the soul of the world," she said, snapping shut the conversation.

Such were the fantastical times.

If only there was a drug powerful enough to ignite his creativity.

Lonely, lost, in those narrow, activity-filled streets, Alex walked past the perfect liaison – well, the perfect one for him. He paused, looked back, paused again, they exchanged glances. And then he kept on walking, thereby destroying his own timeline.

For days he felt out of sorts, annoyed at his moment of cowardice, knowing he had destroyed a river of incident, the correct path.

It didn't matter how many times he walked down the same street, he never saw the person again.

A foolish old man with a seething head in a seething Asian city; he had been there before. These things always hung on fractions of a second.

His woman friend had for days been talking about something called Neuro-Linguistic Programming: a behavioural modification psychotherapy developed in California in the 1970s which at that point he had never heard of.

Wikipedia dismissed the therapy as having been widely discredited; but it was clearly popular in Vietnam. She persisted and he agreed: he would investigate for himself. In any case, he wasn't doing much else, haunted by the surveillance of his hotel room, struggling to be born.

Thus for three days he found himself in a large auditorium with a thousand wildly enthusiastic young Vietnamese listening to a charismatic former Malaysian Indian army officer from Bangkok known as Vas strutting his stuff on stage.

Their motto: "It's all about winning."

Their marketing: "Coach Vas will push you beyond your comfort zones, smash through your emotional and physical pain barriers to activate your inner resources, allowing you to live your true potential."

The man was a master of mass hypnosis. Amid moments of riotous union and profound communion was an extremely aggressive sell of a gradated ten step program costing thousands of dollars, a large amount of money in Vietnam.

Vas grew rich.

His audience grew inspired. Or not.

One of the exercises of the three day introductory program was a piece of homework where one had to write down the five worst experiences for each decade of your life.

He did his homework in the City Star Hotel, and felt immediately discombobulated as a result.

As most of the audience was under thirty, they had rather less homework to do.

The next day was a visualisation exercise. He already thought in pictures, and had no trouble conjuring up images.

You were walking in a forest, you were a at the base of a great tree, you became a giant eagle, you rose up to the very top of the tree where you could look down a vanishing line, each of those trees representing the worst experiences of your life. You flew from one to the other; you absorbed that event into yourself and transformed it into good.

Because of time constraints the audience was only required to pick out one of the five worst events for that decade. Even if the theory worked, that left an awful lot of unresolved events.

Forced to recall everything from youthful suicide attempts to catastrophic loves to the deaths of old friends, he went back to the hotel room feeling extremely disturbed, with nothing but a surveillance team and a honey trap for company.

He wished he had a therapist, but did not.

He chose the honey trap; and went out and got shamelessly drunk in errant company in the red light district of Saigon for a fortnight.

Some were kind enough to warn him: "All hell will break loose."

His sin was to write about something the authorities didn't want written about; their mistake so obvious, it was remarkable the battalions of well-paid experts gracing the bureaucracies had not picked up on it.

His role in exposing a staggering level of incompetence was no sin at all.

He was completely fed up with being harassed.

"I told them to leave him alone," said one of the Watchers on the Watch one Saigon morning, one of the only kindly personnel to ever, in all those years, man the post. "But would they listen?"

As far as Old Alex was concerned, he was observing criminal conduct by the agencies.

And he knew that particular Watcher on the Watch agreed with him.

"We were told to destroy you," one of them later apologised.

Then they brought in the experts.

The story they told him was nothing like the story they told their bosses. The only problem was, they were all on government contracts and he did not know who to trust.

An empath on contract, briefly in Saigon in a busy schedule, for their talents were in high demand around the world, took to spending his evenings in the same roadside cafe. One evening, knowing full well that he had drawn Alex's attention, raised first two, then one finger to his mouth in a shushing gesture: Be quiet, be careful. Tell no-one.

He had seen the gesture before.

A literary device, fiction, a clairvoyant truth, a sure sign the author had lost the plot... On the edge of the Apocalypse, none of it mattered.

Opposite Lucy's, one of them cut through the noise of motorbikes that characterised the Saigon streets, demanding to know: "What are you?" Clear as a bell.

"We are transmission points," he responded, before wishing he had pretended not to hear.

The Saigon streets washed away into the night. "Massage. Massage."

He could not tell friend from foe, and once again took a dive into the ordinary, the very ordinary, destroying his own timeline in a wanton disregard for the many opportunities that presented themselves, anything to avoid detection.

Forbidden to contact him directly, in a divine chuckle one of them said: "I wish we could have just invited him out with us. He would have had a good time."

"Politics, politics. Contract, contract." He heard the words repeatedly but did not know what they meant, a contract for employment, a contract to kill?

More likely the latter, a leftover from the Thailand book when indeed the notorious Thai and Russian mafias pursued him across borders; as fantastical as it would come to seem, sitting there in Newtown, where nothing but low-rent crimes and putrid gossip swirled through indifferent streets.

On his final evening in Saigon he sat by happenstance opposite another Australian on the main strip Bui Vien, characterised by a clutter of bars, Crazy Dog, Drunken Monkey, Lost in Saigon.

The aging renegade, his long hair pulled behind into a rats tail, puffing on a peculiar little marijuana pipe, proffered unprompted: "I'm very disillusioned with my own country. It's a police state."

They agreed to agree as they watched the comings and goings on the street and listened to the clatter of conversation around them.

A foreigner had died in the Love Hotel opposite only the night before; and he heard the story of how the street life swarmed around the ambulance undisrupted as the body was carried out.

Disillusioned Australians were everywhere.

In their own country they just switched off.

Not for the first time, he poured himself onto the plane and back to the Great Southern Land, where he did not want to be.

He slept off the first few days with the help of the Aging Opera Diva's ready supply of sleeping pills.

When he stirred to work, imprinted on a hyper-real world of little more than treachery, all he could feel were tentacles of threat.

Everything was closing in.

That final month of autumn – which truly did herald a winter of discontent – the beginning of a two-month long election campaign, one of the longest campaigns in Australian history, was declared.

The government was determined to bore the population into submission.

THE PLACE WHERE THERE IS NO DARKNESS

DAY THREE of the election, and the campaign was already beginning to go haywire for Mr Harbourside Mansion, as his critics became fond of calling the Prime Minister.

On a grin-and-grip in the seat of Lindsay in Sydney's West in support of sitting member Fiona Scott, it was already obvious how incompetent were his media advisers.

The messaging was all wrong, with a collection of business women assembled to greet the Prime Minister, perpetuating a gender war and a gender divide, an image pushed by a feminist bureaucracy that failed to gel in the community. Did only women count?

The previous Prime Minister Tony Abbott had seen his support amongst males dive as a result of similar antics. An easily achievable 50/50 divide would have perpetrated an image of progressive equality and genuine concern for business people. As it was, it came off as just another taxpayer-funded charade.

All the messaging on cutting company tax and transforming the economy was disastrously misplaced, a misunderstanding of electoral sentiment and an insult to the hundreds of thousands of small business people struggling to survive under insane government imposts.

Literally: flee back to your elitist bubble. You clearly don't belong here. Contempt leaked from every pore.

That afternoon Turnbull cancelled a walk through Penrith's Westfield shopping mall, a set piece of election campaigns amidst the proletariat since the days of Bob Hawke in the 1980s.

As a general news reporter, old Alex had followed them all through the Mall. The job was one of those dregs of the news list, for no one genuinely expected anything interesting to happen.

In the 1980s he watched as people bowled up to "Hawkie" to give him the benefit of their views, in the 1990s to conservative icon John Howard, who even more than his predecessor would politely listen and proceed to do precisely nothing.

It was as close as most of them ever got to an "ordinary voter".

But 2016 was a different era, and with Australia's bombs raining down on the Middle East, killing mujahedeen and their families, it was a far less safe exercise than previously.

It was impossible to secure an entire shopping mall, and extremely easy to lob a bomb from a higher floor into the frantic cluster of the Prime Minister, his many aids, and a curious gaggle of local shoppers.

As the man most directly responsible for Australia's killing of Muslim fighters on the other side of the world, the blood of the martyrs was congealing around Turnbull, whether he liked it or not.

This was no Just War.

Australia's obeisance to America's foreign policy had been backfiring at least since the Vietnam War and was backfiring even now, even in the shopping malls of Western Sydney.

An area which had some of the country's largest and most disenchanted concentrations of Islamic followers was by no means secure.

Whatever the reason, the afternoon events were cancelled without explanation. The public was never going to be told the truth.

As if a set piece specifically designed to illustrate that there was now two very different Australias, on the same day the Australian Federal Police arrested five men trying to flee the country to go and fight with Islamic State.

Such was the success of Australian democracy that people could not even leave if they wanted to. As in the earliest days of the colony, their island home was a prison.

The five men, all of whose passports had been cancelled, travelled 3,000 kilometres in less than four days from Melbourne towing a seven metre outboard-powered dinghy. The men experienced several breakdowns on the way. They were arrested in Cairns on their way to Cape York, the northernmost tip of Australia.

They planned to travel to Indonesia and ultimately on to Iraq and Syria.

Old Alex felt a certain twang of sympathy. He was no jihadist, but he, too, wanted to escape.

The ostensible aim of the government policy to cancel passports was to stop those with predilection and intent acquiring skills in the war zones of the Middle East which they could use back home.

As a number of experts had warned, the policy was likely to backfire, creating a pressure cooker of frustrated jihadists highly prone to the lone-wolf calls of Islamic State.

Security agencies were already preparing for an onslaught of Australian jihadists returning home.

Dr Roger Shanahan of the Lowy institute said there were more than 100 Australians fighting for jihad groups in Iraq and Syria: "Some of them will be seeking to come back to Australia. What their intent when they come back to Australia is, that's going to be another thing that's going to exercise the minds of the security agencies."[265]

A Lowy Institute report, Foreign Fighters in Syria and Iraq: The Day After, co-written by Shanahan, warned:

> The length and intensity of the Syrian and Iraqi conflicts will mean that those foreign fighters who survive will likely be the most operationally experienced, lethally skilled and highly networked group of jihadis to date.
>
> Apart from their appalling human cost, the conflicts in Syria and Iraq have created a number of disastrous legacies. Chief among them has been the generation of a new cohort of jihadist fighters from around the world. Those fighters are now starting to leave those conflicts, a process that will probably accelerate in the coming months and years, taking with them the lethal skills and connections forged in Syria and Iraq. This diffusion of terrorist expertise will pose problems for security services in both Muslim and non-Muslim countries for years to come.[266]

Alex was sitting in that Newtown backyard despairing of the state of

265 Islamic State: Jihadists predicted to return to Australia as IS loses ground in Iraq and Syria, Michael Edwards, ABC, 14 September, 2016.

266 Foreign Fighters in Syria and Iraq: The Day After, Lydia Khalil and Roger Shanahan, Lowy Institute, 13 September, 2016.

Australian politics and pretty much everything else, including a lingering regret at the destruction of his own right path as the spirits struggled to realign the fate lines, when the news came of the five men attempting to flee the country.

Amongst them was Musa Cerantonio, whom he had previously had cause to be fascinated by.

As one of the pre-eminently gifted intellects of contemporary journalism Graeme Wood wrote in his ground-breaking 2015 piece in *The Atlantic*, What ISIS Really Wants, Cerantonio was an integral figure in the global jihad network, his preaching an inspiration to many fighters around the world.

And he also happened to be Australian, forced to remain in Melbourne after previously being blocked from travelling to Syria.

Wood travelled from the US to Melbourne specifically to interview him.

His case echoed the words of Martin Chulov: Australia was far more integral to worldwide jihad than many people originally realised.

Cerantonio was named alongside US-based cleric Ahmad Musa Jibril as one of the two most popular authorities in the world within foreign fighter networks, and one of Islamic State's most significant spiritual authorities.

For three years he was a televangelist on Iqraa TV in Cairo, but he left after the station objected to his frequent calls to establish a caliphate. Later he took to preaching on Facebook and Twitter.

In 2014 Cerantonio and his wife tried to emigrate, but they were caught *en route,* in the Philippines, and deported back.

Australia, which had criminalised attempts to travel to the Islamic State, confiscated Cerantonio's passport.

Wood wrote:

> If Cerantonio were caught facilitating the movement of individuals to the Islamic State, he would be imprisoned.

> So far, though, he is free—a technically unaffiliated ideologue who nonetheless speaks with what other jihadists have taken to be a reliable voice on matters of the Islamic State's doctrine.

> Cerantonio … has the kind of unkempt facial hair one sees on certain overgrown fans of The Lord of the Rings, and his obsession with Islamic apocalypticism felt familiar. He seemed to be

living out a drama that looks, from an outsider's perspective, like a medieval fantasy novel, only with real blood.[267]

Cerantonio explained the joy he felt when Baghdadi was declared the caliph on June 29 and the sudden, magnetic attraction that Mesopotamia began to exert on him and his friends. "I was in a hotel [in the Philippines], and I saw the declaration on television. And I was just amazed, and I'm like, Why am I stuck here in this bloody room?"[268]

The caliphate, Cerantonio said, was not just a political entity but also a vehicle for salvation. IS propaganda regularly reported the pledges of allegiance rolling in from jihadist groups across the Muslim world. Cerantonio quoted a Prophetic saying, that to die without pledging allegiance is to die "jahil", ignorant, and therefore die a "death of disbelief".

Wood conjectured: "Consider how Muslims (or, for that matter, Christians) imagine God deals with the souls of people who die without learning about the one true religion. They are neither obviously saved nor definitively condemned. Similarly, Cerantonio said, the Muslim who acknowledges one omnipotent god and prays, but who dies without pledging himself to a valid caliph and incurring the obligations of that oath, has failed to live a fully Islamic life."[269]

To Cerantonio, Islam had been re-established with the foundation of Islamic State.

Under Australian law, giving allegiance to Islamic State was illegal. But he believed IS leader Baghdadi fulfilled all the requirements to be declared the caliph.

Cerantonio may have been a prisoner of the state, but his influence lived on.

While his Facebook page was blocked, presumably by the Australian authorities, Cerantonio's lectures were readily available on YouTube following his arrest, posted by Stranger Media.

The notion of the stranger had particular relevance in Islam, and echoed loudly in the minds of Australian Muslims, who were often said to feel displaced amongst unbelievers, at odds with the dominant culture, with its

267 What ISIS Really Wants, Graeme Wood, *The Atlantic*, March, 2015.
268 Ibid.
269 Ibid.

multiple travesties of decency and its brazen glorification of sexual freedom aka depravity.

The information website Islamic Religion puts it thus:

> Prophet Muhammad, may the mercy and blessings of God be upon him, said, "Islam began as something strange, and it shall return to being something strange, so give glad tidings to the strangers…"

> Many converts to Islam will tell you about feeling as if they were strangers, before finding Islam. They will speak of feeling that they belonged somewhere else, that their lives were just slightly off centre. They often speak about a vague sense of knowing they were not like everyone else around them, feeling like a stranger in a strange land. Converting to Islam gives one a sense of coming home, of finally being normal, albeit sometimes still in a strange land.[270]

Cerantonio's YouTube presence included sermons on The Final Battle, Fiqh and Sharia. Belief. Law. Some of his sermons were simply clear-eyed expositions of Islamic doctrine. Others were straightforward calls to fight for Allah, Islam and the Islamic State, to know no fear in the face of the infidels, the crusaders, the non-believers, the enemies of the Lord of All The Worlds.

Any Australian teenager, anyone in the world with an internet connection, could access these sermons easily.

It was easy to see why he had become an inspiration to jihadists worldwide.

Cerantonio was an excellent public speaker: concise, compelling, with conveniently interspersed repetition for difficult concepts, as he took his audience with him. In his sermons he came across as clear-eyed and intelligent; his tone was frank, sincere, commonplace, talking as an ordinary person to ordinary people.

But he was no ordinary person.

In the video Who Are The Real Terrorists? posted by Stranger Media, Cerantonio lectured in front of a superimposed Islamic State flag. Giving allegiance to IS was illegal under Australian law. The sermons were also broadcasting on Islamic Path Radio.

---

270 Who Are The Strangers? The Religion of Islam. Posted on IslamReligion 28 March, 2011.

Cerantonio made clear that Blair, Bush and Obama, the crusaders and Zionists, were the true terrorists.

> We see again the mujahedeen in Syria, the ones who are called the terrorists. They are called terrorists for a reason, because it means the ones who are labelling them terrorists are scared of them. They are afraid, they are actually validating them.

> You should know when someone is inflicting fear into the hearts of the enemies of Allah, he is indeed the mujahedeen. He is indeed the one fulfilling the command of Allah.[271]

Cerantonio began his sermon by assuring his clearly devoted audience that they were out of sight of the camera, which only focussed on him, and therefore they need not be afraid.

He recalled the tortures and abuse of the infamous Abu Ghraib prison in Iraq, as well as the rape of "sisters" by American soldiers, and asked: "Is there anyone of us who would not be ready to sacrifice ourselves for our brothers and sisters."[272]

Cerantonio's cry, "We fear none but Allah", was met with a chorus of Allahu Akbar, God is Great.

Looking at the history of Islam, and the origins of the word terror, Cerantonio told his audience:

> Allah is telling us to practice terrorism. Allah says, strike fear into the hearts of the enemies of Allah. No one nation waged jihad like the Prophet, peace be upon him. It is important to know that the Prophet, peace be upon him, intended, clearly, by understanding the verses of Allah, not to allow . . . the enemies of Allah not to fear him. Allah says, let them fear you, strike fear into their hearts. Islam demands that the enemies of Allah are never comfortable. They are meant to be in fear because this is what Allah has commanded. Fear Allah and Allah will grant you victory.

> They are saying the Islamic State, the Islamic State. You find the ones who are truly saying they want an Islamic State and they

271 Who Are The Real Terrorists? Musa Cerantonio, StrangerMedia, YouTube. Posted 2 April, 2013.
272 Ibid.

have no fear, they have no fear. What is there to fear? Death, victory?[273]

Cerantonio warned the enemies of Allah that they do not terrify the Muslims, for there was no reason to be afraid when the crusaders and infidels could be defeated. They were proud to be the followers of Mohammed, and proud to say they were the ones who implemented the words of Allah.

> You know that you fear Islam and terror fills your hearts and we pray to Allah that this terror remains in your hearts until your reign ends and Islam again dominates the worlds. So we as Muslims we don't care what you call us, call us terrorists if you wish. We don't mind because that means you are afraid, and this is the first step. The moment you say this it means victory is near. My dear brothers and sisters, rejoice. The world is rapidly changing. The flag is again being raised. Victory is near.

> My dear brothers and sisters, do not stop praying for the victory of Islam and the Muslims. Do not stop praying for the downfall of these tyrants. I ask Allah to grant us all success. Strike fear into the heart of your enemy. Allow them to fear Allah so that Islam will return to implement justice all over the whole world. Allow the righteous Muslim to return to ruling by your book, to establish the Islamic State so that true justice can prevail. May Allah bless you and protect you all.[274]

Apart from keeping Cerantonio under surveillance, the authorities took no action.

His treatment compounded the impression that there was a state of serious hypocrisy in the authorities' dealings with Islamic fundamentalists; that the public was told one story, while jihadists laughed in their face. As if God himself was laughing, there in the deep, entwining ether of Australian society, a world of shallow purpose. A society ripe for the plucking.

The gods cared little for the truth. Just like bureaucrats they cared for power. Nothing was as it seemed.

In another sermon readily available on YouTube, Jihad Preparation Against

---

273 Ibid.

274 Ibid.

Crusade Invasion of Muslim Lands, presented by Tawheed Carriers, again under the black flag, Cerantonio said:

> Why is it that they are attacking our lands? It is because they want to stop people living by the Book of Allah. You find that Al-Shabab in Somalia, may Allah grant them victory, stood up and said: No more tribalism. No more socialism. We want Islam. So the Americans bombed their lands. The same thing in Afghanistan, the Taliban, may Allah grant them victory. And they are the heroes of the Ummah in these days. These are the Men. They are the men of this Ummah today. Why are the Americans so determined to defeat them, when they have nothing? It is to stop them ruling by the Book of Allah.

Prepare what you can against them.[275]

After being extradited from Queensland to face court Cerantonio and his four colleagues refused to stand for a Melbourne Magistrate – a traditional sign of respect in Australia, across all jurisdictions, for the authority of the court.

The men's lawyer Rob Stary said the refusal to stand was in line with their Muslim faith: "They stand for no one other than Allah."

Amongst the five was aboriginal man Shayden Thorne, who returned to Australia in 2014 after spending more than two years in a Saudi prison for allegedly having terror-related material on his laptop. He was the brother of the Junaid Thorne, who came to the attention of authorities after touring Islamic Centres around the country preaching jihad.

Terror raids were conducted in properties across Melbourne in connection with the five men arrested for attempting to flee Australia – including a raid on the humble home of Musa Cerantonio's mother, with particular attention paid to a tin shed at the rear of the property.

A man at the property said: "If people want to leave the country and they were born here they should have every right to do so. If people don't want to be here, you should let them leave." Neighbour Gordana Zivanovac said: "The boys, everyone, very nice. They always say hello. I'm sorry for the mother."[276]

275 Jihad Preparation against Crusader Invasion of Muslim Lands, Tawheed Carriers
276 Ibid.

Australia's Deputy Prime Minister, Jesuit-educated Barnaby Joyce, waded into the debate, dismissing the men as "clowns and buffoons".

Asked about the national security incident he said:

> It verges on pathos. Breaking down, towing a tinnie along, really and truly. The vast majority of Australian people, despite their creed, despite their colour, despite where they're from, are just looking at this bunch of buffoons saying what on earth are you doing. It's like a Monty Python movie and it's come to an end. Welcome to the constabulary you clowns.[277]

Ridiculing people for their religious beliefs was never a good idea, and a Christian ridiculing a Muslim in the current environment even more so, but that's the way it played.

A group of Australians, with their passports stripped from them and no legal way to leave their island prison, under perpetual surveillance and thereby harassment, with a fundamental religious belief that their destinies lay elsewhere, decided to flee. Who could blame them?

In fact, far from the slur of mad meanderings Barnaby Joyce and his ilk liked to dismiss Islamic fundamentalists with, Cerantonio came across as far more thoughtful, articulate and intelligent than the Deputy Prime Minister.

At the same time, in a string of similar incidents targeting young Muslims, an 18-year-old was arrested in western Sydney for allegedly planning an "imminent" terrorist act, including planning to acquire a firearm.

Police alleged he was exploring military and police targets. Everywhere was a target. Going to McDonald's could be regarded as reconnoitering.

That people could be arrested for even contemplating a crime, if indeed that was what they were doing, demonstrated a fundamental shift in Australian jurisprudence. Innocent until proven guilty was a long way back down the track.

Tamim Khaja, of Macquarie Park in Sydney's north-west, was arrested in Parramatta in Sydney's west at about 10:00am by the Joint Counter Terrorism Team, comprised of officers from the Australian Federal Police, the NSW Police, and other government agencies.

Khaja had previously come to the attention of authorities when, as a 17-year-old student of Epping High School, he was investigated by counterterrorism police for allegedly preaching radical Islam at the school.

277 Details emerge of 30kmh farcical trip to hell, *Courier Mail*, 12 May, 2016.

The young man's passport had been removed by authorities, allowing his alleged jihadist zeal only to be expressed on Australian soil, similar to the five who were arrested fleeing the country.

This time around, police went to great trouble to publicly explain that the removal of passports was essential in safeguarding the country, after considerable contrary opinion that depriving jihadists of the right to travel meant there was only one target left open to them: the homeland.

Even before Old Alex arrived back in Newtown that autumn, he had feared the quiet streets, the lack of profundity, the zero frisson of possibility, the dreary isolation of aging; a virtual shudder in the face of the all too familiar.

And he could hear, he was neither blind nor death, that his Saigon indiscretions, if that is what they were, had followed him back to Australia: a blatant abuse of privacy. But then, as he knew all too well, the Australian government and the thick-headed security officers they employed had zero respect for anybody's privacy or well being.

He remembered those lines in the same garden, those months before: "And if the person cracks or does something stupid? Goes and gets completely smashed?"

"That's when they pounce."

Well, they pounced; and the Psychological Operation against him mounted.

Worn down, in a sense forlorn, still scrabbling to get back on his own timeline, the cliff edge from which he had been driven or had so casually jumped, Alex revisited parts of Sydney which had once held significance.

He walked past one beside the railway line where he and his "partner" and their children had gone to live after declaring bankruptcy more than twenty years before; a concrete garden, a strange old man in the back shed, the sound of trains trundling through the nights… a place where he had felt more depressed than ever before, where his intelligence had gone out feeding through the black nights, once again desperate to escape.

That house where he had been so desperately unhappy was there no longer, a number of the old terraces having been knocked down and replaced with modern apartments.

And then it came to him, that ancient wisdom: "The world is born anew every day."

Day four of election campaign, 12 May 2016, didn't get any better for Malcolm Turnbull, who was forced to deny any wrongdoing when one of his companies from the 1990s warranted him a mention in the Panama Papers, leaked documents which exposed a global scandal of national leaders and prominent figures using tax havens to avoid the taxes of their own country.

Lord Malcolm reiterated that there was no evidence of wrongdoing.

But the class divide could not have been more apparent.

A single mother confronted the Prime Minister with an unanswerable diatribe about the education of her children. Pointing out that his party had increased spending on education got Turnbull precisely nowhere.

In the local cafe at Shellharbour politics finally made it through the usual chatter about football.

"Who's ahead?" one of the gym junkies who gathered there in the morning asked.

"Labor" came the response, met with a brief, disbelieving silence.

Then came the ridicule of the incumbents, who throughout their three year term had blamed their predecessors for the mess the country was in.

"My Auntie Flo crossed the road 150 years ago and it's all her fault," one said.

"We're just a number to them," the milkman delivering supplies to the cafe said, defeat in his eyes and his demeanour, although he had more to be proud of than many of the ne'er-do-wells in politics.

Cloaking themselves in social justice rhetoric, this was the disaster the elites had built, a country where nobody felt well done by.

In Baghdad, more than 90 people were killed in a single day in bomb attacks, news which barely rated a mention; and there were a spate of suicide bombings across the country; a dangerous cauldron of circumstance which Australia had played an role part in creating.

Winter came early and lasted long.

The surveillance got worse. There were cameras everywhere.

He kept locking the back door. The Opera Diva kept opening them. The attic became intensely uncomfortable. He could hear everything.

"They don't have to harass you to harass you."

They thought they had something on him now; there was no privacy and a targeted individual was simply that, a target.

"An abomination", he heard them whispering. There were just as many religious lunatics inside the agencies as out.

But what, in all of this, was the greatest abomination?

The straying hands and fleshly impulses of human frailty, or a country which did not even have the integrity to officially declare war, whose own citizens barely knew anything about the way their billions in taxes were being used, who the bombs were killing, or even why.

He was looking at major misconduct by the agencies, and major incompetence; they would do anything to protect themselves, including destroying a journalist they could not control.

Depressed, he spoke to virtually no one.

It was as if he had laid himself out as bait beside a highway, road kill, and been run over by a truck, uncertain if the strategy had worked.

There in that over-watered, cluttered garden, his fate lines struggled to reknit.

Australians quickly realised that far from offering up heartfelt debates about the future of the country, the election was tedium personified, Australia at its worst.

Lukewarm didn't even begin to describe the tepidity of it all.

The Greens were campaigning on Climate Change. Give us a break. Labor was campaigning on Education. Ditto. The Liberals aka conservatives were campaigning on Economic Management. Ditto. The record of all the parties on all these issues was abysmal.

The nation's memory was being constantly wiped, and in the end, in a failing democracy, no one cared. It made no difference who was in power. They were all as bad as each other.

The set piece of Australian politics, the Budget, designed to set up the Liberal Party for the election campaign, fell flat – with a *Guardian* newspaper poll showing a majority were less likely to vote conservative as a result.

What was most striking was the high level of disengagement of Australians from the political process. His generation had cared passionately about politics, but as Alex could readily sense, most people knew little and cared less. They had stopped believing politicians long ago; and the converging of the political parties as mere fronts for the machinery of government meant few of the political debates related to the daily lives of the citizenry.

The disengagement was dangerous because it was in these incoherent spaces, within a disillusioned populace, that violence, mischief and instability grew.

Within his own life, he dived even more deeply into the ordinary, not wishing to be found. Back in that large white house in Sydney's inner-west, he unusually kept taking sleeping pills to quash consciousness and walked the same quiet streets; 4,249 miles, eight hours and 40 minutes, the distance between Sydney and Saigon.

The crowded clutter, the jolt of unfamiliarity, the spectacular entrance of new landscapes and alluring streetscapes, all gone in the instant of take-off.

The ancient souls who connected to the cluster still marvelled at the modern feat of jet travel. A journey that would once have taken a lifetime, or several lifetimes, even generations, was accomplished in less than a day.

He felt, in those waking dreams, as if he had been on this planet for far too long. He wanted to go home.

The interior reflected the exterior, or the other way around. As one of the last areas of Sydney with any bohemian character, with the prices of houses ensuring a congealed wealth amongst long-term residents, the graffiti seemed even more pointless than last time he had been there.

In the Camperdown Cemetery, founded in 1848 and where some 18,000 people had been buried before it closed in 1942, a Biennale art project was progressively covering the gravestones with white coverings. In a government aka taxpayer-funded exercise by Swedish artist Bo Christian Larsson, seamstresses were employed on site to sew white coverings for the gravestones.

Desecrating a graveyard was now art.

It was meant in part to be a critique of the way social status survived death.

Fade Away, Fade Away, Fade Away, the installation was called. Contracting circumstance.

There were always conversations in the background.

Whether or not he was meant to hear them had become beside the point.

"This job has been a stuff-up from the beginning. I'm out of here. I'm sorry I ever got involved in the first place."

He assumed it was Glen.

"Surveillance doesn't work on someone like this."

"I've got to stop lying to him."

Pull the other one.

The country was one big lie; the greatest threat the truth.

Not that Old Alex could talk. Every chameleon needed a face. After decades of reporting, he wasn't too bad at getting in and out of tight situations himself, shuffling past security guards, looking for all the world like anyone's shambolic old uncle.

It was amazing what people would tell you if they thought you were harmless. He always came back with a story.

Ramadan was upon the face of the Earth, the season of feasting and fighting. World leaders, including Australia's Malcolm Turnbull, wished everyone a happy Ramadan.

Every last one of them knew that hundreds would die in the massacres of the season.

Turnbull kept reiterating: "Australia is the most successful multicultural society on Earth."

Saying so did not make it so.

The government's dire relations with the Muslim minority would briefly, at least on the surface, change with the advent of Turnbull. The multicultural rhetoric shifted up a gear, the rhetoric on terror shifted down.

Under his predecessor Tony Abbott, with the ceaseless "death cult" rhetoric and his one-man war on Islam, relations had never been worse.

Turnbull came in determined to set a new, conciliatory tone. The tone was benighted, the contradictions manifest; he did not understand the world in which he waded.

The bombing of Muslims on the other side of the world did not stop. And with every dead Muslim relations between the Australian government and the country's Muslim minority would grow worse.

Turnbull was about to get a lesson in multiculturalism all of his own making.

His speech welcoming the advent of Ramadan, played on Sydney's Muslim Community Radio, was immediately followed by a song: "He speaks with many meanings, none of them true."

If Turnbull was under the illusion he was amongst friends, he was sadly mistaken.

During the election campaign, on the Prime Minister's official Facebook page, a member of the public posted a link to a sickening picture of what purported to be a mother holding her beheaded four-year-old, another victim of Islamic State. The post was left there for several days before staff finally removed it.

Did no one check these things?

The Prime Minister's staff should have known that anything to do with Islam provoked volleys of sentiment on every public forum in the land, some of it outright poisonous.

The post linked to the Facebook page of Theodore Shoebat, listed as one of the most racist bloggers in America.

It was headlined: "Muslims Take Four Year Old Girl, Behead Her, And Then Force Her Mother To Soak Her Hands In Her Blood."

A man who was paid a million dollars a year couldn't be bothered to ensure that his staff were doing their job on a platform as public as Facebook.

Things got no better on the Prime Minister's government-sponsored website. One post declared: "As a proud Muslim I am happy you allow us to incite violence and crime and conduct jihad in your lands. The Koran contains much hate speech and yet you allow it here in its entirety!!! Especially the many verses stirring up hatred and head chopping for the dirty Kafir, i.e. you.

"Muslims love Aussie cucks!!!

"They are so soft they give credence to all our Jew killing hate. Allahu Akbar – we scream that when we cut your throat, because Muhammad told us. From my family to yours, we will outbreed you, you must accept our higher criminality and our faith."

Another post declared: "If one allows them to set up camp and breed like crazy on Free Welfare they will topple Western Civilization in 30-40 short years. How long did it take to arrive at Western Civilization? and Malcolm Turnbull and company will give it away to Islamists so cheaply who will claim to be victims until they have you by the throat. Jihad by immigration should be stopped in its tracks. The truth is we owe these people nothing, they come here for their own selfish reasons and have been instructed by their leaders and Koran NOT to integrate."

There was plenty more hate speech where that came from; and Old Alex might be all in favour of free speech, but to have this material freely posted on a government-sponsored website in the midst of an election campaign defied belief.

If it was a dog whistle to his right wing supporters, it was an extremely irresponsible one. If it was just incompetence, well that wasn't forgivable either.

In the early days of his reign Turnbull gifted half a million dollars to the

Islamic Museum of Australia for the development of an online research centre; and in a visit observed, according to a media release from his office, "a series of informative exhibits that illustrate the long and rich history of Islamic civilisation and the contribution Muslims have made to Australia. The museum exhibits demonstrate that, throughout our history, Muslims have been at the forefront of innovation, exploration and education and are a vital and integral part of the rich mosaic of Australian society.[278]

The mantra never varied: diversity enriches us all.

The truth lay elsewhere.

The Australian government mismanaged everything, and had badly mismanaged immigration.

The academic, bureaucratic dream of a secular, multicultural paradise was in ruins.

The result had been ethnic division, social chaos, unbridled discontent within large swathes of the population, and an increasing contempt for government evidenced by a dramatic rise in support for anti-immigration parties. And the increasingly authoritarian government crackdown on all dissent in an attempt to hide the truth. In the government's attempts to conceal their own disasters, the people had become the enemy.

Turnbull spoke about fostering resilient communities, increasing the participation of Muslims in all aspects of Australian life, challenging extremist propaganda from those who preyed on vulnerable youths and ensuring that Australians of all backgrounds worked together to uplift the nation. He encouraged Muslim youth to play an active role in strengthening Australia's diverse and tolerant social fabric.

In an official statement, President of the Islamic Council of Victoria, Bayram Aktepe said the Muslim communities of Victoria welcomed the unprecedented visit by an Australian Prime Minister: "Our leaders, and our young leaders of the future, welcome Prime Minister Malcolm Turnbull's fresh tone and positive message regarding the threat of terrorism and challenges of extremism. We look forward to working closely with the Turnbull Government to further enhance our social cohesion and advance this great nation of ours."[279]

---

278 Visit to Islamic Museum of Australia and Islamic Council of Victoria, Media Release, Malcolm Turnbull, 7 March, 2016.

279 Ibid.

Turnbull would later state it was clear at the meeting that young Muslim Australians had an ongoing anxiety about the backlash caused by the violent acts of a small minority of extremists who defame and blaspheme against their faith, and for which the entire Muslim community is often blamed.

> The aim of extremists, including those committing violence through a warped and nihilist interpretation of religion is to divide us and to turn our citizens against each other – but we will not let them win. Acts of terror . . . are perpetrated to divide us along lines of race, religion, sect and sexuality – but that kind of hatred and division must not prevail. We must stand together . . . as one Australian family united against terrorism, racism, discrimination and violence.[280]

In March Australian F/A-18 Hornets dropped 80 bombs on Iraq. In April 71 bombs were dropped. In May, 91.

Once again, no information on casualties or targets was released.

Some of the most vivid imagery to emerge from the two month long election campaign came from conflicting demonstrations between pro-immigration and anti-Muslim groups in Melbourne with, as had occurred the previous year, wild scenes of police tear gassing protesters and fights breaking out between the groups.

The Prime Minister talked of the most successful multicultural society on earth.

On the streets, they rioted.

On their Facebook page a member of the United Patriot Front warned: "Steel yourselves and prepare. Things are going to get ugly."

In Melbourne members of the Party for Freedom, the True Blue Crew and the United Patriot Front, assembled for their eighth confrontation since the previous November.

Many carried large Australian flags.

Police searched protesters for weapons. The state's Police Minister Lisa Neville said: "Victorians have had enough of seeing this sort of incitement of hatred and violence."

When people had no other avenue of expression, were essentially voice-less, they took to the streets.

---

280 Speech at Kirribilli House, Sydney, Malcolm Turnbull, 16 June, 2016.

The anti-Islamic protesters thought they were the true patriots.

They thought, in their hearts, the police actually supported them; that they, too, could not bear to see what had happened to their country.

Every last one of them was now likely to fall victim to the Surveillance State.

Government operatives condemned extremism. But unbeknown to many of the targets, it was those who dreamed of an old Australia who were deemed the extremists.

How sadly disillusioned they would become as they fell victim to a kind of government vigilantism, and all the harassment that in modern-day Australia followed from failing to adhere to the official narrative.

The government line was a ceaseless one of multicultural propaganda and refugee advocacy; billions of dollars worth, entire bureaucratic empires, all dedicated to ignoring the muddling middle ground. The country was paying the price for the arrogance of the elites who had systematically disregarded or dismissed the thousands of Tables of Knowledge dotted across the country, those places where media meant nothing and common sense prevailed.

Where did that extremism lie? With the martyrs prepared to sacrifice themselves for their fellow Muslims and for Allah? Or with those prepared to crush all dissent for a bureaucratic ideology? Who were prepared to destroy their own country in the name of freedom?

Placards included: "Islamic Refugees Not Welcome" and "Stop the Invasion".

On the other side placards read: "Welcome the Mosque" and "Say No To All Racism".

One protestor carried a poster in the Aboriginal colours of black yellow and burnt red with the words: "Not Yours To Reclaim".

To an interviewer Blair Cottrell, Chairman of United Patriots, said: "People come from all across Australia, people come from interstate, people come from everywhere. I think the people here are all willing to fight. I tell them, don't speak violence, but don't fear it."

In angry tones he declared to the gathering: "The English, the Irish, the Scottish, those responsible for building this country up, have nothing, nothing, but their own strict willpower and belief. We will walk in this land again as we did in the beginning. Good luck to anyone who tries to stop us. Let's move."[281]

---

281 Far left, far-right groups rally: Anti-Islam anti-racism groups protest in Melbourne, *The Age*, 26 June, 2016.

The group then marched through central Melbourne chanting: "Aussie pride, nationwide" and "We are taking our streets back".

Beside them, every step of the way, was a line of police equal in number, helmeted and heavily equipped, expecting violence.

More than 100 anti-racism activists had earlier gathered at the steps of Parliament, chanting lines including "No hate, no fear, fascists are not welcome here".

Police struggled to keep the opposing groups apart.

Vashti Kenway, from the Coalition against Racism and Fascism, said: "We want to send a clear message there are individuals and groups, hopefully of a significant amount, who support multiculturalism."[282]

More than 400 police were called in.

The clashes were costing Victorian taxpayers millions of dollars.

This was the Australia the Tables of Knowledge had foretold – and this was just the beginning.

In that early millennial period, as at so many other pivotal points in history, it was characteristic cruelty, indifference to life that came to the fore; and it came on every side of a rapidly devolving situation.

> Many and sharp the num'rous ills
> Inwoven with our frame!
> More pointed still we make ourselves,
> Regret, remorse, and shame!
> And man, whose heav'n-erected face
> The smiles of love adorn, –
> Man's inhumanity to man
> Makes countless thousands mourn![283]

In that ultimately interconnected world, anyone on Earth could watch a ten-year-old boy whose fathers and siblings had been killed in the bombing pick his way through the ruins of Aleppo and say: "The whole world is broken. I never see anybody playing anymore. The entire world has changed from top to bottom."[284]

Analysts warned of the jihad networks running and profiting from the flood of migrants into Europe.

---

282 Violence breaks out after anti-immigration, anti-racist rallies in Melbourne, ABC, 26 June, 2016.

283 Man Was Made to Mourn: A Dirge, Robert Burns, 1794. Off Robert Burns dot org.

284 Aleppo Boy who lost siblings: The Whole World is Broken, NBC, 24 August, 2016.

On the first official day of winter the Australian of the Year, former Army chief, the hopelessly politically correct Lieutenant-General David Morrison, launched a Diversity Council Australia video which aimed to crack down on language which excluded minority groups.

He made news around the country by declaring that the term "guys" should no longer be used in workplaces and he was determined to delete it from his lexicon.

> Exclusive language, gender-based language or inappropriate language, has as much a deleterious or disadvantaged effect as something where you're saying something blatantly inappropriate to another human being, I have now removed that from my lexicon as best I can, I think it's important.[285]

Never mind that most Australians wouldn't know what the word lexicon meant; and that both men and women used the term "guys" in a friendly, gender-neutral and inclusive way.

Meanwhile in Victoria co-founder of the so-called Safe Schools program Ms Roz Ward, a former member of the gay and transgender advisory committee, was suspended after revelations she had described the Australian flag as racist and called for it to be replaced with a red communist flag.

Gay activist Rob Mitchell complained he was sacked from his advisory role after complaining that the Safe Schools program, which began as an anti-bullying campaign, had been hijacked by radical queer theorists determined to deconstruct traditional notions of gender.

The material for the program, which would become compulsory in Victorian secondary state schools in 2018, told teachers not to refer to students as "boys and girls", as the terms were "heterosexist".

George Orwell was very sick while writing his last book *Nineteen eighty-four*, having been diagnosed with tuberculosis, and died in 1950, the year after the book was published. Regarded as one of the great tracts of English literature, in 2016 it would have struggled to find a publisher. It was entirely prophetic:

> We're destroying words--scores of them, hundreds of them, every day . . .

---

285 #WordsAtWork: David Morrison wants Australians to stop saying gender-based terms like 'guys', Andrew Greene and Kristian Silva, ABC, 2 June, 2016.

It's a beautiful thing, the destruction of words.

In your heart you'd prefer to stick to Oldspeak, with all its vagueness and its useless shades of meaning. You don't grasp the beauty of the destruction of words.

Don't you see that the whole aim of Newspeak is to narrow the range of thought? In the end we shall make thoughtcrime literally impossible, because there will be no words in which to express it.

Every year fewer and fewer words, and the range of consciousness always a little smaller. The Revolution will be complete when the language is perfect.

The fifth night of winter and the primary subject of conversation was the weather, with a slow moving low pressure system bringing heavy rains and highs up and down the East Coast.

The national broadcaster led its nightly news with a story on football, followed by another on a lost seven-year-old boy who had been found five days after disappearing in Japan, as if Australia didn't have any lost children of its own; followed by a story on tennis and then another on the continuing controversy in America over the shooting of a gorilla after a child had fallen into its enclosure.

Nothing of substance.

Big Brother was very happy.

The Lie had survived another day.

A person on their own is vulnerable and one of the reasons Alex had been happy enough in the attic was that there were always people around but he was free to come and go. Peter was the most gregarious person he had ever met. Striking up a conversation or catching up on the local gossip was never a problem; and there was always the Carlisle opposite if he wanted company, which he frequently did.

But just like the summer itself, the security and safety he sought was illusory.

Unable to concentrate, one morning Old Alex went down, in that interminable winter full of dark skies and black rain, to park by the sea at Shellharbour and watch the sunrise. Within minutes the police were cruising his vehicle, shortly thereafter demanding to know why he was there.

It was a quarter to six in the morning.

Weren't you even allowed to watch the sunrise these days?

The owner of the cafe where he habitually went to have his morning coffee told him they had seen the police car cruising in the empty main street, bored, nearing the end of their shift, when they had suddenly turned on their flashing lights and headed down to where he was parked.

It was true. He was a Targeted Individual, a TI. He was 64-years-old. What could he possibly be guilty of at that hour of the morning?

The country had become a joke.

He was unflappable, presenting as a doddery old man, unfailingly polite, worried he might not have paid off a parking ticket, giving no lip, and soon enough they left him to sit inside his car, battered by the rain.

That night, Tuesday 9th of August, 2016, was the much touted Australian Census, with a more intrusive array of personal or agenda driven questions than ever before. The Australian government, the creator of the Panopticon Down Under, made repeated assurances that the privacy of the public's data would be protected. If anyone believed them they needed their heads read.

There was no privacy in Australia, none whatsoever.

The Census, once a source of national pride, promptly turned to farce. The website crashed after repeated cyber attacks.

Officials had been releasing warnings that cyber warfare was the next frontier, but whether or not it was terror-related the government did not say.

Instead Turnbull praised the work of the Australian Signals Directorate, claiming they were the best in the world.

The government couldn't even get its messaging straight on this one. The Australian Bureau of Statistics head claimed the scale of the attacks demonstrated they were clearly malicious, while the Minister responsible denied there had even been attacks.

They couldn't lie straight in bed.

What was true was that Australia was a prime target; and the country's politicians had played a major role in making that the case.

There would be considerably worse than cyber attacks to come.

Already disturbed by the new book, the edgy, swirling dreams that inevitably went with it, the coming apocalypse, the deadening manipulation of public discourse he saw all around him, the flak jacket that had to be worn at all times, Alex kept locking the back doors only to have them promptly, dismissively unlocked. There were cameras throughout the house, from the bedroom to the bathroom to the backyard, and there was no privacy. There might have been one solution, to stop writing, but that was no solution at all.

He was reading a book *Spooked: The Truth About Intelligence in Australia*, a collection of essays on the secretive world most Australians knew nothing about, and he left it on the kitchen bench.

One day, taking advantage of a rare burst of sunshine and free time, he went and sat up in Camperdown Park, in front of the graffiti-coated stone wall abutting the cemetery, and idly watched a mother playing with her child, a couple with their chocolate Labrador, a group of students sharing a joint.

He saw and heard everything, he was in that state of mind: the wind curling in the trees, fragments of conversation from the surrounding terrace houses.

A large, surprisingly ugly young woman dressed in the black-tent uniform of the local Goths walked the length of the park, 300 metres or so, to where he was sitting, patted a little dog playing a few feet away from him, and said more than loud enough for him to hear: "You're spooked, aren't you? You're utterly spooked."

And walked back the way she came.

He went back to the Big White House which had briefly passed as a home, where *Spooked* lay prominently displayed.

And thought: "This is fucked."

These people were dangerously incompetent, or deliberately cruel.

"All I can say is that Newtown practises a fringe style of community policing," Glen advised him.

The night was long and once again he felt like prey, sad old prey. He could not sleep, only pretending to be unconscious under an intense gaze.

The next morning, for work, he had to assemble potted biographies of those who had just died in the Orlando massacre in Florida.

The piece was meant to be called 48 Reasons To Stop the Hate, that being the initial number of people named by police as having been killed at the Pulse nightclub, a gay venue.

Decades before, Alex had written his sociology thesis on gay bars. It was easy to imagine the scene inside that bar, as Omar Mateen kept shooting and shooting. The lads were just out to have fun, pick each other up, dance till dawn, relax after a week at work.

He had already read the calls for attacks on gay bars worldwide, the claims of responsibility for the massacre by Islamic State and the celebratory comments of their followers about that "blessed attack on the sodomites":

> A hate crime? Yes. Muslims undoubtedly hate liberalist sodomites, as does anyone else with their fitrah (inborn human nature) still intact. An act of terrorism? Most definitely. Muslims have been commanded to terrorise the disbelieving enemies of Allah. But an act of senseless violence?[286]

Under surveillance, struggling to get the internet working on his laptop, trapped under the attic window, he began to record the deaths.

With each potted biography his blood pressure increased until, as he knew from previous experience, it began to hit dangerous levels.

Alex wrote, or more accurately compiled:

1. Edward Sotomayor, 34, from Sarasota, Florida. Worked as the national brand manager for Al and Chuck Travel, part of America's largest gay owned travel company. A tribute on the company website says Eddie, as he was lovingly known, touched the lives of everyone he came in contact with. "His light will forever shine bright within our hearts."

2. Stanley Almodovar III, 23, Clermont, Florida. Worked as a pharmacy technician. According to his profile, he had previously worked at Walgreens and Target. One tribute on his Facebook page said: "I'll miss you my friend. Stay smiling and make sure you have jokes for me up in heaven!" In a tribute another friend said: "He made me feel it was perfectly fine being who I was."

3. Juan Ramon Guerrero, 22. A student at the University of Central Florida. He worked as a telemarketer. A cousin said he was not the type who liked to go out to parties. He preferred to stay home and look after his niece and nephew. His boyfriend Christopher "Drew" Leinonen was with him at Pulse during the shooting and was also killed.

---

286 *Dabiq*, Volume 13, August, 2016.

That was as far as he got.

He cancelled the job and went straight up to see the pharmacist, who confirmed his blood pressure was dangerously high.

He went back to the attic, threw his passport and clothes into his bag, packed up the car and left, offering no explanation.

Trust no one.

Betrayal was everywhere.

He had long been expecting a similar attack in Australia.

Was it really just a coincidence that Islamic cleric Farrokh Sekaleshfar, who had been preaching in Orlando prior to the massacre, was in Sydney that week, preaching as an honoured guest at an Islamic Centre in Earlwood, a suburb in the city's inner-west?

Sekaleshfar was no outlier. The University of Western Sydney first invited him to Australia two years before. Sekaleshfar had spoken at an Islamic Centre outside Orlando on the subject: "What to do about the phenomenon of homosexuality."

In one video he was quoted as saying: "Death is the sentence. There's nothing to be embarrassed about this. Death is the sentence. We have to have that compassion for people. With homosexuals, it's the same. Out of compassion, let's get rid of them now."[287]

In an interview with *The Australian* newspaper the cleric clarified his comments:

> Just because you find something uncomfortable as a Muslim, you shouldn't feel embarrassed about it – this is law according to Islam. When the judiciary wants to commit the death sentence, they shouldn't do it for the sake of killing the person. Their intention should be, look this person is a sinner ... by killing him he will no longer sin and therefore we are saving him in the hereafter, that's what I mean by it's the compassionate thing to do."[288]

Nowhere was safe.

Australia's dubious military alliances were coming home to roost.

The country was, under the mantle of the War on Islamic State, in mili-

287 Orlando Shooting: gay death cleric Farrokh Sekaleshfar preaching in Sydney, *The Australian*, 14 June, 2016.

288 Ibid.

tary alliance with Saudi Arabia, where women could not swim in a public pool or drive a car.

Homosexuals, apostates, drug users, blasphemers, fornicators, atheists, those accused of sedition or waging war on God, were executed, usually by beheading with a sword, sometimes by firing squad or stoning.

Medieval it might be; but Australia was going right along with it.

Saudi Arabia, with the United States, was a prime prosecutor of the war in Yemen – where thousands had died in the previous months. The haunting images of starving children on nightly television screens were brought to viewers courtesy of Australia's allies.

Along with the neighbouring Arab states, these were the regimes Australia was now in bed with.

That there were now numerous people in Australia, brought in under the mantle of multiculturalism, who believed the same, that gays, lesbians and transgender people, the so-called LGBTQI community, should be put to death, was an obvious consequence of government policy.

Tolerance of intolerance was cowardice: "Unlimited tolerance must lead to the disappearance of tolerance. If we extend unlimited tolerance even to those who are intolerant, if we are not prepared to defend a tolerant society against the onslaught of the intolerant, then the tolerant will be destroyed, and tolerance with them."[289]

All the talk of marriage equality, and the society was going backwards. It was no coincidence that there were now fewer gay bars in Sydney than there had been forty years before.

Every bar was a target for those who believed they would be doing God's work, and showing compassion, by dispatching everyone in them.

The authorities knew this perfectly well.

Venue after venue closed down.

That there were now a significant number of Muslims within the police and security forces who also believed homosexuals and transgender people would be better off put to death was also no secret.

Apps such as Grindr – which had been utilised by the Orlando attacker, Omar Mateen – particularly popular amongst the city's gay men for setting up the short term liaisons which the bedrock of their sexual lives, were

---

289 *The Open Society and its Enemies*, Karl Popper, Routledge, 2002. Originally published 1945.

perfect snitch devices to determine exactly who was doing what to whom when and where, thereby imperilling everybody.

Australia had once been a remarkably tolerant society, the basic attitude being: "I don't care who you fuck, as long as you're not fucking me".

Despite a blizzard of propaganda about diversity and tolerance, by 2016 such blithe, *laissez faire* forms of working class tolerance had disappeared. Nobody liked being told what they could and could not think.

With the debate over marriage equality aka gay marriage running rampant in the media, there were many controversies over the Muslim community's attitudes towards homosexuality, including what was being taught in heavily funded Islamic schools.

Essentially one state creed was conflicting with another.

The principal of Al-Faisal College in Sydney's west, Ghazwa Khan, said they had never had a child who was gay because they were warned against homosexuality in the home.

> We've never had any child who says these things because they are being taught at home how to behave and know that this is not recommended. We've never had this issue at all, we've never had it. I think the students know their limit and they are taught at home what to say and what not to say.[290]

Australia's best known Muslim spokesman Keysar Trad said: "This is something that is clearly spelt out in the Koran and the hadith, that sex is only between a husband and a wife who are of the opposite gender and we have absolutely no mandate to change the grace of God. At school, all kids are told that they should not practise sex until they are married."[291]

The Australian adventure into that godless world of liberality and tolerance was essentially over. Islam dominated public discourse out of all proportion to the two percent of the population Muslims represented, shouldering out discussion of every other ethnic and religious minority and creating deep resentments in the broader population. Sharia law became increasingly more plausible, or feared.

In sections of those ethnic states within states which were the face of multiculturalism it was already operating.

---

290 Ibid.

291 Islamic school 'has never had a child who was gay', Sharri Markson, *The Australian*, 8 August, 2016.

Everything was shifting.

Prime Minister Malcolm Turnbull held an Iftar dinner at Kirribilli House, the traditional residence of the Prime Minister in Sydney, the first ever such event marking the holy month of Ramadan. It was meant to signal a new era of cooperation and conciliation and was a grand affair.

In his welcoming speech Turnbull said he wanted to emphasise to the Muslim community that they were valued and respected and were not viewed through a narrow security prism.

Turnbull had long forgotten the difference between rhetoric and reality, process and substance.

In entertainment tents set up on the lawns of Kirribilli House, which boasted spectacular views across to Garden Island, the Opera House and the Harbour Bridge, the Prime Minister told a collection of the most senior Islamic figures in the country that Muslims were an integral part of an Australian family that rested on the essential foundation of mutual respect and understanding. Every one of us, he declared, is enriched by the culture and the faiths of our friends and neighbours.

> We are the most successful and harmonious multicultural society in the world. Our multicultural success is at the heart of our national identity. It is intrinsic to our history and our character. Every one of us is enriched by the culture and the faiths of our friends and neighbours.

> Australians are not defined by religion or race; we are defined by a common commitment to shared political values, democracy, freedom, the rule of law, all underpinned of course by mutual respect.

> Our humanity and our destiny – each of our destinies – are tied one to all the others.[292]

If only it was all true.

Assembled guests included Sheik Shady al-Suleiman, President of the National Imams Council, who had previously called on God to destroy the enemies of Islam and urged his followers to prepare for jihad. He had previously said he believed AIDS was a "divine punishment" for gays and adulterers should be stoned to death. Old Alex had seen his own friends die of

---

292 Speech at Kirribilli House, Prime Minister Malcolm Turnbull, 16 June, 2016.

AIDS; had watched, as a reporter, an entire generation of some of Sydney's most creative people suffer long, lingering and immensely sad deaths. They were dying before their time. They did not go easily. This was God's will?

Scandals would continue to reverberate in the days following the dinner; including the news that special crockery was trucked in for the event because some Muslims preferred not to eat off plates previously used by infidels.

Every way you walked from the centre of an ideological cloudburst lay fragile sensitivities, multiple contradictions, crystalline creatures who could cut and fray, unmistakable danger.

Repeatedly hunted from his home for the sin of writing the truth and thereby upsetting senior figures in the national security apparatus, driving down country lanes and byways, Old Alex flicked between government-controlled radio channels: a rock station, a classical music station, a local talkback station obsessing about the audience's relationships with their dishwashers... and Radio National, where speaker after speaker warbled on about empathy, compassion for the vulnerable, renewing faith in humanity, intellectual frontiers.

At the various cottages where he sometimes stayed the television also came courtesy of the government-run Australian Broadcasting Commission; and he would occasionally watch in frustration the highly manipulated debates. Show after show – the interviewer, the interviewee, the politicians, lobbyists, activists, academics, every last one of them on the government payroll.

Of genuine community debate there was none.

It was the supreme whitewash. The people were paying for their own indoctrination.

As he once summed it up on a community radio program: "The liars, the lawyers, the bureaucrats and the social engineers have won the day."

They had won the battle, but they did not win the war.

Instead they were destroying the host.

Alex heard the government-funded thugs in the walls of Newtown; flight and fright mechanisms kicked in.

Threat was everywhere.

What could have been a home or at least a bolt-hole had become another prison; in his waking dreams a prism of harsh edges and hostile eyes, of vindictive liars, easily manipulated flash crowds, bullies.

Just as he had done as a child, he walked down the road and never went back.

It was the fifth time he had been made homeless in three years; his house burnt down, hounded, hounded, hounded.

If the public truly knew how their money was being spent the electorate would turn their dislike and distrust of the overlords into plans for revolution.

Plagued, disturbed, distressed by the ceaseless surveillance, Old Alex put up a note at the beginning of the manuscript he was working on, addressed to those he had taken to calling the Watchers on the Watch:

> Please note that I regard this surveillance as harassment, intimidation and abuse. It has gone on for years. It has had extremely negative consequences on my health and well being.
>
> Your actions are illegal.
>
> You may be immune from prosecution for illegal conduct, but this does not protect you.
>
> Nothing in the legislation permits you to harass, bully, intimidate, place under extremely invasive surveillance or invade the places of dwelling of a journalist as you have done to me.
>
> As previously stated, this abuse has gone on literally for years. You have exposed the worst aspects of Australian security and policing.
>
> Cease and desist.

They had forgotten the old truism: point a finger at someone and there are three fingers pointing back.

He wrote to the media office of the Attorney General complaining about the surveillance and asking for the procedures to make a formal complaint. From what he could discern such procedures barely existed, and those which did were, if the bureaucracy was running true to form, deliberate blind canyons, traps, expensive, long winded, complex and time-consuming.

Resolution, much less justice, rarely lay at the end of these processes; and while the bureaucracies might alter their future behaviour, they rarely ever apologised.

Glen, whom he had begun to think of as a friend, said: "It's pathetic, thousands of personnel, billions of dollars. You're just one person. You just have to laugh at them."

A crippled old man with nothing but a laptop… well, that was the way he had begun to think of himself: diminished, shrinking, battered, and bruised.

Frightened as much of having a heart attack as of those who pursued him, Alex arrived on the south coast, at an ordinary suburban house in an excruciatingly quiet suburb, the home of an elderly relative. It was a place which should have been safe, where he should have been free from torment.

Nothing of the kind happened.

All the mad, targeted voices he was meant to hear rose from one of the nearby houses: "Whore of Babylon. Whore of Babylon."

Fundamentalist Christians, fundamentalist Muslims worshipping the same God, condemning the evil spawn of Allah, believing the line: We are the best of people. The mantra of tolerance and diversity which was the government's official narrative did not reach this far into the cabals of the suburbs.

> And the woman was dressed in purple and scarlet, and adorned with gold and precious stones and pearls. She held in her hand a golden cup full of abominations and the impurities of her sexual immorality. On her forehead a mysterious name was written: Babylon the Great, the mother of prostitutes and of the abominations of the earth. I could see that the woman was drunk with the blood of the saints and of the witnesses for Jesus. And I was greatly astonished at the sight of her.…
>
> The beast that you saw was, and now is no more, but is about to come up out of the abyss and go to its destruction.
>
> This calls for a mind that has wisdom.[293]

They should have been frightened, very frightened, as they mumbled incantations before their dark lord.

Transcluscent. Trascendent. W.B. Yeats:

> A shape with lion body and the head of a man,
> A gaze blank and pitiless as the sun,
> Is moving its slow thighs, while all about it
> Wind shadows of the indignant desert birds.
>
> The darkness drops again but now I know
> That twenty centuries of stony sleep

---

293 Revelations 17: 4-9, Berean Study Bible.

Were vexed to nightmare by a rocking cradle,
And what rough beast, its hour come round at last,
Slouches towards Bethlehem to be born?[294]

The centre could not hold. Anarchy had been loosed upon the world; the blood-dimmed tide was rising.

Alex would have put it more prosaically: "Be careful who you pray to."

He could see in his dreams the rising Beast their chanting prayers invoked. Spirits turn on those who unleashed them. Blood lust will be requited, one way or another.

They weren't praying for his soul. They were praying out of fear and for their own selfish redemption, and for him to be damned. They wished to kill that which they did not understand. For them the mystery that passeth all understanding was a plateau of servitude, planked out.

His pursuers had left a mile-wide trail of unethical and incompetent behaviour which any internal review committee should have been able to spot in an instant.

And it led straight to the suited bullies at the top, the same bullies who had tormented him in the schoolyard half a century before; mesmerised by their own power, hated by their staff.

Commercially available advertising technology could target an individual walking past a billboard with words which only they could hear, already tailored from information gleaned by their internet and shopping habits specifically at their interests.

It wasn't such a giant leap to target him.

He discovered, and he wasn't about to explain how, that the authorities had even been picking through an elderly relative's house, snooping through papers, taking photographs. She complained, in the following days, that her contact book with all her codes and contacts, was missing. He wouldn't have put it past them.

Life had gone full circle. He had not felt so dishonoured, so invaded and so deliberately battered since the day when, as a 14-year-old, he had swallowed a bottle of aspirin after school and walked along the beach at Newport in tears, waiting to die. When he didn't die, and went forlornly home, he was belted for being late home from school.

---

294 The Second Coming, W.B. Yeats, 1919.

It was over. They had brought havoc upon themselves, and would continue to do so. If they all lost their jobs it would be too good for them.

He walked free from the fire.

After all the abuse, the invasion, the dishonesty perpetrated by the authorities invading the houses of family members was a step too far. He didn't have any faith left to lose, or he would have lost it all.

It took him some days to calm down.

There was no use appealing to a higher virtue. The base had won.

Or thought they had.

This was a time to rediscover power; not a time to hide.

Take no hostages, know no fear.

Whatever honey trap he may or may not have fallen into, nobody could have cared less except that he was a journalist and a writer; and as he had been doing since childhood, continued to work.

But the times had turned cold, and extremely hostile to the Word, the foundation of civilisation.

Misconduct by the professions, misconduct by the agencies, it was all he could think about.

Journalism had once been a once respected profession, one of its fundamental roles to expose the misconduct of the powerful; but just like the government, journalism had betrayed those it was meant to serve, becoming little more than entertainment, the opium of the masses; even the bombings, the crying children, the riots, the blood spattered bodies and frantic medical teams, all of it was just diversion, patterns on a screen.

The price for compromise, on all sides of the fence, was a loss of credibility, and ultimately an end to the power brought by a respectful citizenry. Instead disbelief reigned.

He complained constantly about the surveillance – which in itself produced a kind of madness. He chanted to the microphone in the car: "Repeat after me. I will never bully, harass or intimidate anyone ever again. I will never lie or spread false rumours about anyone ever again."

Go forth and do good. Help others. Get another job. Find your vocation.

The only journalists to escape this new frontier of social control were the ones singing from the song sheets of the elites; acting as conduits for government propaganda.

On his early morning walks, in storm dark sunrises, the lamp posts appeared as crosses disappearing into a distance of storm bashed eucalypts; a Golgotha of the south.

While the Western oligarchies used the War on Terror as a cloaking mantle to increase by stealth their own wealth and oppress their own peoples, it was a Jesuit, the Soldier of God Pope Francis, who declared the world at war.

The declaration followed the assassination of Jacques Hamel, 85, a French priest butchered at his own alter by two Islamic State supporters.

The attackers shouted Allahu Akbar, God is great, and forced Hamel to kneel.

They reportedly filmed themselves as they recorded a sermon in Arabic.

Then they slit the elderly priest's throat.

A nun present in the church said one of the attackers smiled at her, "a soft smile, that of someone who is happy".

After the killing the two men began discussing the Koran. One of them said "Peace, it's what we want ... as long as there are bombs on Syria, we will continue our attacks. And they will happen every day. When you stop, we will stop."[295]

The local archbishop issued a statement: "I cry out to God with all men of good will."

Pope Francis said: "Let's recognise it. The world is at war. We should not be afraid to speak this truth. The world is at war."[296]

After being cautioned by advisers Pope Francis revised his statement to say that it was a war about special interests, money, natural resources and dominion over people, and claimed that all religions wanted peace.

In response Islamic State published a statement in their official magazine *Dabiq* saying Pope France's claim that Islam was a religion of peace struggled against reality:

> This is a divinely-warranted war between the Muslim nation and the nations of disbelief. Indeed, waging jihad – spreading the rule of Allah by the sword – is an obligation found in the Quran, the word of our Lord. The blood of the disbelievers is obligatory to spill by default. The command is clear. Kill the

---

295 France church attackers smiled and talked of peace, nun says, *The Guardian*, 30 July, 2016.

296 Killing of innocents proof 'the world is at war', says Pope Francis, Lisa Miller, ABC, 28 July, 2016.

disbelievers, as Allah said, Then kill the polytheists wherever you find them. The gist of the matter is that there is indeed a rhyme to our terrorism, warfare, ruthlessness, and brutality. The fact is, even if you were to stop bombing us, imprisoning us, torturing us, vilifying us, and usurping our lands, we would continue to hate you because our primary reason for hating you will not cease to exist until you embrace Islam. Even if you were to pay *jizyah* [tax for infidels] and live under the authority of Islam in humiliation, we would continue to hate you.[297]

Temperatures were below normal across the continent, there in that freezing winter. In his waking dreams, he knew why the planet had become such a focus for the gods. Humans were not called vessels of the soul for nothing. Of all the life scattered through the cosmos, they had proved particularly receptive.

And now was harvest time.

It was natural, as a retired news reporter, that Old Alex would follow with particular interest the failing fortunes of his old profession.

They were all intertwined: the bestial behaviour of the police and the authorities which had been allowed to flourish, the miserably quiet, damp streets, the florid rains, Downton Abbey, the fact that he could not find peace, not even here in this remote outpost at this remote time of life. That with the prevailing use of keylogging technology every word he wrote was used in whispering campaigns against him; in this brutal, smug, dead place where the authorities were using highly dubious techniques to intimidate a reporter.

Ironically, in his own profession and particular field of interest, the media, the most cogent solution came from someone on the government payroll – the same government which had just passed rafts of the legislation destroying the country's once valued freedom of speech.

Graeme Dobell, Journalist Fellow at the Australian Strategic Policy Institute, funded by the Defence Department but not restricted to the propagandistic functions it so often demanded, was scathing of the military's traditional hostility to the media.

Technology had outstripped them, but they were yet to realise it.

A century of Oz military history reveals a tendency to see Oz

---

297 Islamic State answers Pope Francis: Ours is a Religion of War and We Hate You, *Breitbart*, 2 August, 2016.

journalists as only slightly less dangerous than the enemy. An attack from the rear, deploying large headlines, is dreaded.

At the centre of the mindset is secrecy, often an all-purpose shroud. Defence shares the secrecy habit with everybody else in official Canberra.

The standard political and military approach to journalists is to use and abuse. When things go wrong and the going gets tough, the political/military approach shifts gear to shut 'em out and shut 'em up.[298]

The Australian Strategic Policy Institute was funded by the Defence Department but maintained an arms-length relationship with government, allowing its experts to generate ideas without becoming hostage to the political opportunists of the day.

Concurrently with Alex's own travails, attempts to shut him up and shut him down, Journalistic Fellow with the Institute Graeme Dobell made an impassioned, cogent call for change to the military's traditionally hostile approach to the media.

There was history, plenty of history.

In WWI and WWII the shut-up tool was powerful censorship laws.

The military can no longer censor what hacks write or broadcast or tweet. Instead, there's 'media policy'. Control the information flow. Hire lots of Media Minders. Direct the story. Stay on message. Talk about what you want to talk about.

Negative or unwanted yarns are subject to 'damage control' and 'rapid response' and 'clarification'; even a carefully-phrased denial.

Mount the counter-attack of talking points. If something bad happens on your patch, try to shift the news cycle with diversion or feint. Give 'em different, fresh meat—don't look here, look over there at this new, shiny thing.

In Canberra, the shut-up/shut out habit is political practice and bureaucratic custom as well as ANZAC tradition.[299]

---

298 Oz military media policy: shut 'em out, shut 'em up, Greaeme Dobell, The Strategist, 4 April, 2016.

299 Ibid.

The stated reasons for the shut-up shut-out policies of the Defence Department were to protect lives and get accurate information to the Australian people.

The real reasons were to provide political advantage for the government and the Defence Minister, to burnish the image of the government and the Defence Department, to provide embarrassment protection, bury cock-ups and feed the Australian people a diet of government approved messages.[300]

The central purposes of the old strategies had been to coordinate and control information flows in order to serve the power of the day. But as Dobell puts it, hiding information becomes a gamble instead of a judgement call. The next data dump could blow up all those secrets in a single moment.

> Power, though, is dispersing because the Media Age makes it so.
>
> The Media Age is about communication more than control. The creations of communication can overthrow control and subvert secrecy at the touch of a key.
>
> The massive data dump of 'Secrets'—government or business— is a motif of the Media Age. The hacker performs as both criminal and Digital Citizen guerrilla.
>
> Operational secrecy? Media guidelines? Sorry, sir, it's already up and out there—Twittered and videoed and Facebooked and blogged and Instagrammed and YouTubed…and…and… and… [301]

The public wanted to hear, if they thought about foreign wars at all, that they could be proud of their soldiers and they were not dying in vain, that their money was being well spent, the wars in which their country was involved were just, and that the homeland was safer for the sacrifice.

The problem was, the traditional shut 'em up shut 'em out strategies weren't working. Nobody trusted the media anymore, with good reason, and nobody believed a word the politicians said either; instead they had stopped listening altogether.

There was, as Dobell pointed out, a solution to it all. But first the problem

300 Oz Media and the wrong lessons of Afghanistan, Graeme Dobell, *The Strategist*, 9 May, 2016.
301 Defence confronts the Media Age, Graeme Dobell, The Strategist, 16 May, 2016.

had to be understood, and Dobell began with a quote from Marshall McLuhan: "Electric circuitry has overthrown the regime of 'time' and 'space' and pours upon us instantly and continuously the concerns of all other men.[302]

Dobell went on to use the example of Afghanistan, regarded as the most secretive war in Australian history, to illustrate that traditional tactics of dealing with the media no longer worked.

In Afghanistan 41 soldiers died and more than were 300 seriously wounded, essentially in secret. Thousands more would suffer some degree of psychological damage for the rest of their lives.

Those lucky enough to return were not embraced by a grateful nation, who knew nothing about their deeds.

The enormous expenditure of resources and the energies of young soldiers building schools and mosques for Afghanis, promptly looted by the Taliban, would have been better off spent on Australia's crumbling infrastructure.

Surveys showed the majority of Australians did not support the country's involvement in this virtually invisible war and did not regard the loss of life as justifiable.

But their political masters were happy. They got away with it, unfortunately. And the only way they got away with it was through concealment.

From his own standpoint, the war was already on. Like any other soldier, Alex was forced to pray for protection. There was no Desmarquet to help him now.

As Dobell, a journalist of 45 years standing, wrote, the Media Age had been dawning since the middle of the 20th Century, yet institutions failed to adapt, their every attempt at concealment and at exerting greater control over information failing. His sarcasm could equally be applied to the intelligence and security wings of government.

> It's a tribute to the ability of the Defence Department and the Australian Defence Force to fight old wars that that so much effort is still concentrated on the traditional foe, The Press or News Media.

The fear of hacks reaches towards phobia. Be on guard against

---

302 *The Medium is the Massage: An Inventory of Effects*, Marshall McLuhan and Quentin Fiore, Penguin Books, 1967.

monsters that feed on inaccuracy and misrepresentation. Disclosure is dangerous. Uncoordinated messages will be punished.

Striking that, there's not much emphasis on the speedy deployment of maximum truth firepower to occupy the Information high ground and triumph in the Media Age battle.

Instead of communication, the core Defence message is about coordination and control. These are the tactics for old battles not the new frontiers that have already arrived.[303]

The wars the bureaucracy's were fighting, against truthsayers, journalists, purveyors of information and believers in the public's right to know, using the panopticon, Psyops, social engineering, financial lures, threats, strategic alliances, tranches of restrictive legislation, the creation of a compliant and ill-informed population, by targeting individuals, crushing dissent, defunding and destroying the country's arts sector, and by procuring much of the country's media and sources of information into government controlled hands, all the effort was wasted.

Whatever secrets the Defence Department and the security agencies held – and most of them were about their own dysfunctional bureaucracies, over-paid public servants, misplaced programmes and abject wastes of public money – a world where it was impossible to lie was dawning.

As Dobell advised the government, their wildly inflated phobias about journalists, that mighty monster called The Press, were misguided and serving them poorly in a rapidly evolving environment.

The hack world is unravelling at warp speed.

The beast evolved to become the Media—big and rich newspapers, television and radio. That time and those riches are now gone.

The mighty Media creatures of the 20th Century will not survive.

The mass audience is splintering and the mass that was once mass Media is going with it. The behemoths of The Press are lesser beasts as their readers and markets dash away through digital portals. The digital disruption dominates.

303 Defence and the Media Age Pt 1, Graeme Dobell, *The Strategist*, Australian Strategic Policy Institute, 16 May, 2016.

The dismal state of Australian internet and of the country's telecommunications, deliberately engineered to keep the population suppressed, was about to be transformed.

The blue rotating circle, the buffering symbol which was Australians most common experience of the internet, the best known and most frustrating symbol in Australia, would be replaced.

Google was well advanced in its plans to put low orbiting satellites and drones around the world, to bring high quality internet to the entire Earth's population, including the remotest parts of Australia.

The world was already at a stage when billions of individual users acted as more than customers, they function as Digital Citizens. Billions of Digital Citizens; the mark of their citizenship the smartphone they carry.

> The Enlightenment marked the shift of the people from being subjects to citizens; the Media Age creates customers who demand the rights of Digital Citizens.
>
> The Media Age changes the game in fundamental ways. Journalism and journalists will not disappear . . . But the digital comets have hit. The atmosphere is changed forever. New realities throb. Competing media realities rise.
>
> These Digital Citizens have the tools and reach once controlled by the Media; today you don't need a TV station to be a broadcaster, nor own a printing press to be a publisher.[304]

Now was the time for a New Enlightenment.

The developing communications power that billions of Digital Citizens would shortly hold was just one example of the fluidity and creative destruction surging through the Age.

The old techniques of working through press offices with a known set of contacts in the mainstream media, many of whom were happy enough to be kept on a leash in return for stories, or the even more tried and true tactic of deny, deny, deny, then obfuscate, could no longer work. Nor would the tried and true tactic of diversion: look over there, a bright, shiny thing, just what your editor wants: a new story.

The diminished state of the media had for a time served the government well.

---

304 Ibid.

Unlike days of yore, no news organisation could any longer afford the months it sometimes took for an experienced journalist or teams of journalists to disclose malfeasance and misconduct in public administration.

Once official media releases were regarded with little more than suspicion.

By the time Alex left full time work, most newsrooms were happy to snap up government releases as the story of the day.

Journalists of the new millennium had very short attention spans, and were expected to churn out multiple stories every day.

Throughout his career Old Alex had stubbornly insisted, whenever he could get away with it, on doing only one story a day.

In his later years, he would argue with his Chief of Staff that you could write one story a day well, or slap your byline across half a dozen lightly rewritten press releases. Take your pick.

The bosses weren't always impressed by his truculence.

He didn't much care. He had been beyond caring before they were even born.

But for both the government and the media it was all backfiring.

By failing to take the stick to government, the media lost credibility, respect, and profitability, with sales in steep decline.

On the converse, by ceaselessly churning out propaganda and refusing to engage with their critics or justify their programs, governments lost support.

The arguments applied to war as much as they did to social policy.

And it was all about to change.

Dobell argued that on the battlefield, the soldier would run slap bang into a Digital Citizen on every corner, over every rise.

That Citizen had the capacity to bear witness, to record, to broadcast, to report, to proclaim – to speak truth to power at the touch of a button.

As Dobell noted, the Afghanistan War, Australia's longest and most secretive of wars, would be the last war the Australian Defence Force fought where it would not be surrounded by Digital Citizens all armed with smartphones.

The Afghanistan War was fought in remote villages amongst poor populations, many of whom could not afford smartphones or in situations so remote the technology did not work.

The war had little public support, in reality, apart from spasms of a reflexive and ill-informed nationalism, no support.

The consent, if it could even be called that, at least the lack of coordinated opposition, was only achieved through the cloak of extreme secrecy which had characterised Australia's military involvement in Iraq, Syria and elsewhere.

There would be no more helicopter battleships machine-gunning down innocents without the world instantly knowing.

The corporal might have the gun but the Digital Citizen had media clout.

With the cheapening and ubiquitous spread of the technology, the Army could no longer conduct their wars without being filmed.

Already most of the images of injured and crying children as a result of Western supported bomb attacks which were flooding the internet and the nightly news coverage of the Middle East came from smartphones. With each injured child, with each fresh outrage, indignation increased. People wanted to know one basic question: Why? And why is my country, my tax dollars, supporting this?

The solution: Truth with Speed.

It sounded simple, but for the Defence Department, the Australian Defence Force, the national security agencies, and for almost all of the government apparatus, local, state and federal, straddling Australian society, it was entirely revolutionary.

> The communications demands of the Media Age are so diverse and complex that only a simple answer will suffice.

> This is back-to-basics meets back-to-the future. Head to the bedrock of first principles while everything else in the Media Age goes into the flux capacitor.

> Express the essence in six words: speak truth, always. Speak fast, always.

> Maximum truth. Maximum speed. Always. Hyphenate the motto to show how the two concepts merge: truth-with-speed.

> Truth up front, but speed nearly as important. The Media Age puts a rocket under the adage that a lie dashes round the world while truth is still pulling on its trousers.[305]

---

305 Defence confronts the Media Age, Graeme Dobell, *The Strategist*, 23 May, 2016.

Truth-with-speed would strike at government control. Essentially it was the same world the saints so desired: a world where it was impossible to lie; a world where, as in the case of Iraq, Syria and Afghanistan, it would have been impossible to take the country to war on a lie.

The control imperative of government would have to be revised, the increasingly totalitarian impulses of Australian government to control all information and to manipulate the general public into accepting depleted levels of debate would have to be abandoned.

The power to control and disseminate government-sponsored lies was already being blown away by the Media Age and the all-seeing phones of billions of Digital Citizens – five billion mobile devices and counting.

> The call for less political control and bureaucratic obfuscation is about responding to the meaning of our era as much as any commitment to openness. The openness is overrunning everything of its own accord.

> Embrace truth-with-speed not as a gift or a concession but as an acknowledgement of the environment that has arrived.

> Ever more information flows from ever more sources. To censor or limit information or to speak slowly merely vacates the arena and allows other voices to define the issue or define you.[306]

Alex thought: "Interesting in theory."

And when it came to war, the perpetual war in which Australia was now engaged, the people might just go along – if they could be convinced it as a so-called "just war", in defence of the homeland.

But all the recent conflicts with which Australia had been involved had been anything but just, and had neither protected the country nor made it safer.

The point of the secrecy, propaganda and the deliberate creation of high levels of public indifference had been to provide a cloak for conflicts with which the public would never have agreed if they had been told the truth: that the gains were minimal or non-existent, the motives did not relate to the defence of the populace but to defence contracts, the costs were extremely high, the morality unconscionable.

---

306 Ibid.

And that by engaging themselves in a crusader war, in a cauldron of collapsing circumstance, they had endangered themselves.

If Dobell's theory was to be embraced – and if as he argued, with the proliferation of mobile devices and so-called citizen journalists, governments ultimately had no choice – then the nature of the conflicts and operations with which the country was engaged would also ultimately have to change.

As every conflict of the past half century had hammered home, and as the war on terror morphed into a war on the people's right to know, that would be a very good outcome.

Seven days after the winter solstice, and the Murdoch Empire proved once again what a wonderful friend of the government it was – and how seriously irresponsible had become the nation's terror coverage.

Best selling Sydney tabloid *The Daily Telegraph* bannered outside the state's newsagents the taunting jibe: AUSSIE TERROR CRY BABY: JIHADI WEEPER CELL.

Even for the Murdoch press it was a new low.

The front page headline read: "Exclusive: ISIS, ISIS BABY CRY-HARD JIHADI."

The story itself concerned an Australian Islamic State fighter, Mohammad Ali Baryalei.

Suffering heat stroke, he had become distressed after watching several of his comrades, including his commander, die that day in fierce fighting. In tweets to a friend in Australia he recorded how he had just seen a man "blown up in front of my eyes man" and that "pieces were flying left right and centre... At first I started crying. I was just ... that day I don't know ... we got smashed man."

Baryalei was said to have suffered abuse at the hands of his father and left home at the age of 17, later working as a nightclub bouncer in Kings Cross, an area of Sydney Old Alex had known for half a century.

He was named as a co-conspirator in a 2013 terrorism plot to film a person being beheaded in Martin Place some seven weeks before he was reported killed in Syria.

Australia entered its final month of winter.

Malcolm Turnbull re-entered the official Canberra residence, the Lodge, a far less impressive dwelling than his own home on Sydney Harbour.

He had narrowly won a two-month election campaign, and acted as if it was a great victory; for he knew from his own polling it was touch and go, and he had been likely to lose.

The images Old Alex had in his head, of a grim-faced Malcolm and a smiling Opposition leader Bill Shorten, which he thought might mean Turnbull was about to lose office, turned out to be true in a different sense.

Shorten acted as if his Labor Party had won, exhibiting broad smiles as he did a victory lap of the country.

While each passing day the mantle of high office Malcolm Turnbull had sought all his life fitted more and more uneasily, and he became increasingly grim-faced.

With the Battle of Lies aka the election finally over, they both promptly settled back into their comfortable, well paid sparring positions; while the sickness of the country as a whole, and the sickness of the political class, was everywhere evident.

The optimistic "Jobs and Growth" platitude heard hundreds of times during the Election, so clearly a lie from Malcolm Turnbull's body language, turned overnight into rhetoric more befitting a Doomsday Cult.

Treasurer Scott Morrison warned of an impending Depression.

The conservatives had won six out of the eight last elections. They were more to blame for the present situation than anybody.

Although he had not done so in decades, Alex thought of that old poem from school days:

> We are the hollow men
> We are the stuffed men
> Leaning together
> Headpiece filled with straw. Alas!
> Our dried voices, when
> We whisper together
> Are quiet and meaningless
> As wind in dry grass
> Or rats' feet over broken glass

The poem ended, of course, with those famous lines:

> This is the way the world ends
> This is the way the world ends

This is the way the world ends
Not with a bang but a whimper.[307]

It was not Malcolm Turnbull who was the most striking winner of that winter election.

Anti-Muslim anti-multicultural politician Pauline Hanson stormed home in the election with her One Nation Party gaining four Senate seats, and granting her party, in conjunction with other independents, the balance of power.

Previously dismissed and mercilessly ridiculed as far right, racist, unsophisticated and xenophobic; after more than two decades in the public spotlight her time had come.

This time around the very same conservative politicians who had done their best to destroy her queued up to gift her legitimacy, saying she should be treated with respect – clearly struck by the fact she had garnered half a million votes.

It was a trigger point. From that moment on, her views would gain increasing currency.

In her first maiden speech to parliament literally twenty years and four days before, Senator Hanson said:

> We now have a situation where a type of reverse racism is applied to mainstream Australians by those who promote political correctness and those who control the various taxpayer funded 'industries' that flourish in our society servicing Aboriginals, multiculturalists and a host of other minority groups. In response to my call for equality for all Australians, the most noisy criticism came from the fat cats, bureaucrats and the do-gooders. They screamed the loudest because they stand to lose the most—their power, money and position, all funded by ordinary Australian taxpayers.[308]

The country's failure to debate the social transformations being imposed on the country and the government-run media's ceaseless spruiking of bureaucratic agendas had left a gaping hole in the polity. The refusal to countenance opposing views, the refusal by the country's new ruling castes

---

307 *Poems 1909-1925*, T.S. Elliot, Faber & Faber, 1937.

308 Pauline Hanson's 1996 maiden speech to parliament: Full transcript, *The Sydney Morning Herald*, 15 September, 2016.

of tertiary educated elites to treat the views of ordinary, uneducated people with respect, all of it came home to roost.

> The problem is we have not had leaders with the foresight or the intestinal fortitude to cast aside political correctness. They have failed to discard old treaties and agreements that are not in our best interest and have signed new ones giving away our sovereignty, rights, jobs and democracy. Their push for globalisation, economic rationalism, free trade and ethnic diversity has seen our country's decline. This is due to foreign takeover of our land and assets, out-of-control debt, failing infrastructure, high unemployment or underemployment and the destruction of our farming sector. Indiscriminate immigration and aggressive multiculturalism have caused crime to escalate and trust and social cohesion to decline. Too many Australians are afraid to walk alone at night in their neighbourhoods. Too many of us live in fear of terrorism.

> Now we are in danger of being swamped by Muslims, who bear a culture and ideology that is incompatible with our own.[309]

Hanson went on to repeat the criticism of Islam as incompatible with liberal society; it did not believe in democracy, freedom of speech, freedom of the press, or freedom of assembly. It did not separate religion and politics. It had a political agenda that went far outside the realm of religion, regulating Muslims' social and domestic life, their legal system and politics – their total life.

The Greens walked out of the Senate as she spoke, garnering to themselves little but contempt. That was the point of democracy, the right to hold different views, not to turn your back on half a million voters.

Old Alex had covered Hanson's town hall meetings twenty years before. The thing that had struck him the most was that far from being the bunch of redneck whites he had expected, many of her most ardent supporters were migrants.

They were proud to be New Australians, and angry at the direction of the country away from integration towards multiculturalism.

In the Australia they had adopted as their own, all you had to do was work hard and say you loved Australia and you were accepted.

---

309 Transcript: Pauline Hanson's 2016 maiden speech to the Senate, ABC, 15 September, 2016.

No longer: the country's immigration, set at historically high and many believed unsustainable levels, had become the hottest button issue of the time.

Now welfare systems and public housing created ethnic enclaves where work was optional. The all-pervasive public media ran story after story about refugees and Muslims, and entirely ignored the mainstream.

The bureaucracy had spent many billions of dollars promoting multiculturalism, thereby creating mounting resentment.

Visible tensions rippled across the social landscape, but far worse lay beneath the surface.

A poll by research group Essential showed that 62% agreed with the view that Hanson spoke for ordinary Australians; 65% agreed with the statement that she spoke about issues other politicians were too scared to tackle. Taking into account the "Don't Knows", at 49% per cent larger numbers supported her call for a ban on Muslim immigration than opposed it.[310]

There were many portents, in those darkening days.

A French backpacker shouted "Allahu Akbar" as he stabbed to death a British backpacker, Mia Ayliffe-Chung, 21, from Derbyshire.

The killing took place at Shelley's Backpacker Hostel, about 100 kilometres southeast of Townsville, a comparatively remote location popular with young people fruit-picking on the surrounding farms.

The knifing frenzy, in which several people were injured, lasted for hours. The insanity was spreading – even into these remote, idyllic locations in The Great Southern Land.

As Alex continued his nomadic drift along the east coast of Australia, he was drawn to the picturesque, rundown frontages of abandoned shopfronts.

Telegraph Point's Butcher and Grocery Stores, where he spent a month, were just one example: their walls collapsing, vines growing over the roofs, the entire scene speaking of a country destroyed.

It was not just the psychological impacts of mass surveillance, the increasing secrecy of government, the cloaking of power, concealment from those they were meant to serve, that made the era so disturbing.

It was what was being done behind all those closed doors; and, just as you could tell much from the surface of a pond, the tentacles of dread which malformed the once laughing spirits of place, destroying even the trace memory of happy families.

---

310 Ban on Muslim Immigration, Essential Report, 21 September, 2016.

Echoes of the Vietnam War, one of Australia's greatest American-led military follies, would travel through that year one more time.

More than 1,000 Vietnamese veterans travelled to the site of the Battle of Long Tan in South Vietnam, where 18 Australians and more than 250 Viet Kong died, to mark the 50th anniversary of what came to be seen as an Australian victory.

Concerned at the reaction of locals to an event which was quickly taking on an air of celebration, the Vietnamese government shut down access to the site. Australia's Department of Foreign Affairs had previously assured Vietnamese officials that it would be a small and respectful memorial.

Planned events included a gala dinner and a concert featuring much-loved singer of the era Little Pattie. The event was seen as a way for veterans to come to terms with the events of the past. All those decades later, many still bore the psychological wounds of battle, compounded by the hostility with which they were greeted on returning home from the controversial war and the prolonged indifference of the Australian government to their welfare.

Veteran Affairs Minister Dan Tehan described the cancellation as a "kick in the guts".

The locals still call the conflict "The American War" and mark its end with nationwide celebrations.

Alex visited an elderly man on a property outside Telegraph Point. As the sky darkened into night, he pointed to a bright light hanging high over the hills and asked: "What's that? A satellite?"

"All money it's a drone," the 84-year-old farmer replied. "It's been there for about a year. It will move a bit through the night, and sometimes has a red or greenish tinge. Different lights. My grandson, when he's here, aims a laser at it."

"What are they looking for?"

The two of them both shrugged and agreed, "they" were watching everything.

He remembered, for some reason, the words of a good Muslim he had met in Lightning Ridge two years before: "The biggest thieves in this country are the government."

Everywhere, an unfolding disaster. By the final day of winter 3,000 thousand refugees had drowned on the trip to Europe. One Syrian father, speaking of his drowned children, said: "They woke me every day to play. Everything is lost."

The war had not been mentioned in the entire election campaign – a conflict which was having profoundly negative consequences for the country domestically and internationally. But war was the government's first order of business.

Turnbull would continue the belligerent, militaristic mistakes of his forebears, and never rise to the occasion history delivered to him.

In the wake of the Chilcot Report and the clear counterproductive consequences of Australia's decades' long involvement in Iraq and Syria, it felt little more than criminal and immoral misconduct; and history was likely to see it so.

As commentators had been warning, Islamic State rose from the ashes of the US invasion of Iraq; but as the bombings continued, casualties rose, chaos spread and terror metastasised, something far worse could rise in its wake. •

The train was accelerating towards collision – with a hubris-laden captain at its helm.

Turnbull, who surely must have secretly longed to return to his natural hunting grounds, the wealthy cocktail circuit of Sydney's eastern suburbs where he had been universally popular, rose grim-faced to address the nation. He recited Islamic State's attacks against civilians across the Middle East and Africa, resulting in the deaths of thousands, mainly Muslims. In July 80 people were killed and 230 injured by suicide bombers in Kabul.

> Since the Parliament last met on 5 May the world has witnessed a seemingly constant barrage of terror attacks. Nice (84 killed, 201 injured); Orlando (49 killed); a Church in Normandy where a priest was slain by a teenager; and 47 killed at Ankara airport and 23 in Dhaka, with both attacks specifically aimed at foreigners. The list goes on.

> In the last year alone, there have been around 40 Islamist terrorist attacks against the West or western interests. These attacks have resulted in over 700 deaths. Many of these are assessed to have been directed or inspired by Daesh.[311]

Journalists called the world's most famous terror group Islamic State. Politicians alone called them Daesh, a feeble attempt to conceal religious affiliation.

---

311 National Security Statement on Counter-Terrorism, Parliament House, Canberra, Prime Minister Malcolm Turnbull, 1 September, 2016.

In Australia there had been three terrorist attacks over the past two years, in each occurrence the attacker claiming allegiance to Islamic State. The government claimed a further ten attacks were thwarted.

In the same period, 47 people had been charged as a result of 18 counter-terrorism operations around Australia.

> In order to defeat this despotic and barbaric movement we are working closely with our friends and allies to destroy it at its core: – its so-called "caliphate" in Syria and Iraq.
>
> To promote Australia's safety our first objective must be to expel Daesh from its occupied territories and destroy its pretensions of statehood.
>
> This is why a 400-member Australian Defence Force Air Task Group is conducting airstrikes over Daesh strongholds in Iraq and Syria, and a similar number of ADF personnel are training and assisting Iraqi ground forces.[312]

Australia was there because America was there. No other reason.

Why bother to maintain the lie?

Why treats the people like fools?

Just as President Obama had done in the US, Turnbull put the best possible gloss on a devolving situation, boasting of military gains and territorial losses.

Against a group which did not even exist two years before.

Talk of the defeat of Islamic State was entirely premature.

IS had become the biggest story on Earth, there were now affiliates around the globe, and the loss of a few kilometres of empty desert or a strategic retreat from already bombed-out ruins of cities meant little. As the situation continued to devolve, the reality behind the boastful, glossy messaging of the West would, if Alex's waking dreams held true, be swept away in a single day.

Former Army chief and now head of the National Security Institute Peter Leahy, noted that there was more discussion about Johnny Depp's dogs being deported after the actor breached Australia's quarantine laws than there was about Australian soldiers in Afghanistan and Iraq.

There was no endgame.

---

312 Ibid.

Islamic State had risen from and been empowered by Western intervention, its soldiers were clothed and equipped Western goods, the fruits of conquest, and news of its demise was entirely premature. The group was metastasising rapidly, gaining ground in Libya, Afghanistan, Yemen, northern Nigeria, Bangladesh, Indonesia and the Philippines.

> The destruction of the caliphate will not be easy nor will it signal victory in the so-called war on terror. The caliphate may go but the ideology behind it will remain.

> Nor will it do much to calm the maelstrom enveloping the broader Middle East. Violence is everywhere and it is clear that cultural, read religious, differences are driving much of the fighting.

> By the presence of our troops in the region, we are involved.

> Do the radicals have a strategy? You bet they do. They know what they want and have a long-term view – they are engaged in a cosmic battle between good and evil. In case you are unsure, we are the evil ones.

> They are operating on multiple fronts including in our homelands, where they assault us daily with propaganda exhorting their followers to join their fight or attack us at home.[313]

Leahy said IS were adaptable, changed their tactics to suit dynamic battlefields and were equipped with a powerful ideology. Meanwhile the West was nowhere near even having a coherent strategy, and Australia's soldiers in Iraq and Syria were on a "set and forget" mission – where Australian politicians, usually with a good deal of flag-waving fanfare, send them on an overseas mission, and then promptly forget them.

The soldiers' lives remain at risk; the politicians head off to the next function in their chauffeur-driven cars.

Undeterred by the cautions emanating from some of the country's most qualified military strategists that the war was at best futile, Turnbull announced legislation to grant additional killing powers to the Australian Defence Force.

---

313 We need a political plan on the war on terror, Peter Leahy, *The Australian*, 31 May, 2016.

More than a decade of disastrous, and extremely expensive, military intervention, and the PM was determined to continue down a path of no return.

Essentially Australian law made it illegal to either target or kill civilians in a war zone, and defence personnel could be charged if found guilty. Such niceties over "collateral damage" had never bothered their American ally, and Turnbull was keen to loosen the restrictions.

> It meant that the ADF's targeting base in Iraq and Syria was restricted, and we could not operate as freely as our coalition partners. So I can announce that the Government has reviewed its policy on targeting enemy combatants and earlier this year made an important decision to ensure our forces are empowered to act against Daesh in Iraq and Syria – to the maximum extent allowed by international law.

> And we will move quickly to introduce the necessary amendments to the Commonwealth Criminal Code that will bring our domestic laws into line with international norms.

> This means that ADF personnel will be supported by our domestic laws. They will be able to target Daesh at its core – joining with our coalition partners to target and kill a broader range of Daesh combatants – which is consistent with international law.[314]

Bravery behind a lectern would get Malcolm Turnbull precisely nowhere. Making it easier for the Australian military to kill civilians without being charged with war crimes did the country and the soldiers themselves no good whatsoever.

As the German philosopher Fredrich Nietzsche so famously said: "Whoever fights monsters should see to it that in the process he does not become a monster. And if you gaze for long into an abyss, the abyss also gazes into you."

In May the Australian military dropped 91 bombs on Iraq, in June 67, in July, 52. The government did not release casualty estimates.

"You still have a good beard," Alex said cheerfully to a Muslim man while out on one of his early morning walks along the shores of Lake Illawarra.

The man smiled proudly.

---

314 Ibid.

The first words he ever said to Mustafa, back in those warmer days of the previous year, were: "You have a good beard."

And that was that, they had been saying hello to each other ever since.

Mustafa had just come, as always, from morning prayers at the local mosque.

His group had bought the old Uniting Church building, and he invited Alex to attend.

"An infidel like me is welcome?" Alex asked.

"Of course," came the reply, with only a moment's hesitation.

Obviously, if he chose the correct path and attended the mosque, he would not stay an infidel for long, not with the power of Allah's message.

"So much trouble now, what do you think about all this?" Alex asked.

Mustafa made a kind of swirling shrug towards the sky.

"It is the God. He controls everything."

They agreed that all was crazy, the Muslims, Christians and Jews fighting although they all had the same grandfather, Abraham.

"We worship the same God," Mustafa said, and they parted, the sunrise painting the lake a vivid, dark pink.

That same day more than 70 people were killed and 100 injured in Pakistan by a suicide bomber. Both the Taliban and Islamic State claimed responsibility.

There were deplorable ironies in the media-saturated world in which Old Alex swam, and which he knew so well.

The government propagandists pushing the agendas of the military were so blunt and unsophisticated, their efforts were bound to backfire.

Brendan Nicholson, Defence writer for Murdoch's *Weekend Australian*, was embedded with an RAAF flight team and wrote an adulatory Top Gun-style piece spilling off the front headlined: "Raining Down A Fiery Justice".

The rich benefited from war; and Murdoch's many hundreds of newspapers and television outlets worldwide had been uncritical supporters of the Iraq War; and in Australia they remained in close connection with the government's militarism.

Alex was not alone in seeing Murdoch's lathering for war as an abuse of power, and the journalists who sang to script as having abandoned any semblance of journalistic principle.

The skies above Iraq are a complex tangle of drones, fighter planes and hi-tech wizardry. On an RAAF mission, I see it all at close quarters.

Forty seconds after two RAAF jet fighters drop their bombs from 20,000 feet, the projectiles slam through the roof of a building near the Iraqi town of Ramadi, obliterating an Islamic State weapons team.

As the eruption of smoke and dust clears, images gathered by the jet fighters confirm the bombs have gone "high order" and detonated as planned.

Kelpie One and Kelpie Two, the call signs of the pilots of the F/A 18A "Classic" Hornets of the Royal Australian Air Force, turn away in search of more targets.[315]

There followed another 4,600 words in the same vein.

Nobody died in those puffs of smoke so far below; no children lost their fathers, no one was maimed for life; there were no moral quandaries in an unending war.

But however much the exercise cost the Australian taxpayer, the gotcha euphoria of the propagandists was short-lived.

That same weekend the Royal Australian Air Force was forced to admit it was involved in the killing of more than 60, later upgraded to 80, Syrian troops and wounding more than 100 others in a botched bomb strike which was meant to be targeting Islamic State.

Russia called a meeting of the UN Security Council in response to the fiasco.

Syria insisted the US led attack was deliberately aimed at supporting Islamic State as part of a push to unseat President Bashar al-Assad. The Defence Minister and the Australian Defence Force were forced to deny supporting Islamic State.

Cartoonist Ron Tanberg called it, with an air force captain bawling out to RAAF pilots: "You're supposed to kill the bad guys." And comes the response: "It's difficult to tell the difference."

Front woman, the never forthcoming, robotic Defence Minister Marise

---

315 Raining Down A Fiery Justice, Brendan Nicholson, *The Weekend Australian*, 17-18 September, 2016.

Payne, refused to give any detail of the RAAF's involvement in the killing of scores of soldiers: "We will continue in an appropriate, measured way with the international coalition, to do what is required, but there has been no hold as such put on Australia activity."[316]

At an excruciating press conference, she refused to answer the following questions:

> Were Australian jets actually physically bombing at the time or were the Australian planes in a support role?
>
> What proportion of the planes that were deployed at the time were Australian in relation to Coalition?
>
> Would you describe Australia's role as a leading role in the operation?
>
> What particular planes did we have in that operation?
>
> Do you know, initially at least, what went wrong, how you could mistake 60 Syrians and what you thought was a Daesh border position as you said?
>
> A communications problem?
>
> The operation was tracking the target for, you know, a period of time beforehand. How did they get it so wrong?[317]

Payne billed herself as the Senator for Western Sydney, an area where hundreds of thousands of her constituents bitterly opposed Australia's morally bankrupt incursions into an imploding Middle East.

In that storm-tossed winter, underneath the sound of wind whipping against the thin sheet of glass that passed for a window, Alex woke up one morning dreaming of being trapped high up in a 90-storey building. Walls were collapsing, sheets of flame enveloped the apartment from which he was trying to escape.

He did not even know there was such a thing as a 90-storey skyscraper in Australia and so, using the remarkable technology of the period, he simple Googled it.

---

316 No pause in Australian air strikes on Islamic State despite fatal blunder against Syrian forces, David Wroe, *The Sydney Morning Herald*, 19 September, 2016.

317 Minister for Defence Press Conference transcript, Sydney, 19 September, 2016.

There was only one, the Eureka Building in Melbourne, Australia's tallest skyscraper.

It was a prime terrorist target.

Facial recognition software and extra patrols around major landmarks such as the Sydney Opera House and the Sydney Harbour Bridge made them difficult targets.

But the Eureka building, completed in 2006, was a residential tower. Although built post 9/11, the architectural plans were drawn up well before that date, and without a terrorist attack in mind.

One of the country's busiest buildings, people of all types came and went day and night.

An attack simply would not be that difficult.

Alex had no way of knowing whether the dream was a premonition or not. He had been wrong before, but when he looked at images of the building he felt an immense sadness.

That was the point of terror. Every non-believer was a target; every mass gathering a potential mass casualty event, every landmark simply a place which was yet to be bombed. The Islamists had achieved their goal. The infidel had been made uncomfortable in their own homes. Nobody knew where or when the next attack would be, all anyone knew was that it was coming, as night followed day.

The only recourse for survival, the only avenue to safety was to surrender to the will of Allah the Most Merciful; as many Christians now declared: "We worship the same God."

Alex dreamed constantly of being attacked as the world erupted into flames.

Still in the grip of winter, came the news that was Australia was third on the Islamic State hit list, equal with the United Kingdom, after the United States and France.

Far from the glossy talk of victory and loss of territory, a Homeland Security Committee Report, Terror Gone Viral, recorded that Islamic State had become the preeminent global terror threat: "The total number of casualties from the group's anti-Western attacks more than doubled in just the first half of this year. At least 875 people have been killed or wounded in 2016 alone—more than the combined total from 2014 and 2015 (750 people)—

and in just the past year the average number of casualties per attack jumped from 48 to 58."[318]

Not long afterwards, IS made lengthy tribute to Abu Mansur al-Muhajir, an IS fighter hailing from Melbourne who had been previously jailed for his role in plots to blow up the Melbourne Cricket Ground. He had been arrested in one of Australia's largest terror operations, Pendennis.

In the magazine Rumiyah, Islamic State then made specific call for Lone Wolf attacks in Australia:

> Therefore, O lions of the Ummah, and those living in Australia in particular, follow the path of these righteous souls for there is no other path. The Khilafah has called for you to mobilize from your dens to alleviate the pain afflicting the hearts of the Muslims by striking the kuffar in their homelands. It is only from the hikmah of Allah that he has scattered you around the earth and in the various lands of the Crusaders to see which of you are best in deeds. So here before you are the doors of jihad – unhinged, and in their lands! Light the ground beneath them aflame and scorch them with terror.
>
> Kill them on the streets of Brunswick, Broadmeadows, Bankstown, and Bondi. Kill them at the MCG, the SCG, the Opera House, and even in their backyards. Stab them, shoot them, poison them, and run them down with your vehicles. Kill them wherever you find them until the hollowness of their arrogance is filled with terror and they find themselves on their knees with their backs broken under the weight of regret for having waged a war against the believers, and by Allah's will, and then through your sacrifices, this Ummah will be victorious.[319]

The same magazine featured an article titled The Kafir's Blood is Halal for You: So Shed It.

"There are multiple plots across the country," a voice said, again.

The first to act on the renewed call for lone-wolf attacks on Australia was 22-year-old Ihsas Khan, who yelled "Allah Akbar", God is Great, "someone

---

318 Terror Gone Viral, House Homeland Security Committee Majority Staff Report, 2014-2016.

319 Among the Believers are Men: Abu Mansur al-Muhajir, Rumiyah, 1st Edition, September,2016.

is going to die tonight" and "you killed my brothers and sisters in Iraq" as he knifed a 59-yer-old local resident Wayne Greenhalgh in the south-western suburb of Minto.

"Terror in Sydney Suburbs" read the newspaper banners.

The attack occurred on the eve of memorial events for the collapse of the Twin Towers. Ten Australians were amongst the 2996 people who died that day.

Malcolm Turnbull said:

> Let me say something too about 9/11 and its links to what happened yesterday in Minto. At one level they seem very different, 15 years apart, very different events. But connecting them both is a violent Islamist ideology which perverts the religion of Islam and seeks to destroy and threaten our way of life. What also is consistent or common between them is heroism. We remember, when we mourn those who died in the 9/11 attacks we also honour the heroism of those who rushed to the aid of the victims in New York and in Washington – the heroes of that hour. We honour them.

> You know in Minto yesterday there was an owner of some premises who sheltered the 59-year-old man who was assaulted. There was a bystander who confronted this assailant with his knife and managed to keep him at bay until the police arrived. Then there were the police who defended public safety courageously, brought the assailant under control and placed him under arrest. So we honour those heroes of today, just as we honour the heroes of 9/11.[320]

There was no mention of the invasion of Iraq and the hundreds of thousands who subsequently died, nor any mention of the many thousands of Islamic State fighters and their families who had been massacred by Western bombs, including Australian bombs.

In reference to the Minto attack Michelle Grattan, a legend of Australian journalism, asked: "Do you think that there is some reluctance from the Muslim community in particular to come forward with information when the situation may be ambiguous, they worry what might happen to relatives if they approach the authorities?"

---

320 Press Statement, Prime Minister Malcolm Turnbull, 11 September, 2016.

To which the Prime Minister replied:

> We are a big, successful – very successful – multicultural nation.
> The most successful multicultural nation in the world . . . That
> multicultural nation includes many Muslims, we have people
> from every possible faith and race and background and so forth.
> We have a common cause in protecting ourselves and protecting
> our neighbours and that is why cooperation is very important,
> as you've heard Director Generals of ASIO say again and again,
> that collaboration and engagement with the Muslim commu-
> nity is a very important part of it.[321]

At the Tables of Knowledge scattered across the country there was nothing
but contempt for their political leaders; stubborn, resentful, disillusioned,
increasingly embittered.

The once staunch Labor voters who populated those tables, the builder's
labourers, concreters, plasterers, truckies, electricians, carpenters, mixed
with subsiding alcoholics in poor health, switched their vote.

A year or two before, few of them would have ever admitted publicly their
politically incorrect support for Senator Pauline Hanson.

Now, they were the protest vote, and they supported her to a man, or
woman.

Some of it was vicious: "I can't wait to watch Pauline string up the first
rope."

But the vast majority of it was simply the voices of people who had had
enough; sick of a country where nothing worked, where everything was
expensive, where government mangled into every part of their lives, where
fat cats and politicians stole their taxes, where their opinions and their hard
work were regarded as of no account.

The identity politics of the day, refugees, lesbian mothers, aboriginals in
custody, ignored the muddling middle.

Not one politician stood up and declared to ordinary workers: "I am
going to make your life better."

The social engineers, their tertiary acquired group think theories failing to
take in the real world, had reaped what they had sowed: contempt.

One of the Australia's most esteemed writers, Richard Flanagan, delivered
a heartfelt condemnation of the country in which he dwelled:

---

321 Ibid.

Every day we hear grim and grimmer news that suggests we are passing through the winter of the world. Everywhere man is tormented, the globe reels from multitudes of suffering and horror, and, worst, we no longer know with confidence what our answer might be. And yet we understand that the time approaches when an answer must be made or a terrible reckoning will be ours.

Resentment curdled everywhere.

A petition went up for returned soldiers, sent to war by the very government which now ignored them:

When you slip into your warm bed tonight, over 100 veterans of Iraq and Afghanistan wars will sleep rough in parks around Australia. Cold, hungry and suffering Post Traumatic Stress Disorder as a result of service to their country, these brave veterans deserve better. They need a place to shower, to eat, to sleep and to talk to other veterans who understand what they are going through. But where do they go? How can the government justify spending millions and millions on refugees yet forget those who were prepared to lay down their lives for the country they love???[322]

The horsemen wheeled out onto the plains of Dabiq.

And when he had opened the fourth seal, I heard the voice of the fourth beast say, Come and see. And I looked, and behold a pale horse: and his name that sat on him was Death, and Hell followed with him. And power was given unto them over the fourth part of the earth, to kill with sword, and with hunger, and with death, and with the beasts of the earth.[323]

The drones flew overhead.

Western bombs rained down on crying children.

The massacres grew worse.

Nobody thought it was going to end. Talk of a World War was everywhere in the wind.

So the angel swung his sickle over the earth and gathered the

322 Veterans Affairs: Homeless Heroes, Petition by Anthony Williams, Change dot org.
323 Revelation 6: 7-8, King James Bible.

grapes of the earth, and he threw them into the great winepress of God's wrath. And the winepress was trodden outside the city, and the blood that flowed from it rose as high as the bridles of the horses...[324]

In those waking dreams which continued to haunt Old Alex, the attempts by those who had sent him and hundreds of others like him to rescue a race from an apocalypse, to avoid the gifting of billions of souls to the Dark Lords, stood on the precipice of failure.

The world had ignored the warnings of the town criers.

The Enlightenment had failed.

Time was running out.

The books he had loved as a youth began to recycle rapidly through his brain. Ask not For Whom the Bell Tolls, it tolls for thee.

The policies and procedures were in place, the rules and regulations drafted.

The place had been prepared. The plane was on the tarmac.

There was a gap in the air, that intake of breath prior to calamity.

We will meet in the place where there is no darkness, in the middle of the torture chamber.

But it would all avail the torturers nought; their feeble souls the flashes of light at the edge of a firestorm, barely existing before they were gone, destroyed in the maelstrom they themselves had helped created.

Above, as it had done all year, the sky burned.

---

324 Revelation 14: 19-20, Berean Study Bible.

ACKNOWLEDGEMENTS

I would like to thank Peter Binning, Leigh Dayton, Max King and family, Peter van de Voorde, Nola Stapleton, Kylie Pickett, Cara McDougal, Tim Cribb, Tony Candito and Simon Parker for their hospitality and support during the writing of this book.

I would also like to thank Jessica Bell for her always superb cover designs and Stafford Sanders for his sympathetic and painstaking editing.

And last but not least, Anthony Reale, owner of the Village Fix in Shellharbour. His excellent coffee and convivial company saw me through the final drafts.

ABOUT THE AUTHOR

The first money William John Stapleton ever made out of writing was in 1974 when he was co-winner of a short story competition held by what was then Australia's then leading cultural celebration, the Adelaide Arts Festival. He graduated from Macquarie University in Sydney in 1975 with a double major in philosophy and anthropology and did post- graduate work with the Sociology Department at Flinders University. His articles and fiction have appeared in a range of magazines, newspapers and anthologies. Stapleton joined the staff of The Sydney Morning Herald in 1986. In 2004 he moved to The Australian, leaving after 15 years. As a general news reporter in Sydney John Stapleton, or "Stapo" as he was widely known, covered literally thousands of stories: from the funerals of bikies, children and dignitaries to fires, floods, droughts and demonstrations of all kinds. In 2000 he helped found the world's longest running father's show, Dads On The Air. After leaving The Australian at the end of 2009 he established A Sense of Place Publishing while traveling in S.E. Asia. His books include Thailand: Deadly Destination, Terror in Australia: Workers Paradise Lost, Hunting the Famous, and Chaos at the Crossroads: Family Law Reform in Australia.

A collection of John Stapleton's journalism can be found here:
http://thejournalismofjohnstapleton.blogspot.com.au/

www.ingramcontent.com/pod-product-compliance
Lightning Source LLC
Chambersburg PA
CBHW060308030426
42336CB00011B/975